China Law, Tax & Accounting

This series provides practical overviews, suggestions and advice on the main issues concerning law, tax and accounting in China. Each topic is investigated in depth from a professional point of view, and will, where possible, include the opinions of CPAs and Lawyers. These books provide useful tools for understanding the Chinese law, tax and accounting systems, they are written by professionals, for professionals. Every book in the series includes an appendix with the relevant laws and regulation and, where possible, the main interpretation of the Supreme Court of China.

More information about this series at http://www.springer.com/series/13914

Giovanni Pisacane · Lea Murphy
Calvin Zhang

Arbitration in China

Rules & Perspectives

Springer

Giovanni Pisacane
GWA Law, Tax & Accounting
Shanghai
China

Calvin Zhang
GWA Law, Tax & Accounting
Shanghai
China

Lea Murphy
GWA Law, Tax & Accounting
Shanghai
China

ISSN 2365-628X ISSN 2365-6298 (electronic)
China Law, Tax & Accounting
ISBN 978-981-10-0683-8 ISBN 978-981-10-0684-5 (eBook)
DOI 10.1007/978-981-10-0684-5

Library of Congress Control Number: 2016934024

Printed on acid-free paper

This Springer imprint is published by Springer Nature
The registered company is Springer Science+Business Media Singapore Pte Ltd.

Contents

Presentation

This piece wishes to provide the reader with a general overview of the practice of arbitration in China from the perspective of a foreign business operator. It was drafted keeping in mind the possibility that the foreign business operator is present in China either directly, or through a company incorporated and existing under the laws of China.

Aside from the option of submitting disputes to arbitration administered by Chinese institutions, the (rather problematic) option of having arbitration conducted in China under the rules of a foreign arbitration institution, or having arbitration carried out without relying on any institution, will also be examined. Proceedings at non-Chinese arbitration institutions, as well as the recognition and enforcement abroad of arbitral awards rendered in China are not covered in this short guide.

This piece is not meant to thoroughly deal with every issue that might arise when arbitrating in China; rather, care was taken to cover the most important issues. This guide addresses both the practical needs of business operators as well as provides more technical insights for foreign legal counsel evaluating arbitration in China.

The order of topics in Chaps. 1–6 reflects, as closely as possible, the normal sequence of events in an arbitration. After an *Introduction* dedicated to general definitions and issues, the following chapter deals with the drafting of the arbitration agreement touching on the main issues that a business operator and his legal counsel should keep in mind at this stage. The chapter on *Jurisdiction* explores the problems that may arise when a party to the arbitration agreement, disregarding said agreement, applies to Chinese courts for a ruling. An overview of procedural rules governing arbitration at the main Chinese arbitral institutions is provided. Finally, a chapter on *Recognition and Enforcement* deals with the problems related to the setting aside of an arbitral award rendered in China, as well as with the enforcement procedure to be followed in the event the losing party does not voluntarily comply with the award. Chapters 7 and 8 respectively address sample arbitration proceedings and the most common questions regarding arbitration in China.

Chapter 1
Introduction to Chinese Arbitration Law

1.1 Why Choose Arbitration for Business Disputes in China?

Arbitration is a popular choice among foreign enterprises doing business in China. Solving disputes through arbitration has several advantages:

(i) It is possible—albeit within certain limits—to entrust the solution of disputes to a subject of one's own choice which then allows for the selection of more professional and technical arbitrators;
(ii) An arbitral award is usually easier to enforce in China than a foreign court ruling;
(iii) Arbitration proceedings are characterized by confidentiality and can reach a resolution faster than if the issue was to be litigated in court.

1.2 Legal Sources Governing Arbitration in China

Arbitration is regulated in China by the following:

(a) National provisions
Arbitration is governed primarily by the PRC Arbitration Law (1994; hereafter, "AL") and by the PRC Civil Procedure Law (first issued in 1991; the latest reform was made in 2012; hereafter, "CPL"). Some provisions formulated by the Supreme People's Court (hereafter, "SPC") enjoy the same binding force as the statutes that they interpret.

G. Pisacane et al., *Arbitration in China*,
China Law, Tax & Accounting, DOI 10.1007/978-981-10-0684-5_1

It is worth mentioning here, the *Interpretation of the SPC on Some Questions Concerning the Application of the Arbitration Law of the PRC*, issued in 2006 (hereafter, the "Arbitration Law Interpretation" or "ALI"). The Arbitration Law is the main and general statute regarding arbitration, but not the only one. Special provisions are also contained elsewhere, for example, in Article 55 of the PRC Copyright Law,[1] in Article 34 of the PRC Law on Consumers Protection[2] and in Article 47 of the PRC Product Quality Law.[3]

(b) International conventions
Since 1986, China has been a party to the *New York Convention on the Recognition and Enforcement of Foreign Arbitral Awards*; it has acceded in 1992 to the *Washington Convention on the Settlement of Investment Disputes Between States and Nationals of Other States*. Moreover, China has signed bilateral investments treaties (BITs) with some 100 countries,[4] as well as judicial cooperation treaties with some 30 countries.[5]

(c) Rules of arbitration institutions
China presently has approximately 200 arbitration institutions. The main Chinese arbitration institution by volume of administered cases is CIETAC—*China International Economic and Trade Commission*—founded in 1956 under the China Council for the Promotion of International Trade (CCPIT).[6] CIETAC has its main seat in Beijing and sub-commissions in Tianjin and Chongqing.

---

[1]Article 55 of the PRC Copyright Law: "*Any dispute over copyright may be settled through mediation, it may also be submitted to an arbitration body for arbitration under a written arbitration agreement between the parties or under the arbitration clause in the copyright contract.*

Any party may take legal proceedings directly in a People's Court where there is neither a written arbitration agreement between the parties nor an arbitration clause in the contract".

[2]Article 34 of the PRC Law on Consumers Protection: "*In case of disputes with business operators over consumer rights and interests, consumers may settle the disputes through the following approaches*:

1. *to consult and conciliate with business operators*;
2. *to request to consumer associations for mediation*;
3. *to appeal to relevant administrative departments*;
4. *to apply to arbitral organs for arbitration according to the arbitral agreements with business operators*;
5. *to institute legal proceedings in the people's court*".

[3]Article 47 of the PRC Product Quality Law: "*Where a civil dispute over product quality arises, the parties concerned may seek a settlement through negotiation or mediation. Where the parties are unwilling to resort to negotiation or mediation, or the negotiation/mediation fails, they may apply to an arbitration organization for arbitration as agreed upon between the parties. Where the parties fail to reach an arbitration agreement, or the arbitration agreement is invalid, they may file a suit directly with a people's court*".

[4]The countries with which China signed a BIT were 101 as of November 15, 2011 (see the list published by the Chinese Ministry of Commerce: http://english.mofcom.gov.cn/article/bilateralchanges/201309/20130900300306.shtml).

[5]A list updated to 2014 published (in Chinese) by the Ministry of Justice mentions 34 agreements, including those only governing extradition: see http://www.moj.gov.cn/sfxzws/node_218.htm.

[6]Official English website: http://www.cietac.org/index.cms.

SHIAC[7]—*Shanghai International Economic and Trade Arbitration Commission* and SCIA—*Shenzhen Court of International Arbitration*[8]—are former branches of CIETAC, which split from it in 2012. Another institution worth noting is BAC—*Beijing Arbitration Commission*,[9] founded in 1995 following the entry into force of China's Arbitration Law. Every arbitration institution has its own arbitration rules, which will be cited throughout this book as necessary.

1.3 Types of Dispute, Types of Arbitration and Types of Award in the Chinese Legal System

Chinese law is peculiar in that it largely ignores the parameters of seat of arbitration and nationality of arbitration (as they are known in other legal systems) in its classification of both types of arbitration and types of award. A basic distinction of arbitrable disputes must be drawn between disputes that fall entirely within the scope of the Chinese legal system and those disputes which involve foreign elements.

A dispute is deemed to be "*foreign-related*" where any of the following conditions are satisfied:

(a) One or more parties are foreign nationals, stateless persons, natural persons having their domicile outside of China, or legal persons/other organizations having their legal seat outside of China.

- Note that all legal persons incorporated and existing under the laws of China are regarded as "Chinese persons" in this sense, regardless of the fact that they have been incorporated or are invested in or controlled by foreign entities. Therefore, as long as all its remaining elements fall within the scope of the Chinese legal system, a dispute having a Sino-foreign Joint Venture (JV), a Wholly Foreign-Owned Enterprise (WFOE) or a Foreign-Invested Partnership Enterprise (FIPE) as a party will be deemed to be a "domestic" one.

(b) The legal circumstances originating, modifying or terminating the civil relationship between the parties have taken place in a foreign country;
(c) The object of the dispute is located in a foreign country.[10]

---

[7]Official English website: http://shiac.org/English/.

[8]Official English website: http://www.sccietac.org/web/index.html.

[9]Official English website: http://arbitrator.bjac.org.cn/en/.

[10]Article 304 of the *Opinions of the Supreme People's Court on Some Issues Concerning the Application of the Civil Procedure Law of the People's Republic of China* (1992).

Domestic disputes, i.e., disputes not involving any foreign element, can only be submitted for arbitration to a Chinese arbitral institution (so-called *domestic arbitration*). Arbitration agreements submitting disputes with no foreign-related elements to the jurisdiction of a foreign arbitration institution are consistently held to be invalid in the current practice, leading Chinese courts to deny the enforcement of awards resulting from such agreements under Article V (1), Item 1 of the New York Convention.

The People's Courts, in denying the validity of such arbitration agreements, usually refer to general norms that draw a distinction between the treatment of domestic cases and foreign-related cases such as those contained in Civil Procedure, Contract, and Arbitration Law. Article 304 of the *SPC Opinions on Some Issues Concerning the Application of the PRC Civil Procedure Law* establishes a similar norm in stipulating that "*A civil case where one or both parties are foreign or stateless persons, foreign enterprises or organizations, or the legal facts establishing, modifying or terminating the civil relationship existing between the parties has taken place abroad, or the target of the lawsuit is located abroad, shall be a foreign-related one*".

The Supreme People's Court explicitly references this point in its *Provisions Regarding the Handling by the People's Courts of Cases Involving Foreign-Related Arbitrations and Foreign Arbitrations (Draft for Comment)* of 2003. According to Article 20 of these *Draft Provisions*, "*When one of the following circumstances is present, upon request of one of the parties, a People's Court shall deem an arbitration agreement to be ineffective:* [...] *(7) national parties have agreed on submitting to arbitration abroad a dispute not featuring any foreign-related element*".

However, as of today, there seems to be no provision in force actually stipulating that domestic disputes cannot be arbitrated abroad: the judgments issued by the courts do not provide a any specific explanation. In 2014, the No. 2 Intermediate People's Court of Beijing denied enforcement of an arbitral award rendered by a Korean arbitration institution in a dispute involving only Chinese elements. After quoting various norms providing for arbitration in civil and commercial disputes, the court simply concludes: "[...] *But the law in no way allows for national parties to submit a dispute devoid of any foreign-related element to a foreign arbitrator*". The underlying reasoning seems to be that anything not expressly allowed must be deemed forbidden.[11]

Where a dispute involves one or more elements falling outside the scope of the Chinese legal system, the parties then have a choice: the dispute can be submitted either to a Chinese arbitration institution (so-called *foreign-related* arbitration) or to a foreign arbitration institution (so-called *foreign* arbitration). Note that

---

[11] *Beijing Chaolai New Sports Leisure Co., Ltd. v. Beijing Suowangzhixin Investment Advisory Co., Ltd.*, [2013] Er Zhong Min Te Zi No. 10670, Beijing No. 2 Intermediate People's Court, January 20, 2014.

Hong Kong, Macau and Taiwan are considered as foreign legal environments for this purpose: Hong Kong and Macau by virtue of the principle "one country, two systems".

Chinese rules on the recognition and enforcement of awards establish a "double-track system", whereby different provisions apply to domestic awards and foreign awards. A *domestic award* is an award issued by a Chinese arbitral institution: this kind of award can be the result of either domestic arbitration or foreign-related arbitration.

Domestic awards are regulated:

(i) If the award results from domestic arbitration, by the Arbitration Law in general or;
(ii) If the award results from foreign-related arbitration, by Chapter VII of the Arbitration Law and, lacking provisions in such Chapter, by the other relevant provisions of the same Law.

A foreign award, on the other hand, is an award issued by a foreign arbitral institution. The difficult issues in this respect are those concerning the recognition and enforcement of foreign awards rendered in China (i.e., awards rendered in China by arbitrators chosen according to the rules of a foreign arbitration institution) (see § 5.2, d).

1.4 The Distinction Between "Domestic Arbitration Institutions" and "Foreign-Related Arbitration Institutions"

It is worth mentioning the distinction, which is made between Chinese arbitration institutions into "domestic arbitration institutions" and "foreign-related arbitration institutions", even though it is now largely obsolete. Until fifteen or twenty years ago, domestic disputes—i.e., disputes with no elements falling outside the parameters of the Chinese legal environment—could only be arbitrated by arbitration institutions qualified as "domestic", while disputes involving one or more foreign elements had to be arbitrated by "foreign-related arbitration institutions" (mainly CIETAC).

As of today, this distinction has mostly no meaning. Domestic arbitration institutions were allowed to hear foreign-related cases by a State Council *Notice* issued in June 1996.[12] Likewise, foreign-related arbitration institutions today can hear purely domestic cases as well. A ground-breaking role was played by CIETAC which led the way in this area between 1998 and 2000 by gradually expanding its jurisdiction into domestic issues, in order to keep its position as China's leading

[12] *Notice of the General Office of the State Council on Some Notable Issues Concerning the Execution of the PRC Arbitration Law*, issued by Guobanfa No. 22 [1996] of June 8, 1996.

arbitration institution. The 1998 CIETAC Arbitration Rules expanded the jurisdiction of CIETAC to encompass disputes involving foreign invested companies, which, if all other elements are domestic as well, count as "domestic disputes" (see § 1.3). Its competence on such matter was cemented in the Arbitration Rules of 2000: Article 2 provides that CIETAC shall have jurisdiction over "*other domestic disputes, which the parties have agreed to submit to arbitration by CIETAC*".

The effect of this is that the parties are no longer bound to submit domestic disputes to domestic arbitration institutions and foreign-related disputes to foreign-related arbitration institutions. However, this does not mean that choosing a domestic institution is equivalent to choosing a foreign-related institution. However, there are some important differences, which a foreign party should consider when drafting an arbitration agreement:

(i) Domestic arbitration institutions submit requests for evidence preservation measures to the competent basic-level People's Court (Article 46 AL), while foreign-related arbitration institutions forward such requests to the competent Intermediate People's Court (Article 68 AL), which usually has more expertise than a basic-level court in dealing with foreign-related issues.

(ii) The Arbitration Rules of foreign-related institutions provide for proceedings in English and/or other foreign languages, whereas most domestic institutions conduct their proceedings solely in Chinese.

(iii) The arbitrators of domestic arbitration institutions can only be chosen between "righteous and upright persons" presenting one or more of the requisites set forth by Article 13 AL (see § 2.5 b); Article 67 AL sets a less restrictive rule for foreign-related arbitration institutions, which "*may appoint arbitrators from among foreigners with special knowledge in the fields of law, economy and trade, science and technology,* etc.", with no further prerequisites.

(iv) In general, traditionally foreign-related arbitration institutions have a greater experience in dealing with issues involving foreign parties.

Chapter 2
The Arbitration Agreement

2.1 Definition

An arbitration agreement is an agreement by which the parties decide that they shall submit to arbitration any disputes, existing or future, concerning their relationship. For a Chinese person—keeping in mind, the definition of a "Chinese person" as found in § 1.3—, (validly) stipulating an arbitration agreement is the only way to subtract the relevant disputes from the jurisdiction of the People's Courts: therefore, a careful drafting of the arbitral agreement is essential.

An arbitral agreement can be stipulated in two ways (Article 16(1) AL):

(a) *Arbitration clause* incorporated in the contract
(b) Separate *arbitration agreement*

2.2 Conditions for the Existence and Validity of an Arbitration Agreement

An arbitration agreement must satisfy certain substantive and formal requirements in order to be considered existent, valid and, therefore, legally binding. The lack of one or more of the conditions that are enumerated below is sufficient for a People's Court to deny the existence of a (valid) arbitration agreement and therefore, to accept a case, thereby frustrating the intention of the parties to submit their disputes to arbitration (see § 3). The People's Courts, in deciding whether or not they have jurisdiction over a certain case, tend to apply a rather restrictive interpretation of these requirements. Because of this it is often the case that they find the necessary elements of the agreement are absent. It is therefore necessary to carefully draft the arbitration agreement, so as to avoid any requirement to be deemed as not satisfied.

G. Pisacane et al., *Arbitration in China*,
China Law, Tax & Accounting, DOI 10.1007/978-981-10-0684-5_2

2.2.1 *Conditions for the Arbitration Agreement to Be Deemed* Existing

An arbitration agreement will only be created by the express intent of the parties to arbitrate. Additionally the subject matter to be submitted to arbitration and the appointment of the specific arbitration institution must be clearly indicated (Article 16(2) AL). Under Article 18 AL, the parties can make up for the lack of one or more of the following conditions by stipulating a supplementary agreement.

(a) *Expression of the intention to apply for arbitration* (Article 16(2) no. 1 AL).
(b) *Indication of the subject matter to be solved through arbitration* (Article 16 (2), no. 2 AL). The subject matter must be *arbitrable*: see § 2.2.2, (a).
(c) *Designation of an arbitration institution* (Article 16(2), no. 3 AL).
This is the condition, which causes the most problems for the validity of arbitration agreements. Although the Arbitration Law does not explicitly state so, it is commonly believed that the requirement of designation of an arbitral institution excludes the possibility of recognizing so-called ad hoc arbitration in China. The definition "ad hoc arbitration" refers to arbitration not administered by an arbitral institution (such as the International Chamber of Commerce or, for China, CIETAC, SHIAC, etc.). Of course, ad hoc arbitration can per se be freely carried out; however, if the losing party does not implement the measures established in the arbitral award of its own accord, then the winning party will not be able to apply to the People's Courts for its enforcement (see also § 5.2, (c)).

Nevertheless, the Supreme People's Court has declared that the parties shall be deemed to have designated an arbitral institution when:

(i) The name of an institution is indicated in an unclear way, yet it is possible to determine such institution (Article 3 ALI);
(ii) The arbitral agreement only makes reference to certain arbitration rules, and not to an arbitration institution, yet it is possible to infer the designated institution (Article 4 ALI);
(iii) The arbitral agreement makes reference to a particular place and only one arbitration institution is present in that particular place (Article 6 ALI).

Where the arbitration agreement designates more than one institution and there is no subsequent agreement as to what arbitration institution will have jurisdiction, the arbitration agreement shall be deemed invalid (Article 5 ALI); the same happens if the arbitral agreement makes a reference to a place in which more than one arbitration institution is present and there is no subsequent agreement as to which institution will have jurisdiction (Article 6 ALI).

Lastly, an arbitration agreement referring the matter solely to the parties' discretion whether to apply to an arbitration institution or to the People's Courts shall be deemed invalid. However, such an arbitration agreement shall not be invalid if one party applies for arbitration and the other party does not object, by invoking said invalidity of the arbitration agreement, before the first hearing of the arbitral tribunal (Article 7 ALI). Regardless, it is a good practice when drafting an arbitration clause to always designate an arbitral institution in a clear and precise manner, so as to avoid any possible doubt, which might lead to the agreement being declared invalid by a court.

2.2.2 *Circumstances Making an Arbitration Agreement* **Invalid** *(Article 17 AL)*

An arbitral agreement is deemed to be invalid where one of the following circumstances is present. Generally, in transnational practice, the arbitral tribunal itself will evaluate the validity or invalidity of the arbitration agreement; by contrast, the power to decide this matter is also vested in the People's Courts in the Chinese system (Article 20 AL; see also § 3).

(a) *The agreed matters for arbitration exceed the range of arbitrable matters as specified by law* (Article 17, no. 1 AL).
The PRC Arbitration Law provides a somewhat problematic definition of arbitrable matters. According to its Article 2, "*Contractual disputes and other disputes over rights and interests in property between citizens, legal persons and other organizations that are equal subjects may be arbitrated*". This provision, if read literally, excludes all non-property related matters from the scope of arbitration; this then casts doubt on the arbitrability of disputes involving torts and—according to some—intangible property.
In practice, it is generally possible for the parties to an arbitration agreement to raise both property-related claims and non property-related claims.[1] Nevertheless, given the tendency of both arbitration institutions and State judges to expand the scope of their jurisdiction, one must take into account the possibility that, while an arbitration tribunal accepts a case not strictly related to property, a judge, based on a strict interpretation of the Arbitration Law, may consider the same case to fall outside the scope of arbitrable matters and therefore assume jurisdiction over it.
The Arbitration Law introduces a (albeit uncertain) limit to the scope of arbitration that does not have an equivalent in many foreign jurisdictions.

[1]GU Zhenlong, *Some Considerations on Parties' Self-Determination in the Arbitration Law* (关于仲裁法中当事人意思自治的几点思考), 2012, in the legal database *pkulaw.cn*, Ref. Code CLI.A.073818.

Compare, for example, Article 806 of the Italian Civil Procedure Code, according to which, in principle, the only non-arbitrable disputes are those involving non-negotiable rights (*diritti indisponibili*). Also compare Section 1029, Paragraph 1 of the German Civil Procedure Code, which is very clear in specifying that arbitration can regard a legal relationship "*that is contractual or non-contractual in nature*". Likewise, Article II (1) of the New York Convention makes a reference to "*a defined legal relationship, whether contractual or not*".[2]

Interestingly, the *Notice on Managing Arbitration of Securities and Futures Contract Disputes According to Law* jointly issued by the Legal Affairs Bureau of the State Council and by the China Securities Regulatory Commission in January 2004, specifies that the disputes arising between subjects of the securities and futures market regarding the trade of securities and futures fall within the scope of "civil and commercial disputes between equal civil subjects" and are therefore, arbitrable. Although this specification was probably not indispensable from a technical point of view, it does give a significant indication of the policy followed by the Chinese government in the last decade with regards to arbitration: the cited *Notice* aims to encourage recourse to arbitration for disputes involving trade in securities and futures, to take advantage of its flexibility, confidentiality, and (comparatively) low cost.[3]

The following matters are not arbitrable owing to a specific statutory provision:

(i) Issues concerning marriage, adoption, guardianship, support and succession (Article 3, no. 1 AL);

ii) Issues that are to be handled by administrative organs as established by law (Article 3, no. 2 AL).

(b) *One party to the arbitration agreement has no capacity for civil conducts or has limited capacity for civil conducts* (Article 17, no. 2 AL).

(c) *One party coerced the other party into concluding the arbitration agreement* (Article 17, no. 3 AL).

2.2.3 Formal Requirements

The arbitration agreement must be stipulated in writing; otherwise, it will held to be non-existent under Article 16(1) AL. The requirement of written form is held to be satisfied:

[2] *Ibidem*.

[3] See ZHU Sanzhu, "Legal Aspects of Commodity and Financial Futures Market in China", in *The Brooklyn Journal of Corporate, Financial and Commercial Law*, 2009, 3 (2), 377–430.

(i) Where the agreement has been concluded by means of letter, telegram, fax, electronic data exchange or e-mail (Article 1 ALI);
(ii) Where the arbitral clause is included in general contract conditions, as long as these have been duly incorporated in the contract (Articles 39 and 40 of the PRC Contract Law).

2.3 Autonomy or Severability of the Arbitration Agreement

Regardless of the form through which it is expressed—arbitration clause or separate agreement—the arbitral agreement is commonly understood, in transnational practice, to be *autonomous* and *severable* from the main contract to which it refers. The amendment, rescission, termination or invalidation of the main contract does not affect the arbitration agreement, which remains valid and enforceable.

This principle, which has its *raison d'être* in the will to preserve the existence and the effectiveness of arbitration agreements, is enshrined in Article 19(1) AL. Nevertheless, a long time passed before this principle found correct and consistent application by the People's Courts. Some authors have remarked that, all through the 90s and well into the new millennium, many rulings passed by Chinese courts unduly restricted or expanded the application of the principle of autonomy of the arbitration agreement.[4]

The courts are at times unduly restrictive in that, if the main contract had not entered into force—resulting, for example, from the lack of an administrative approval—, then the arbitration clause was find not to be binding on the parties. By contrast, a misunderstanding of the principle of autonomy of the arbitration agreement sometimes leads to excessively expansionist decisions: in *Hong Kong Longhai v. Wuhan Zhongyuan*,[5] the Intermediate People's Court of Wuhan held that the arbitral clause, being autonomous from the main contract, was not binding on the assignee of the contract.

With the Arbitration Law Interpretation of 2006, the Supreme People's Court put an end to the uncertainty of the courts by setting out that an arbitration agreement shall remain valid and enforceable even when the main contract has been revoked or has not yet taken effect. If the arbitration agreement refers not to a contract, but only to an agreement to contract, its validity and enforceability shall not be affected by the fact that no contract is stipulated afterwards (Article 10 ALI).

However, the principle of autonomy does not create two distinct expressions of contractual will; one related to the main contract and one to the arbitration clause.

---

[4]See, for example, Kun Fan, *Arbitration in China: A Legal and Cultural Analysis*, 1st ed., Oxford, Hart Publishing, 2013, pp. 31–34.

[5]*Hong Kong Longhai Co. v. Wuhan Zhongyuan Scientific Co.*, Wuhan IPC, [1998] n. 0277.

This means that a third party assignee cannot say he did not expressly agree to the separate agreement in order to avoid the arbitration clause; the intent to contract on the terms of the main contract also encompasses the arbitration agreement. As a result, the arbitration agreement is generally held to be binding on the assignee of the main contract (Article 9 ALI; see also the following paragraph).

Currently, the principle of severability of the arbitration agreement is also enshrined in the arbitration rules of the most important institutions (Article 5(4) CIETAC; Article 5(5) SHIAC; Article 10 SCIA, though referring to "independence", not to "autonomy" or "severability"; Article 5 BAC, referring to "separability").

2.4 Scope of the Binding Force of the Arbitration Agreement

As with other agreements (i.e. privity of contract), parties will only be bound by an arbitration agreement where they have expressly consented to it. There are some exceptions to this rule, which, being exceptions, tend to be interpreted by the People's Courts in a restrictive way.

(a) The entity generated by the merger or demerger of previously existing entities is bound by the arbitration agreements entered into by its predecessor(s) (Article 8(1) ALI), unless the opposite is expressly agreed when stipulating the arbitration agreement;
(b) The arbitration agreement stipulated by a deceased person is binding on the persons succeeding the deceased (Article 8(2) ALI), unless the opposite is expressly agreed when stipulating the arbitration agreement;
(c) Where any creditor's rights or debts are assigned or transferred, in their entirety or partially, the arbitration agreements related to such rights or debts are binding on the assignee or transferee, unless:
    (i) The parties have expressly agreed to the contrary;
    (ii) The assignee or transferee has clearly objected to the arbitration agreement;
    (iii) When agreeing to the assignment or transfer of the relevant rights or debts, the assignee or transferee was clearly unaware of the existence of an arbitration agreement separate from the main contract (Article 9 ALI).
(d) Where a legal entity changes its name or legal form, the legal entity resulting therefrom shall be bound by the arbitration agreements entered into by its predecessor.

2.5 The Choice of Arbitrators

The PRC Arbitration Law theoretically emphasizes the *free will of the parties* as to every aspect of the conduct of arbitration. Parties to the agreement are free to choose arbitration as a method of dispute resolution (Article 4 AL), to choose the arbitration institution (Article 6 AL), as well as arbitrators (Article 31 AL). However, in practice, this principle suffers a number of limitations.

(a) No recognition of ad hoc arbitration
The parties are not totally free to submit their disputes to any person, or group of persons, that they deem to be professional and trustworthy: it is required that arbitration in China is administered by a recognized arbitration institution (see § 2.2.1 (c)).

(b) Requirements of arbitrators
While in transnational practice a prospective arbitrator does not need to meet any particular requirements in order to be appointed as an arbitrator, Article 13 of the PRC Arbitration Law establishes some rather strict requirements. Chinese arbitration institutions can only appoint their arbitrators among "righteous and upright persons"; such persons, in addition, must possess one of the following qualifications:

(i) To have been engaged in arbitration activities for at least eight years;
(ii) To have worked as a lawyer for at least eight years;
(iii) To have served as a judge for at least eight years;
(iv) To have been engaged in legal research or legal education, possessing a senior professional title; or
(v) To have acquired knowledge of law, being engaged in the professional work in the field of economy and trade or other related fields, possessing a senior professional title or having an equivalent professional level.

(c) Panels of arbitrators
The names of the arbitrators of each institution are recorded in ad hoc registers; although the Arbitration Law does not expressly say so, it is commonly thought that the parties can choose arbitrators only among those included in the register of arbitrators of the relevant institution (the so-called *compulsory panel system*).
CIETAC, SHIAC and SCIA are all exceptions to this rule: the arbitrators for proceedings to be held at these institutions can be chosen among persons not included in the panels of arbitrators. Article 26 of the CIETAC Arbitration Rules provides that previous approval by the Chairman of the institution is needed in order to appoint an arbitrator from outside the panel of arbitrators; Article 21 of the SHIAC Arbitration Rules and Article 28 of the SCIA Arbitration Rules further specify that the arbitrators must in any case meet the requirements set forth by the law (see point b of this paragraph). Article 18 of the BAC Arbitration Rules, on the other hand, maintains a more restrictive

approach and does not make any provision as to the appointment of arbitrators from outside the official panel.

Given these requirements, it is usually not possible to appoint arbitrators that are technical specialists in a given field as the rules dictate the individual must have an expertise in law or economics. However, given the abundance of arbitrators listed in the panels of the main arbitration institutions—over one thousand for CIETAC; around eight hundred for SHIAC; around five hundred for SCIA and BAC—, in most cases it is possible to choose an arbitrator having some experience in cases regarding a certain technical topic.

Note also that neither the Arbitration Law nor the rules of the premier arbitration institutions contain any restrictions as to the nationality of arbitrators. After the application for arbitration, when the arbitration tribunal is formed, there will be an option between a three-arbitrator tribunal and a sole-arbitrator tribunal. If the tribunal is composed of three arbitrators, each party will select one and the remaining one will be chosen jointly by the parties or appointed by the Chairman of the arbitration institution. If there is a sole arbitrator, he will be chosen jointly by the parties or appointed by the Chairman of the arbitration institution (see § 4.7).

Keeping in mind these rules, it is common practice to establish right away in the arbitration agreement:

(i) The number of arbitrators—one or three—forming the tribunal (if no choice is made, the tribunal will be composed of three arbitrators);
(ii) The nationality of the arbitrator to be chosen jointly by the parties or appointed by the Chairman of the arbitration institution.

With regards to the second point, making a selection of this nature is imperative for foreign business operators given that when parties cannot agree, the institution has an tendency to appoint Chinese arbitrators which may pose linguistic difficulties in certain cases.

2.6 The Choice of the Seat of Arbitration

The parties are free to choose the place where the arbitration will have its seat. In the absence of any express provision by the parties, the seat of arbitration will generally be the place where the arbitration institution has its seat: for example, Beijing for CIETAC (Article 7 of the Arbitration Rules) and BAC (Article 26), Shanghai for SHIAC (Article 7), Shenzhen for SCIA (Article 4). An arbitral award is deemed to have been made at the seat of arbitration determined pursuant to these rules; therefore, the concept of "seat of arbitration" governs such fundamental issues as the court having jurisdiction for any preservation measures (see § 4.5), and for an action to set aside the award (v. 4.1), etc.

2.7 The Choice of the Substantive Law Applicable to the Dispute

It is advisable to determine from the very beginning of a contractual relation the substantive law pursuant to which the arbitral tribunal will decide any disputes arising from the said relation, keeping in mind the following observations.

(a) Disputes not involving any foreign element
If there is no "foreign element" to the case (see the definition provided in § 1.3) Chinese law will be applicable without an option for the parties to choose an alternative.

(b) Disputes involving a foreign element
As for disputes involving one or more foreign elements, it is possible for the parties to choose the applicable law (Article 126 of the PRC Contract Law; Article 3 of the PRC Law on the Laws Applicable to Foreign-Related Civil Relations). Chinese law will govern the following situations, regardless of whether an alternative applicable law was indicated in the arbitration agreement:

(i) Contracts on the incorporation of a Sino-foreign Joint Venture (Article 126 of the PRC Contract Law);
(ii) Contracts on the exploration and exploitation of natural resources to be carried out in China (Article 126 of the PRC Contract Law);
(iii) Contracts on the transfer of shares in a Sino-foreign Joint Venture or in a Wholly Foreign-Owned Enterprise (Article 8, no. 4 of the *SPC Provisions on Some Issues concerning the Application of Law in Hearing Foreign-Related Contractual Dispute Cases Related to Civil and Commercial Matters* of 2007);
(iv) Contracts on the operation by a foreign person of a Sino-foreign Joint Venture (Article 8, no. 5 of said SPC Provisions);
(v) Contracts on the purchase by a foreign person of shares in a non-foreign-invested Chinese enterprise (Article 8, no. 6 of the SPC Provisions);
(vi) Contracts on the subscription by a foreign person of a capital increase in a non-foreign-invested Chinese Limited Liability Company or Company Limited by Shares (Article 8, no. 7 of the SPC Provisions);
(vii) Contracts on the purchase by a foreign person of assets of a non-foreign-invested Chinese enterprise (Article 8, no. 8 of the SPC Provisions);
(viii) Other contracts to which Chinese law mandatorily applies.

Where the parties do not expressly make a provision as to the law applicable to their contract, the provisions of the PRC Law on the Laws Applicable to Foreign-Related Civil Relations apply. This Law has a general nature and its provisions are superseded by any different special provision (Article 2). As a general principle, the "the law that is most closely connected with the foreign-related civil relation" shall apply to a foreign-related civil relation (Article 2): the various

Chapters of the Law specify this principle as to particular cases. Below is a non-exhaustive list of the main rules:

(i) Issues concerning the legal capacity, the capacity for civil conducts and the rights relating to personality of natural persons are decided according to the law of the place of habitual residence (Articles 11 and 12);
(ii) Issues concerning the legal capacity and the capacity for civil conducts of legal persons, as well as their organizational structure and shareholder rights, are generally governed by the law of the place of registration; however, the law of the principal place of business may be applicable where such place is different from the place of registration (Article 14);
(iii) Rights (*in rem)* in immovable property are regulated by the law of the place in which the property is situated (Article 36);
(iv) Rights (*in rem)* in movable property are regulated by the law of the place in which the property is located, at the moment of the relevant legal fact (Article 37); if the property is in transit, the law of the destination of transportation applies (Article 38);
(v) Contracts are generally governed by the law of the habitual residence of the party whose obligation is most characteristic of the contract or by the law presenting the closest connection with the contract (Article 41);
(vi) Employment contracts are governed by the law of the place in which the employee works or, if such place cannot be determined, by the law of the place where the employer has his main place of business (Article 43);
(vii) Issues regarding tortious liability are decided pursuant to the law of the place where the tortious act occurs; if the parties have common habitual residence, tortious liability is governed by the law of common habitual residence (Article 44);
(viii) Issues regarding product liability are generally governed by the law of the place of habitual residence of the victim (Article 45);
(ix) The content and ownership of intellectual property rights are governed by the law of the place where protection is applied for; the transfer and license of intellectual property rights are governed by the rule on contracts (see point (*v*); Article 49).

2.8 Arbitration *ex aequo et bono*

Arbitration can be conducted *ex aequo et bono*, i.e. it is governed by the principles of equity as opposed to the substantive laws of a jurisdiction; However, Chinese law does not provide for this possibility.

Pursuant to Article 7 AL, "disputes shall be resolved on the basis of facts, *in compliance with the law* and in an equitable and reasonable manner". Therefore, arbitration according to law seems to be the rule in China. This provision aims at protecting the legitimate rights and interests of the parties, in light of a developing arbitration culture in China.

As we shall see in chapter 5, Chinese arbitration law contains the following distinction:

- Awards resulting from domestic arbitration can be refused enforcement on the grounds of violation of law;
- Awards deriving from foreign-related arbitration cannot be refused enforcement on such grounds. This may then indicate that in practice an award in equity is more easily admissible for foreign-related disputes than for domestic disputes.

To summarise this point; arbitration can be conducted in equity, as long as: (i) the parties have so consented expressly and in writing and (ii) the award does not run counter to mandatory law provisions and to public policy (Article 69(3) BAC; Article 56 of the Rules for Arbitration in the Shanghai FTZ).

2.9 The Choice of the Language of Arbitration Proceedings

The parties to the arbitration agreement are generally free to choose the language of the proceedings; absent any choice by the parties, the proceedings are conducted in Chinese (Article 81 of the CIETAC Rules; Article 60 of the SHIAC Rules; Article 6 of the SCIA Rules). Article 72 of the BAC Rules contains a slight variation: absent any choice of the parties as to the language of proceedings, the proceedings are conducted in Chinese and/or in any other language or languages chosen by the arbitral institution or by the arbitral tribunal.

Chapter 3
Jurisdiction

Given that arbitral jurisdiction has its roots in the arbitration agreement (see § 2.1), to decide on arbitral jurisdiction essentially means to determine:

- Whether or not there is a (valid) arbitration agreement, according to the criteria described in § 2.2, which implies the need to keep in mind the possibility of an objection to jurisdiction when drafting the arbitration agreement;
- Whether or not the parties to the dispute being submitted to arbitration are actually bound by the arbitration agreement (see § 2.4).

The standard transnational practice here is characterized by the *principle of competence-competence*; deciding on jurisdiction is first of all the prerogative of the arbitral tribunal. In most legal systems, the decision made by the arbitral tribunal as to the jurisdiction can be subject to judicial control. In these instances, such judicial control is exercised before the issuing of an arbitral award, with the party objecting to the arbitral jurisdiction applying directly to the courts for a ruling as to this point (*concurrent control*). Generally the arbitral tribunal can continue its proceedings without having to stay them, even when an objection to its jurisdiction has been raised with a court. In certain other systems, judicial control on the jurisdiction of arbitrators can only be carried out after an award on jurisdiction has been rendered (*negative effect of competence-competence*).

The Chinese provisions on this matter differ greatly from the standard practice elsewhere. First of all, the power to decide arbitral jurisdiction is attributed to both the *arbitral institution* (not the tribunal itself) and to the People's Courts (Article 20, AL). More precisely, the Arbitration Rules of the main Chinese arbitration institutions provide that the institution can authorize the arbitral tribunal to determine jurisdiction as it sees fit (per Article 6(1) CIETAC Rules; Article 6(1) of the SHIAC Rules; Articles 11(2) and 12 of the SCIA Rules; Article 6(4) of the BAC Rules).

However, there is a certain cautiousness in the application of these provisions as they may be seen as conflicting with Article 20 AL. It is also worth noting that none of these provisions specify when it is "necessary" to authorize the arbitral tribunal

G. Pisacane et al., *Arbitration in China*,
China Law, Tax & Accounting, DOI 10.1007/978-981-10-0684-5_3

to decide on jurisdiction. Therefore, it is not advised to rely too certainly on these provisions when formulating one's arbitration strategy.

The party objecting to the jurisdiction of the arbitral tribunal can therefore choose to raise its objection with either the arbitral institution or the People's Court. Where the matter is referred to both the arbitral institution and the court, the latter shall give a ruling (Article 20 AL). When the People's Court accepts the case, it should inform the concerned arbitral institution, so as to enable it to stay its proceedings (*SPC Reply on Several Questions Regarding the Determination of the Validity of Arbitration Agreements* of 1998).

A People's Court, however, cannot accept the case when:

(i) The objection to jurisdiction has been raised after the first hearing of the arbitral tribunal has begun (Article 20 AL) ; or
(ii) The arbitral institution has already made a decision as to jurisdiction (Article 13 ALI, according to which, in addition, a People's Court shall not accept an application to set aside the decision made by an arbitral institution as to jurisdiction).

The obvious concern for a foreign operator involved in a dispute in China is that a People's Court will carry out their examination in an excessively strict manner. This could call into question the validity of the arbitration agreement, as well as the scope of its binding force. Alternatively the court could give itself jurisdiction over the case, which would further frustrate the agreement, and in doing so, deprive the operator of the advantages of arbitration (see § 1.1). Regardless of the final decision of the People's Court on who has jurisdiction over the case, proceedings might be initiated with the court with the only objective of taking advantage of the stay of arbitral proceedings. This may provide opportunity for the other party to implement measures aimed at making a prospective award impossible to enforce (for example, transfer of assets and funds; bankruptcy; etc.).

Chapter 4
Procedural Rules of Arbitration

4.1 Sources Governing Arbitration Procedure

The foundations of arbitration procedure in China are set out by the Arbitration Law, which applies to all categories of arbitration, be it domestic, foreign-related or foreign. The Arbitration Rules of each arbitration institution contain more detailed provisions but they still must operate within the confines of the statutory provisions.

The PRC Civil Procedure Law dedicates to foreign-related arbitration a chapter—Chapter 26—, as well as two provisions—Article 224 and Article 237—not included in that Chapter. Most of these provisions actually concern the action of the People's Courts (enforcement of awards and granting of interim measures); only two articles, 271 and 273, deal with the delimitation and the coordination of judicial lawsuits and arbitration proceedings. Therefore, the reality of the situation is that the Civil Procedure Law does not regulate arbitration procedure.

From another point of view, although the discipline of arbitration proceedings is autonomous and clearly distinguished from civil procedure, it must be borne in mind that the former are administered by a Chinese institution and, therefore, are inevitably exposed to the "environmental" influence of the latter.

In practice, arbitration proceedings are generally less cumbersome and more predictable than an action within the People's Courts. However, choosing to arbitrate does not then provide for the application of procedural rules identical to those of a foreign operator's home jurisdiction as one might expect.

The most remarkable features of Chinese arbitration procedural rules will be pointed out where relevant in the course of this chapter.

G. Pisacane et al., *Arbitration in China*,
China Law, Tax & Accounting, DOI 10.1007/978-981-10-0684-5_4

4.2 Application for Arbitration

By applying for arbitration, a party submits a dispute or a claim to arbitration, subject to the terms of the arbitration agreement. The application for arbitration must be submitted to the arbitration institution designated in the arbitration agreement. The arbitration proceedings will then start from the day of submission (see Article 11 CIETAC; Article 10 SHIAC; Article 14 SCIA). Differently, proceedings under BAC are deemed to commence on the day of acceptance of the case by the institution (Article 8(3) BAC).

An application for arbitration must set out the details of the claimant and of the respondent, the arbitration claims with the relevant facts and reasons. The relevant evidence, as well as a copy of the arbitration agreement, must be attached to the application (Article 23 AL; Article 12(1–2) CIETAC; Article 11(1–2) SHIAC; Article 15 SCIA; Article 7(1) BAC). When applying for arbitration the claimant must also deposit an advance on arbitration fees (Article 12(3) CIETAC; Article 11 (3) SHIAC; Article 21 SCIA; Article 7(2–3) BAC).

4.3 Acceptance of the Application for Arbitration (Articles 24–25 AL; Articles 13 and 15 CIETAC; Article 12 SHIAC; Article 17 SCIA; Articles 8–9 BAC)

If the application is found to be formally correct and the case is accepted, then the arbitral institution will notify both parties of this acceptance (this is called "Notice of Acceptance"/"Notice of Arbitration" depending on the institution). The institution will serve both claimant and respondent a copy of the application for arbitration and its related attachments. The BAC Regulation further states that the institution sends to the respondent a specific "Request for Submission of Defence".

On the other hand, if the situation arises where the arbitration institution finds the application to be formally incorrect or incomplete, it will request the applicant to complete or correct it within a set time. If the mistakes and/or gaps in the application are not rectified within this time, then the application will be treated as though it was never submitted. Under the Arbitration Rules of CIETAC (Article 13 (4)), SHIAC (Article 12(3)) and BAC (Article 1(4)), the arbitration institution, after accepting the case, appoints one or more members of its personnel to take charge of the administrative and procedural matters related to the case.

4.4 Statement of Defence and Counterclaims

The respondent, upon receiving the application for arbitration, must submit a written statement of defense, as well as any counterclaims, within the time limit specified in the relevant arbitration rules (Articles 25(2) and 27 AL).

The time limit is calculated starting from the day in which the respondent receives the notice of arbitration or, in the case of BAC, the request for submission of defense. The limits are as follows:

- 45 days for CIETAC (Articles 15–16)
- 45 days for SHIAC (Articles 13–14)
- 30 days for SCIA (Articles 18–19)
- 15 days for BAC (Article 10–11)

The deadline for submission of the statement of defense can be deferred upon the respondent's request and if justified reasons are provided. However, the arbitral tribunal can accept statements of defense and counterclaims filed after the time limit has expired at its own discretion.

It is worth specifying that the statement of defense is the first and last opportunity for the respondent to object to the existence of an arbitration agreement. Where a party affirms the existence of an arbitration agreement and the other does not deny this during the exchange of the application for arbitration and in the statement of defense, *the agreement is deemed to be existing* (Article 5(2) CIETAC; Article 5(3) SHIAC; Article 9(2) SCIA; Article 4(3) BAC). If the respondent then submits counterclaims, he must pay an advance on the arbitration fees.

4.5 Representatives of the Parties for Arbitration Proceedings

The parties and their legal representatives can appoint one or more representatives for the handling of matters related to arbitration by forwarding to the arbitration institution the related Power of Attorney (Article 29 AL). The Arbitration Rules of CIETAC (Article 22), SHIAC (Article 17) and SCIA (Article 23) specify that the representatives *ad litem* can be foreign nationals, while the BAC Arbitration Rules (Article 17) do not expressly provide for this possibility. It is therefore advised to have joint counsel and defense consisting of Chinese and foreign lawyers so as to capitalize on the specific jurisdictional expertise of the former as well as the communication skills of the latter.

4.6 Interim Measures

A party may request the arbitral tribunal to adopt interim measures aimed at preserving property and evidence (Articles 28, 46, 68 AL). However, neither the arbitral tribunal nor the arbitral institution have the power to grant such measures: the arbitral tribunal must forward the request to the competent People's Court, which the only authority which can grant such requests (Article 28(2) AL; Article 272 CPL; Article 23 CIETAC; Article 18 SHIAC; Article 24 SCIA; Article 16 BAC).

Where the issue is property preservation, the appropriate court will be that of the place where the property is located or where the respondent is domiciled. For the preservation of evidence, the People's Court where the evidence is located has jurisdiction. One should keep in mind that it is generally not possible, under Chinese law, to obtain interim measures, which entail specific performance of a contract or cease and desist orders.

4.7 Formation of the Arbitral Tribunal (Articles 30–33 AL; Articles 24–31 CIETAC; Articles 19–25 SHIAC; Articles 26–31 SCIA; Articles 18–20 BAC)

As mentioned above, an arbitral tribunal is composed of one or three arbitrators; if the parties have not formulated any provision as to this point, the arbitral tribunal is composed of three arbitrators.

Where the parties have opted for a sole arbitrator, the arbitrator is jointly selected by the parties or is appointed by the Chairman of the arbitral institution (if he is entrusted for this purpose by the parties). Where the tribunal is to be composed of three arbitrators, each party selects one. The third individual is then jointly selected by the parties or appointed by the Chairman of the arbitral institution.

Arbitrators can be chosen, first of all, from the panels provided by the arbitral institution. The arbitrators' registers of CIETAC, SHIAC, SCIA and BAC include a large number of non-Chinese arbitrators, as well as Chinese arbitrators who are fluent in one or more foreign languages. There is also an option to choose arbitrators outside the panels, under the conditions described in § 2.5, (c).

The parties must select arbitrators, or entrust the arbitral institution to appoint arbitrators, within a certain time limit; the Arbitration Rules of CIETAC, SHIAC, SCIA and BAC all set this term at 15 days from receipt of the Notice of Arbitration (see § 4.3). If the parties fail to comply with this time limit, the Chairman of the arbitration institution will appoint the relevant arbitrators.

Once the arbitral tribunal has been formed, the arbitral institution sends a notification thereof to both parties. Until the arbitral tribunal has been formed (pursuant to the rules described above), all the procedural actions that should be taken by it are carried out by an organ of the arbitration institution: the Arbitration Court for CIETAC, the Secretariat for SHIAC, the Secretary General for SCIA and the Board for BAC. For example, the decision to postpone the time limit for submission of the Statement of Defense or of counterclaims (see § 4.4) and the actions related to the granting of interim measures (see § 4.6).

4.8 Withdrawal of Arbitrators and Challenge to Arbitrators

4.8.1 Provisions of the Arbitration Law (Articles 34–37)

An arbitrator has an obligation to withdraw—and the parties have a right to challenge him—in any of the following circumstances:

(i) The arbitrator is a party in the case or a close relative of a party or of an agent in the case;
(ii) The arbitrator has a personal interest in the case;
(iii) The arbitrator has other relationship with a party or his agent in the case which may affect the impartiality of the arbitration;
(iv) The arbitrator has privately met with a party or agent or accepted an invitation to entertainment or gift from a party or agent (Article 34 AL).

Any challenge to an arbitrator must be submitted before the first hearing of the arbitral tribunal. The Chairman of the arbitration institution will decide the outcome of the challenge or, if he is an arbitrator in the same case, the Board of the institution will.

4.8.2 Provisions of Arbitration Rules (Articles 31–33 CIETAC; Articles 25–27 SHIAC; Articles 31–33 SCIA; Articles 21–23 BAC)

Each arbitrator, upon appointment, must issue a declaration disclosing any circumstances that might raise doubts as to his independence and impartiality. The parties may challenge an arbitrator:

- Based on the circumstances disclosed by the arbitrator in the said declaration, within 10 days from receiving it;
- Based on other reasonable doubts as to the independence and impartiality of the arbitrator, within 15 days from receiving the notice of formation of the arbitral tribunal (or, if the party found out a reason for challenging an arbitrator after that notice, within 15 days from the day when the party found out such reason, but in any case not after the end of the last hearing of the arbitral tribunal).

The Chairman of the arbitration institution decides on the challenge; however, where the challenged arbitrator voluntarily withdraws from his position, or the other party agrees with the challenge, the concerned arbitrator ceases to be a member of the arbitral tribunal with no need for a decision by the Chairman. The arbitrator who has withdrawn or has been successfully challenged, or that cannot, for any other reason, perform his functions, is substituted by a new arbitrator, selected or appointed pursuant to the same rules followed for his selection or appointment.

4.9 Hearings (Articles 39–48 AL; Articles 35–47 CIETAC; Articles 29–43 SHIAC; Articles 34–47 SCIA; Articles 24–30 BAC)

Arbitration proceedings are generally conducted orally, through hearings; however, the parties may agree to have them conducted in written form. There are no public hearings; therefore, the whole arbitration is carried out in camera, unless there is an express and joint request by the parties for an alternative arrangement. For the substantive law applicable to the dispute, see § 2.7; for the language of proceedings, see § 2.9.

4.10 Multi-party Arbitration

Just like a civil trial, arbitration proceedings can involve more than two parties. In the majority of cases this would be when from the very beginning of the arbitration there are more than one claimant or more than one respondent. Obviously, when this is the case, there must be an arbitration agreement binding all the parties involved.

Secondly, multi-party arbitration can be the result of the joinder of an additional party in an arbitration that originally involved only one claimant and one respondent. The arbitral tribunal, upon evaluating the necessity of the joinder, decides whether or not to approve it. For the details of the discipline, we refer the reader to the arbitration rules of each institution (Article 18 CIETAC; Article 31 SHIAC; Article 35 SCIA; Article 13 BAC). The CIETAC and BAC Rules only make a reference to the joinder requested by one of the original parties to arbitration proceedings; the SHIAC and SCIA Rules also take into account the joinder requested *motu proprio* by the additional party. Generally, when the additional party is bound by the arbitral agreement—see, e.g., the indications set forth in § 2.4—, then it will not be necessary to obtain such third party's consent to the joinder; on the other hand, where the third party is not a party to the arbitral agreement, his express written consent will need to be presented as evidence of his intent to be bound by the arbitration agreement.

Multi-party arbitration entails the application of particular rules as to the formation of the arbitral tribunal (Article 29 is CIETAC; Article 24 SHIAC; Article 16 SCIA; Article 19.6 BAC). The basic principle is the application of the rules described in § 4.7, with each side of arbitration—claimant side and respondent side—collectively counting as one subject. Where one side of the arbitration cannot come to a consensus on the selection of an arbitrator, the deadlock will be solved by the arbitration institution.

4.11 Evidence

As a rule, the interested party must provide evidence. However, the arbitral tribunal can gather evidence of its own accord when it deems it necessary. Technical advice can also be requested where appropriate, in order to solve technical issues. (Articles 43–44 AL; Articles 41–44 CIETAC; Articles 37–39 SHIAC; Articles 41–44 SCIA; Articles 32–37 BAC).

Arbitration proceedings carried out in China, in a similar fashion to Chinese judicial proceedings, are generally characterized by a greater preference for written evidence and a relatively low degree of familiarity with oral evidence. Furthermore, there are rather stringent rules as to the authentication and translation of documents, applying both to documents used as evidence and to other written documents. These prerequisites are subject to variations according to the kind of claim, to the type of evidence and, in some cases, even according to the arbitrator handling the case.

The following observations can be of some use:

- The People's Republic of China is not a party to the Convention of The Hague Abolishing the Requirement of Legalization for Foreign Public Documents of 1961; therefore, the so-called *apostille* is not valid in China.
- In general, powers of attorney signed abroad by a foreign person must be notarized and legalized by the competent Consulate of the People's Republic of China. All written evidence coming from abroad and using a foreign language must be notarized and translated into Chinese unless a different language for the arbitration has been selected.
- Documents proving the existence of a foreign legal person—mainly, incorporation or registration certificates—must be legalized. In this general situation, a remarkable albeit limited exception is given by the certificates of registration of trademarks issued by the competent foreign authorities, which are accepted in China with no need for legalization pursuant to Article 6-*quinquies* of the Paris Convention for the Protection of Industrial Property.

4.12 Default of the Parties (Art. 25, 42 AL; Art. 15, 39 CIETAC; Art. 13, 35 SHIAC; Art. 18, 39 SCIA)

If the respondent does not submit a Statement of Defence within the relevant time limit, this will not affect the proceedings. However, if a respondent does not appear at a hearing that has been notified to him, or he leaves a hearing before it is over (without the permission of the arbitral tribunal), then a default award may be given. When a claimant, without justified reason, does not appear at a hearing he has been notified of, or he leaves a hearing before it is over (without the permission of the arbitral tribunal), the application for arbitration is deemed revoked.

4.13 Withdrawal of the Application for Arbitration and Termination of Arbitration Proceedings; New Application for Arbitration (Art. 46 CIETAC; Art. 43 SHIAC; Art. 47 SCIA)

At any time either party is able to withdraw its claims and/or counterclaims. Where it becomes impossible to continue arbitration proceedings for a cause attributable to one of the parties, the arbitral tribunal may consider that such party has withdrawn its claims. When the claims of one party are wholly withdrawn, the arbitral tribunal can still render an award as to the other party's claims. Where all the claims and counterclaims of both parties are wholly withdrawn, the arbitral tribunal can terminate the proceedings.

Although neither the Arbitration Law nor the Arbitration Rules of the main arbitration institutions contain any specific provision on this point, it seems that the party having withdrawn the application for arbitration or having obtained in any other way the termination of arbitration proceedings can newly apply for arbitration against the same respondent and with the same claims. Article 50 AL, governing the withdrawal of the application for arbitration resulting from conciliation suggests that this is the case: where onc of the parties later repudiates conciliation, that party *may apply for arbitration again in accordance with the arbitration agreement*.

4.14 The Award (Articles 53–57 AL; Articles 48–55 CIETAC; Articles 44–51 SHIAC; Articles 50–56 SCIA; Articles 46–52 BAC)

Under CIETAC Arbitration Rules, the award must be rendered within 6 months from the formation of the arbitral tribunal, whilst under BAC Arbitration Rules it must be rendered within 4 months from such date. The Arbitration Rules of SHIAC and SCIA make a distinction between disputes involving foreign elements—including disputes involving Hong Kong, Macau and Taiwan—and disputes that do not involve foreign elements. For the former, the award must be rendered within 6 months of formation of the arbitral tribunal; for the latter, the time limit is reduced to 4 months. The award is effective starting from the date in which it is rendered, regardless of which time period is applicable. Arbitral awards are generally not appealable.

The arbitral award is made according to the opinion of the majority of arbitrators. If the arbitral tribunal does not succeed in forming a majority opinion, then the opinion of the presiding arbitrator will prevail. The award specifies the arbitration claims it refers to, the relevant facts, the reasons for the decision and the results of the award itself and the facts of the case. The reasons for the decision can be omitted where the parties jointly so request. Where certain facts come to light before others, the tribunal can render partial awards related to those facts.

4.15 Summary Procedure (Articles 56–64 CIETAC; Articles 52–59 SHIAC; Articles 57–64 SCIA; Articles 53–59 BAC)

Summary arbitration procedure applies, under CIETAC Arbitration Rules:

(i) To cases where the amount in dispute does not exceed RMB 5,000,000, unless otherwise agreed by the parties;
(ii) To cases where the amount in dispute exceeds RMB 5,000,000, but one party requests arbitration to be conducted with the summary procedure and the other party expressly consents in writing.

Equivalent rules apply under SHIAC, SCIA and BAC Arbitration rules, but the threshold is instead set at RMB 1,000,000.

Summary procedure at CIETAC, SHIAC and SCIA features the following main differences in comparison with the ordinary procedure:

(i) Unless the parties agree otherwise, the arbitral tribunal is composed of a sole arbitrator;
(ii) The arbitral tribunal decides whether or not to conduct the arbitration through hearings, considering the views expressed by the parties on this point;
(iii) The award is rendered within 3 months from the formation of the arbitral tribunal.

On the other hand, "expedited procedure" at BAC presents the following main features:

(i) As is the case with CIETAC, SHIAC and SCIA, unless the parties agree otherwise, the arbitral tribunal is composed of a sole arbitrator;
(ii) The award is rendered within 75 days from the formation of the arbitral tribunal;
(iii) A reduction of arbitration fees applies.

4.16 Combination of Arbitration with Conciliation or Mediation (Articles 49–52 AL; Article 47 CIETAC; Article 41 SHIAC; Articles 48–49 SCIA; Articles 42–43 BAC)

The arbitration law of the PRC, as well as the Rules of all the main arbitration institutions, contain provisions on combining arbitration with conciliation or mediation. As far as the English terminology goes, CIETAC Rules and BAC Rules mention "conciliation", while the Rules of SHIAC and SCIA make a reference to "mediation"; however, the Chinese versions of all these documents refer to 调解 (*tiáojiě*). Significantly, the Arbitration Law and the SCIA Rules use a different wording for settlement made autonomously by the parties (和解, *héjiě*) and settlement by the arbitral tribunal or by a mediation institution (调解, *tiáojiě*). For the sake of simplicity the following description will generically refer to "conciliation".

The basic prerequisite to start conciliation during the course of arbitration proceedings is the consent of both parties as to such choice.

Conciliation can be conducted by the arbitral tribunal or by the parties themselves. When the parties entrust the arbitral tribunal to settle their dispute, the tribunal carries out the relevant proceedings in the manner that it considers most appropriate.

The tribunal terminates conciliation proceedings and resumes arbitration proceedings in two cases:

(i) Either party so requests (i.e., case of subsequent lack of the consent of both parties to conciliation); or
(ii) The tribunal believes that further efforts to mediate will be futile.

On the other hand, where the parties do not wish to have conciliation proceedings carried out by the arbitral tribunal, they may proceed autonomously to conciliation. In this case, the CIETAC Rules provide that the CIETAC may assist them in the manner that it considers most appropriate.

If conciliation is successful, arbitration proceedings come to an end either by withdrawal of the parties' claims (see § 4.12) or by the arbitral tribunal rendering an award (or a conciliation statement) incorporating the terms of the settlement. More specifically, where the parties have reached conciliation by themselves, they may request the arbitral tribunal to render an award incorporating the terms of their agreement or, if an arbitral tribunal has not yet been formed, they may request the arbitration institution to form an arbitral award in order to render such an award. Both ways of terminating conciliation/arbitration tend to ensure that the parties will respect the outcome of proceedings. For the same purpose, under the Arbitration Rules of CIETAC and SHIAC, where conciliation is successful, the parties are under an obligation to sign a written settlement agreement.

If conciliation fails, the arbitral tribunal resumes arbitration proceedings, up to the rendering of an arbitral award. Any opinion, view, statement or proposal expressed by either party during conciliation proceedings cannot be subsequently used when arbitration is resumed as grounds for any claim, defense or counterclaim. The spirit of this rule requires the parties to enter into conciliation with a genuine and sincere wish of settle their dispute and not with a view to disloyally collecting "trial weapons" against the other party.

Although only the BAC Arbitration Rules explicitly say so, it is to be considered as a general rule that any additional costs resulting from conciliation/arbitration, as opposed to "pure" arbitration, are to be borne by the parties.

4.17 Arbitration Under the SHIAC Shanghai Pilot Free Trade Zone Arbitration Rules

The Shanghai Pilot Free Trade Zone, established in September 2013, features, in comparison to the overall Chinese system, more flexibility with regards to some topics which are crucial for foreign trade, exchange and investment.

In 2013 SHIAC, with a view of administrating arbitrations for disputes related to the Free Trade Zone, established the Free Trade Zone Court of Arbitration. Following this, it issued the China (Shanghai) Pilot Free Trade Zone Arbitration Rules, which introduce specific procedural rules for arbitration conducted by SHIAC in the FTZ.

In particular, an emergency procedure is foreseen for interim measures requested between the acceptance of the case by the court and the formation of the arbitral tribunal (Article 21 FTZ Regulations). The interested party can request the formation of an emergency tribunal composed by one arbitrator, to be appointed by SHIAC, who can order interim measures binding on the parties. The FTZ Rules provide for a summary procedure (Articles 63–70) and a procedure for small claims (Articles 71–78); a mixed mediation-arbitration procedure is also contemplated (Articles 50–53).

The parties can also decide to submit to arbitration, under the FTZ Rules, cases having no factual relation with the Free Trade Zone (Article 3). Submitting a dispute to arbitration under the FTZ Rules is even more advantageous if one considers the judicial treatment of the awards resulting therefrom. As a matter of fact, quite significantly, the Shanghai No. 2 Intermediate People's Court, competent for the judicial review of the arbitration awards issued by SHIAC, followed up on the publication of the FTZ Arbitration Rules by issuing two documents: the *Shanghai No. 2 Intermediate People's Court Opinions on Judicial Review and Enforcement of Arbitration Cases Applying China (Shanghai) Pilot Free Trade Zone Arbitration Rules* and the *Shanghai No. 2 Intermediate People's Court Interpretation of the Opinions on Judicial Review and Enforcement of Arbitration Cases Applying the China (Shanghai) Pilot Free Trade Zone Arbitration Rules*.

Under Article 7 of the *Opinions*, when a party applies for a ruling on the validity of an arbitration agreement submitting disputes to the FTZ Arbitration Rules or for setting aside of an award rendered under said Rules, normally the Intermediate People's Court consults with the parties within 15 days from the filing of the case and passes a ruling within one month from the same date (instead of within two months, as set forth by Article 60 AL).

Article 8 of the *Opinions* provides for an expedited schedule for small claims. In urgent cases, a decision as to property preservation measures is issued by the Intermediate Tribunal within 24 hours—and not 48 hours as before—upon payment of a deposit by the party requesting them (Article 6 of the *Opinions*). The Tribunal will examine an application for enforcement of an arbitral award issued under the FTZ Regulations on the same day on which it is filed. Where the property of the involved goods is made clear by the evidence presented by the parties, the necessary investigations must start within 24 hours (Article 15 of the *Opinions*).

4.18 Costs of Proceedings and Trial Expenses

4.18.1 Arbitration Fees

Arbitration fees are calculated in relation to the amount in dispute. Where, during the proceedings, the real disputed amount is ascertained results to be different from the amount initially indicated by the parties, the real disputed amount is taken into account for the purpose of determining the fees. Arbitration fees are calculated according to a bracket system: the following chart shows the admission fees and procedure fees applied by CIETAC, SHIAC and SCIA as of January, 2015.

Disputed amount (RMB)	*CIETAC*				*SHIAC/SCIA*			
	Domestic dispute		Dispute involving foreign elements		Domestic dispute		Dispute involving foreign elements	
	Adm. fee	Proced. fee	Adm. fee	Proced. fee	Adm. fee	Proced. fee	Adm. fee	Proced. fee
500.000	13.550	12.000	10.000	20.000	13.550	11.000	10.000	17.500
1.000.000	18.550	19.500	10.000	40.000	18.550	18.500	10.000	35.000
5.000.000	38.550	38.000	10.000	150.000	38.550	37.500	10.000	135.000
10.000.000	63.550	58.000	10.000	225.000	63.550	58.000	10.000	210.000
50.000.000	263.550	143.000	10.000	625.000	263.550	143.000	10.000	610.000
100.000.000	513.550	218.000	10.000	875.000	513.550	218.000	10.000	860.000

4.18.2 Trial Expenses and Allocation of Arbitration Fees (Article 52 CIETAC; Article 47 SHIAC; Article 66 SCIA; Article 51 BAC)

In the Chinese legal system, generally, the losing party is not condemned to the payment of trial expenses: trial expenses are in principle to be borne by the party that has incurred them, regardless of the result of the case. Consequently, the Arbitration Law does not set out any provision on this point.

The rules of the main arbitration institutions are a significant exception in this context. Pursuant to the Arbitration Rules of CIETAC and SHIAC, the arbitral tribunal can give a discretionary award whereby the losing party shall pay to the other party the "reasonable expenses" incurred for the arbitration. The actual award will be context specific and will turn on the facts of the given case.

SCIA Arbitration Rules provide that trial expenses and arbitration fees are borne, in principle, by the losing party. However, the arbitral tribunal, after considering the specific circumstances of the case, can decide to apportion such expenses and fees between the parties. Under BAC Arbitration Rules, arbitration fees are borne in principle by the losing party, but the tribunal can decide to apportion them between the parties. With regards to trial expenses, the tribunal can decide in the award that the losing party shall pay reasonable expenses to the winning party.

Chapter 5
Recognition and Enforcement of the Arbitral Award

An arbitral award is final and is not subject to appeal (Article 9(1) AL); parties are under an obligation to spontaneously comply with it (Article 62 AL). However, the losing party might disregard this obligation. This Chapter deals with the cases in which the losing party does not spontaneously comply with the arbitral award, and discusses: (i) the action for the setting aside of the award, weapon of the losing party, and (ii) the action for recognition and enforcement of the award, weapon of the winning party.

5.1 Application for Setting Aside of the Award

By applying to have the award set aside, the interested party requests a judge to annul the award. The application is filed with the judiciary of the country in which the arbitral award has been rendered; this distinguishes the action for setting aside of the award from the action for recognition and enforcement of the award, which is necessarily brought before the judiciary of the country in which enforcement is sought.

The application for setting aside an award must be filed within 6 months from the date in which the award has been notified to the interested party (Article 59 AL) at the Intermediate People's Court of the place in which the relevant arbitration institution has its seat (Article 58(1) AL).

For an award resulting from domestic arbitration, the grounds for setting aside are set out in Article 58 of the Arbitration Law; for awards resulting from foreign-related arbitration, the grounds for setting aside are set out in Article 274 of the Civil Procedure Law.

It should be noted that when the grounds for the setting aside of an award are found to be present, a Chinese judge *must* set aside the award (Article 58(2) AL). This feature distinguishes Chinese arbitration law from international practice, where

G. Pisacane et al., *Arbitration in China*,
China Law, Tax & Accounting, DOI 10.1007/978-981-10-0684-5_5

the judge, upon finding that grounds for the setting aside of an arbitral award are present, usually has the *power*, but not an *obligation*, to set it aside.

5.1.1 *Awards Resulting from Domestic Arbitration*

An award resulting from domestic arbitration must be set aside when one of the following circumstances is present (Article 58(1) AL):

(i) There is no [valid] arbitration agreement: the agreement must be deemed non-existent or invalid, or is not binding on one of the parties of the arbitration proceedings (see respectively § 2.2 and § 2.4);
(ii) The matters decided in the award exceed the scope of the arbitration agreement or are beyond the arbitral authority of the arbitration commission (so-called grounds of ultra vires);
(iii) The formation of the arbitration tribunal or the arbitration procedure was not in conformity with the statutory procedure;
(iv) The evidence on which the award is based was forged;
(v) The other party has withheld the evidence which is sufficient to affect the impartiality of the arbitration; or
(vi) The arbitrators have committed embezzlement, accepted bribes or committed malpractices for personal benefits or perverted the law in the arbitration of the case.

Claims on the grounds of points (iv), (v) and (vi) entail the re-examination of substantive issues such as evidence and the application of law. Note also that, pursuant to Article 58(3) AL, a People's Court must set aside an arbitration award if it "violates public interest".

5.1.2 *Awards Resulting from Foreign-Related Arbitration*

An award resulting from foreign-related arbitration must be set aside if one of the following circumstances is present (Article 274(1) CPL):

(i) The parties do not have an arbitration clause in the contract or have not subsequently reached a written arbitration agreement;
(ii) The party against whom the application for enforcement is made was not given notice for the appointment of an arbitrator or for the inception of the arbitration proceedings or was unable to present his case due to causes for which he is not responsible;
(iii) The composition of the arbitration tribunal or the procedure for arbitration was not in conformity with the rules of arbitration; or

(iv) The matters dealt with by the award fall outside the scope of the arbitration agreement or which the arbitral tribunal was not empowered to arbitrate on such matters.

Therefore, when deciding whether there are grounds for setting aside an award resulting from foreign-related arbitration, a judge *only reviews it as to its procedural aspects*: Article 274 CPL does not mention any circumstances regarding the merits of the awards. Much like domestic award, a People's Court must set aside a foreign-related arbitral award if its enforcement violates "the social and public interest [of the country]" (Article 274(2) CPL).

5.2 Application for Recognition and Enforcement of the Award

An application for recognition and enforcement of an arbitral award must be filed within 2 years from the time limit given to the losing party to perform the obligations established in the award. This should be filed with the Intermediate People's Court of the place where the party against which enforcement is sought has its domicile or of the place where the involved property is located (Article 224(2) CPL).

The party applying for enforcement must submit the original award and arbitration agreement or notarized copies thereof, as well as evidence supporting its claim.[1]

There are only limited grounds on which an award can be denied recognition, and therefore, enforcement. Article 237 CPL details these for cases of awards from domestic arbitration, whilst Article 274 CPL relates to foreign-related awards. Foreign awards are governed by the principle of reciprocity as well as international treaties signed by the People's Republic of China.

5.2.1 Awards Resulting from Domestic Arbitration (Article 237(2) CPL)

The People's Court responsible for enforcement can review the *merits* of the award. Enforcement must be denied—once again, this is not left to the judge's discretion—when one of the following circumstances is present:

(i) The parties have not stipulated an arbitration clause in the contract or have not subsequently reached a written arbitration agreement;

[1]Articles 20–21 of the *Regulations of the SPC on Certain Issues Concerning Enforcement by the People's Courts (for Trial Implementation)* of 1998.

(ii) The matters being arbitrated exceed the scope of the arbitration agreement or the authority of the arbitration agency (so-called grounds of ultra vires);
(iii) The formation of an arbitration tribunal or the procedure of arbitration is not in conformity with the legal procedure;
(iv) The evidence on which the arbitral award is based is falsified;
(v) The other party has concealed from the arbitral tribunal sufficient evidence to affect the impartiality of the arbitral award; or
(vi) The arbitrators have committed embezzlement, accepted bribes, practiced favouritism for personal advantages or twisted the law.

Moreover, a People's Court must deny enforcement of an arbitral award if such enforcement would "contradict the social and public interest" (Article 237(3) CPL).

5.2.2 Awards Resulting from Foreign-Related Arbitration (Art. 274 CPL)

The grounds for denying enforcement coincide with the grounds for the setting aside of the award (see § 5.1.2). The enforcement of arbitral awards takes on a peculiar nuance where the concerned party applies for enforcement in China only as a second recourse, after failing to obtain enforcement in a foreign country.

The Shanghai No. 1 Intermediate People's Court, in the *Retech case*, (decided on November 17, 2008), has addressed some aspects of this particular situation.[2] Notably, this case has been included as Case No. 37 in the eighth batch of *Guiding Cases* issued by the SPC on December 18, 2014,[3] which indicates that the reasoning in the case is looked upon favourably by China's highest jurisdiction.

According to the "Main Points of the Adjudication" published by the SPC, "*Where a party applies to a court of* [the People's Republic of] *China to enforce a foreign-related arbitral award that has come into legal effect and discovers that the party against whom the enforcement application is filed or its property is* [located] *within the territory of China, the PRC court thereupon has enforcement jurisdiction*

[2]*Shanghai Jwell Machinery Co., Ltd. v. Retech AG*, [2008] Hu Yi Zhong Zhi Zi No. 640-1, Shanghai No. 1 Intermediate People's Court, November 17, 2008.

[3]Starting in 2010, the Supreme People's Court has issued several batches of *Guiding Cases*, with the main purpose of increasing the quality and the uniformity of the judgments rendered by the People's Courts across China. As to the guiding value of these cases, it has been said that "[…] *the existing guiding cases are of 'quasi-compulsory enforcement power,' secondary to the "compulsory enforcement" of laws. In other words, they are* 'de facto *binding,' rather than 'de jure binding*" (Liao Wanchun of Guangdong High People's Court, as quoted in *Southern Weekly*, January 12, 2012, at http://www.infzm.com/content/67395).

The first batch of *Guiding Cases* was issued on November 26, 2010, upon publishing the *Provisions of the Supreme People's Court on Case Guidance*; the latest one was issued on April 15, 2015. As of May 18, 2015, the Chinese legal system can count with a total of 52 guiding cases, issued in ten batches.

over the case. The limitation period for a party to apply to a [PRC] *court for compulsory enforcement should be calculated from the date on which the party against whom the enforcement application is filed or its property is discovered to be* [located] *within the territory of China*".[4]

5.2.3 Foreign Awards

To our knowledge, as of today no foreign arbitral award has ever been enforced in China by invoking the *principle of reciprocity*. From a practical point of view, the enforcement of foreign awards is based only on the international treaties stipulated by the People's Republic of China, with the New York Convention of 1958 being the main treaty.

When acceding to the Convention, China made a *reciprocal reservation* (China only recognizes and enforces the awards rendered in other countries being parties to the Convention) and a *commercial reservation* (China only recognizes and enforces awards concerning disputes which would qualify as "commercial" under Chinese law).

Under Article V (1) of the New York Convention, enforcement of a foreign award *can*—but does not *have to*—be denied based on the following grounds, which must be raised by a party:

(i) Incapacity of a party to the arbitration agreement or invalidity of the said agreement;
(ii) The party against which enforcement is sought did not receive proper notice of the appointment of an arbitrator or of the arbitral proceedings, or was otherwise unable to take part in the proceedings for causes not attributable to it;
(iii) The arbitral tribunal dealt with a dispute not covered by the arbitration agreement or matters exceeding the scope of said agreement;
(iv) The arbitral tribunal was not formed in accordance with the agreement of the parties or, lacking such agreement, with the law of the country where the arbitration has taken place;
(v) The award has not yet become binding on the parties, or has been set aside or suspended by the competent authority of the country in which it has been rendered.

As to the circumstances set forth at point (iv), it is worth mentioning two rather curious rulings passed by the Intermediate People's Court of Chengdu (Sichuan) in 2008.

According to its common interpretation, the requirement that the arbitral tribunal should be formed in accordance with the parties' agreement—or, lacking an

[4]Translation by the *Stanford Law School China Guiding Cases Project*: http://cgc.law.stanford.edu/guiding-case-37/.

agreement by the parties, with the law of the country where arbitration takes place—refers to considerable deviations from the correct procedure. The circumstance to which the parties most commonly refer to when invoking this ground is the lack of compliance by the arbitrators with the arbitration agreement or the applicable law in deciding as to their own jurisdiction.

In *PepsiCo v. Sichuan Pepsi*[5] and *Pepsi China v. Sichuan Yun Lu*,[6] both decided on April 30, 2008, Chengdu IPC denied recognition and enforcement of two arbitral awards rendered in Sweden, motivating its decision as follows. Pursuant to the arbitration agreement, the parties, before applying for arbitration, must attempt to settle their dispute through negotiation. According to Chengdu IPC, *the evidence presented by PepsiCo and Pepsi China could not establish that they had issued any notice to resolve the dispute through consultation, nor that consultation had been carried out for the requisite number of days. The awards must accordingly be refused enforcement because the arbitral proceedings were not in accordance with the parties' agreement*. Scholars have noted that these rulings, being rather weak in their legal reasoning, may actually be guided by other interests.[7]

Under Article V (2) of the New York Convention, enforcement can be denied by the competent court of its own motion if: (i) the award regards matters that are not arbitrable under the law of the country in which enforcement is sought and (ii) the enforcement is deemed to be contrary to the public policy of that country.

The PRC Arbitration Law does not specify whether foreign awards resulting from ad hoc arbitration are recognizable in China (the Chinese legal system does not recognize ad hoc arbitration: see § 2.2.1 (c)); however, the People's Courts usually grant the *exequatur* to this kind of awards, in compliance with China's obligations under the New York Convention.

Although Hong Kong and Macau are not foreign countries, which makes it impossible to apply the New York Convention, a practically equivalent discipline is set forth, respectively, by the *Arrangement Concerning Mutual Enforcement of Arbitral Awards between the Mainland and the Hong Kong Special Administrative Region* of 2000 and by the *Arrangement Concerning Mutual Enforcement of Arbitral Awards between the Mainland and the Macau Special Administrative Region* of 2007.

The recognition of awards rendered in Taiwan is governed by the *SPC Provisions on the People's Courts' Recognition of Civil Judgments Made by Courts in the Taiwan Region* of 1998, which, however, only applies to the cases in which the permanent domicile or habitual residence of the person requesting enforcement, or the property concerned, are located in mainland China, Hong Kong or Macao.

[5] *PepsiCo Inc. v. Sichuan Pepsi-Cola Beverage Co., Ltd.*, [2008] Cheng Min Chu Zi No. 912 (Chengdu IPC, April 30, 2008).

[6] *PepsiCo Investment (China) Ltd. V. Sichuan Province Yun Lu Industrial Co., Ltd.*, [2008] Cheng Min Chu Zi No. 36 (Chengdu IPC, April 30, 2008).

[7] Kun Fan, *Arbitration in China: A Legal and Cultural Analysis*, Hart Publishing, 2013, pp. 107–108.

5.2.4 *Foreign Arbitral Awards Rendered in China*

Another issue concerns awards rendered within the territory of the People's Republic of China as a result of arbitration proceedings administered by a foreign arbitral institution (think of an arbitration clause providing for "arbitration in Beijing under the ICC Arbitration Rules").

According to some authors, "arbitration institutions" under the Arbitration Law cannot include foreign institutions. As we have seen in § 2.2.1, Article 16 AL, in its commonly accepted interpretation, requires the agreement by which the parties opt for arbitration in China to designate an arbitration institution.

When read in connection with Article 10 AL (*Arbitration commissions may be established in municipalities directly under the Central Government and in cities that are the seats of the people's governments of provinces or autonomous regions. They may also be established in other cities divided into districts, according to need. Arbitration commissions shall not be established at each level of the administrative divisions.* [...]), it seems to require the designation of a *Chinese* arbitration institution. It then follows that the agreement providing for arbitration in China under the rules of a foreign arbitration institution must be invalid. Besides that, as arbitration is a form of professional service, any foreign entity would need an ad hoc administrative authorization in order to conduct arbitration in China.

In the past it was extremely improbable, for an arbitral award rendered in China by a foreign institution, to obtain enforcement. The Supreme People's Court has repeatedly declined to validate this kind of arbitration agreement. In the *Züblin* case, the Court found an arbitration clause reading: "arbitration: ICC Rules, Shanghai shall apply" to be invalid for lack of designation of an arbitration institution pursuant to Article 16 AL.[8] Similarly, in 2006, Wuxi (Jiangsu) IPC refused enforcement of an arbitral award resulting from that arbitration clause under Article V (1) of the New York Convention, as the award was deemed to be affected by the invalidity of the said clause.[9]

In 2009 the Supreme People's Court, in *Xiaxin Electronics*, denied the validity of an arbitration agreement indicating ICC Rules as the applicable rules and Xiamen (Fujian) and Brussels as the seat of arbitration, as no arbitration institution was deemed to have been designated under Article 16 AL.[10]

In contrast with the stance taken by the Supreme People's Court in *Xiaxin Electronics*, the Intermediate People's Court of Ningbo (Zhejiang), in the *Duferco* case (2009), granted the enforcement of an award rendered in Beijing as a result of arbitration proceedings conducted under the ICC Rules.

---

[8] *Züblin International GmbH v. Wuxi Woco-Tongyong Rubber Engineering Co., Ltd.*, [2003] Min Si Ta Zi No. 23, Supreme People's Court, July 8, 2004.

[9] *Züblin International GmbH v. Wuxi Woco-Tongyong Rubber Engineering Co., Ltd.*, [2003] Xi Min San Zhong Zi n. 1, Wuxi IPC, July 19, 2006.

[10] *Xiaxin Electronics Co., Ltd. v.. Société de Production Belge AG*, Supreme People's Court [2009] Min Min Di Zi No. 7.

Significantly, the Supreme People's Court has avoided dealing with this issue in its Arbitration Law Interpretation of 2006. A very important development in this context, has been witnessed in the *Longlide* case, in which the SPC deemed an award rendered in Shanghai by the International Court of Arbitration of the International Chamber of Commerce to be valid under Article 16 AL and enforceable.

The concerned arbitration clause stated: "*Any dispute arising out of or in connection with this Agreement shall be submitted to ICCICA, with one or several arbitrators appointed according to the ICC Arbitration Rules, for arbitration pursuant to the ICC Arbitration Rules. The place of jurisdiction shall be Shanghai and the language shall be English*". The SPC expressed its view in a reply to a report made by the Anhui High People's Court under the so-called *Report System* (see § 5.4).[11]

This ruling definitely represents a remarkable step in the opening of the Chinese legal environment to foreign arbitration institutions. However, several issues remain to be addressed. For example, it is not yet clear whether an arbitration agreement rendered in China by a foreign arbitration institution should count as a domestic award or a foreign award and, therefore, whether it should be enforced under the PRC Civil Procedure Law or the New York Convention.

Another problematic point here is given by the procedural rules that have to be followed by the foreign arbitration institutions operating in China. Regardless of whether the law is interpreted as allowing foreign arbitration institutions to operate in China or not, some points of arbitration law were clearly drafted not taking into account the possibility of foreign institutions conducting arbitration in the PRC.

A prime example of this would be that to claim for an award rendered in China to be set aside, there must be a filing with the Intermediate People's Court of the place in which the relevant arbitration institution has its seat (Article 58(1) AL). If a foreign institution has made an award, then what is the appropriate location to file the claim to have the award set aside?

What court will be competent for setting aside an award issued under the auspices of a foreign institution, given that such institution has its seat outside of China?

Considering that the view expressed by the Supreme Court in the *Longlide* case (despite being authoritative) has no binding value in Chinese law, to subscribe a clause entailing arbitration in China by a foreign institution is not yet a full proof solution to the issues related to foreign awards.

[11] *Reply of the SPC regarding the Dispute on the Validity of an Arbitration Agreement between Anhui Longlide Packing and Printing Co., Ltd. and BP Agnati S.R.L.*, [2013] Min Si Ta Zi No. 13, 25 March 2013. The *Reply* was then published in the *Guide on Adjudication of Cases involving Commercial and Maritime Affairs*, Volume 26, 125–129.

5.3 Fraudulent Measures Put into Effect by the Losing Party in Order to Prevent the Enforcement of the Award

The following chapter will move away from the legal issues strictly pertaining to enforcement itself and instead look at some of the 'collateral' legal issues. In some instances, the losing party may implement fraudulent measures with a goal of preventing the enforcement of an award. This would usually entail getting rid of the company's assets, declaring bankruptcy etc., all whilst the arbitration proceedings are underway.

The attitude of the Chinese legal system towards this type of behaviour seems to have evolved in recent years.

The *Revpower* case is a well-known example of the use of such fraudulent measures. After obtaining an arbitral award against Chinese company SFAIC, in Stockholm, U.S. company Revpower applied for enforcement with the Shanghai No. 2 Intermediate People's Court. It took the court almost two years to decide on the enforcement as SFAIC had meanwhile challenged the arbitration tribunal's jurisdiction before the same court. When the Shanghai Intermediate People's Court eventually granted enforcement of the award,[12] approximately two and a half years had passed since the enforcement application. During this period, SFAIC had successfully applied for bankruptcy, making it impossible for Revpower to enforce the judgment. This case is not an anomaly with many other cases of this kind having taken place in China during the 90s.[13]

In this situation, an interesting development is seen in the *Cargill* case, decided in last instance by the Supreme People's Court on August 22, 2012.[14] Under a settlement agreement reached in 2005 during arbitration and incorporated in an award by the Federation of Oils, Seeds and Fats Associations, Fujian Jinshi Vegetable Oil Producing was obligated to pay a sum of USD 13 million to Cargill in a fixed number of instalments. Furthermore, it was under an obligation to mortgage all of its assets as a security for the payment of such debt. Since the losing party did not spontaneously implement the award, in 2006 Cargill applied for recognition and enforcement of the award; the following year, the Intermediate People's Court of Xiamen (Fujian) granted enforcement.

---

[12] *Revpower Ltd. (Hong Kong) v. Shanghai Far East Aerial Technology Import & Export Corp. (SFAIC)*, Shanghai No. 2 Intermediate People's Court, March 1, 1996.

[13] See, among other cases, *Norbok Cargo Transport Services Co. Ltd (Hong Kong) v. China Navigation Technology Consultation & Services Company (China)*, Beijing Intermediate People's Court, August 26, 1992; *Nautilus Transport & Trading Co., Ltd. (Hong Kong) v. China Jilin Province International Economic & Trade Development Corp. (China)*, Dalian Maritime Court, April 25, 1997.

[14] *Cargill International S.A. v. Fujian Jinshi Vegetable Oil Producing Co., Ltd.* et al., [2012] Min Si Zhong Zi No. 1, Supreme People's Court, August 22, 2012.

Meanwhile, Jinshi took a series of measures aimed at making the award ineffective. This essentially involved the transfer of all its assets to companies belonging to the same group (and controlled by members of the same family) for a price markedly lower than their real value. Cargill reacted by filing a lawsuit with the High People's Court of Fujian, in order to have the transfer agreements voided. Finally, in the judgment of last instance, the Supreme People's Court declared the mentioned agreements to be void and ordered the concerned property to be returned to Fujian Jinshi.

The case has been included in the eighth batch of *Guiding Cases*, issued by the SPC on December 18, 2014, as Case No. 33. The "Main Points of Adjudication" published by the SPC are as follows: "*1. Where a debtor transfers* [its] *principal property to an affiliate company at a clearly unreasonably low price and the affiliate company, with knowledge of the debtor's indebtedness, does not actually pay consideration* [for the principal property], [a court] *may determine that the debtor and its affiliate company have colluded in bad faith and have adversely affected the interests of* [the debtor's] *creditors.* [The court] *should then determine that the related property transfer contract is invalid.*

2. The provision of Article 59 of the Contract Law of the People's Republic of China is [also] *applicable to situations where a third party is the owner of the property* [covered by that provision]. *Where a creditor enjoys* [only] *an ordinary claim against a debtor,* [a court] *should, in accordance with the provision of Article 58 of the Contract Law of the People's Republic of China, order the property obtained through an invalid contract to be returned to the original owner of the property.* [The court] *cannot, based on the provision of Article 59, directly order that the debtor's property obtained by the debtor's affiliate company through a contract that is the result of "collusion in bad faith and that adversely affects the interests of a third party" be returned to a creditor.*[15]

5.4 Obligations of Intermediate People's Courts in the Case of Refusal of Enforcement of a Foreign or Foreign-Related Award: The So-called *Report System*

In order to combat the resistance of the Intermediate People's Courts with respect to the enforcement of arbitral awards ruling in favour of foreign parties, the Supreme People's Court established a report system in the 1990s. The resistance here partly stemmed from local protectionist attitudes.

[15] Translation provided by the *Stanford Law School China Guiding Cases Project*: http://cgc.law.stanford.edu/wp-content/uploads/2015/03/CGCP-English-Guiding-Case-33.pdf.

Under the *Report System*, if an Intermediate People's Court intends to refuse enforcement of a foreign award or of an award deriving from foreign-related arbitration, before ruling on the issue it must inform the High People's Court above it of the situation. If the High People's Court also finds that enforcement is not to be granted, it must refer the issue to the Supreme People's Court for approval. The Intermediate People's Court cannot refuse enforcement until the Supreme People's Court has given its approval.

It is arguable that the described system is transitional in nature. Undoubtedly, it fights the unwillingness of lower courts to grant the enforcement of awards ruling in favour of foreign parties not by tackling its actual causes, but simply by making denial of enforcement more cumbersome.

5.5 Coordination of Proceedings for Setting Aside an Award and Proceedings for its Enforcement

Chinese arbitration law mainly contains two provisions aimed at avoiding practical conflicts between judgments on the setting aside of awards and judgments on their enforcement.

Where one party applies for recognition and enforcement of an award and the other party applies for the setting aside of the same award, enforcement proceedings must be stayed until a ruling on the setting aside is passed (Article 64 AL). Moreover, the judge responsible for the enforcement cannot refuse such enforcement based on grounds that have been unsuccessfully invoked for the setting aside of the award (Article 26 ALI).

Chapter 6
A Recent Cause of Turmoil in the Landscape of Chinese Arbitration: The So-called "CIETAC Split"

Until the "CIETAC Split" in 2012, today's SHIAC and SCIA were the sub-commissions of CIETAC respectively in Shanghai and Shenzhen. CIETAC had other two sub-commissions, located in Tianjin and Chongqing, which did not split and therefore are still its sub-commissions as of today.

In May 2012, a series of internal tensions—including the issuance of new Arbitration Rules which strengthened the power of CIETAC Beijing in a way that the sub-commissions viewed as excessive—led to the Shanghai and Shenzhen sub-commissions "declaring independence" from CIETAC. The two former sub-commissions maintained their old names until October, 2012 and April 2013, when, respectively, CIETAC Shenzhen became SCIETAC (afterwards also SCIA) and CIETAC Shanghai became SHIAC. CIETAC Beijing issued a series of declarations contrasting the split and, after some time, established new sub-commissions in Shanghai and Shenzhen.

The CIETAC split caused a remarkable problem as to the interpretation of existing arbitration clauses designating "CIETAC Shanghai", "CIETAC Shenzhen" or using other similar expressions: after the split, should they be deemed to refer to SHIAC and SCIA—the entities originally referred to by the clause, now established as separate institutions—or to CIETAC Beijing (and its new Shanghai and Shenzhen sub-commissions), according to the letter of the clause?

Actual answers to this question came not so often from the involved arbitration institutions themselves—which were naturally inclined to assume jurisdiction over any case they were presented with, lest they deny their own legitimacy—, but rather from the action of the People's Courts deciding on arbitral jurisdiction and enforcing arbitral awards.

In practice, the party challenging the jurisdiction of a certain arbitral institution or the enforcement of its award could argue in two ways. First of all, the party claimed that the involved institution had no jurisdiction over the case, as it was not the one originally chosen by the parties; this objection, if successful, led to the competing arbitration institution being deemed as having jurisdiction (i.e., CIETAC

G. Pisacane et al., *Arbitration in China*,
China Law, Tax & Accounting, DOI 10.1007/978-981-10-0684-5_6

Beijing—or its Shanghai/Shenzhen sub-commission—instead of SHIAC/SCIA, or the other way around).

Secondly, the party could claim that the arbitration clause in question was invalid under Article 18 of the PRC Arbitration Law, as it did not clearly indicate an arbitration institution; this claim, if successful, led to the People's Court assuming jurisdiction over the case. In fact, one major consequence of the split was to potentially void all arbitration clauses making a reference to "CIETAC Shanghai/Shenzhen", or using similar expressions, by causing them to be unclear as to the designation of an arbitration institution.

The attitude of the People's Courts as to this point was initially uncertain. More than one piece of research has illustrated the back and forth of Chinese courts through of four cases.[1]

In *Hong Kong Jia v. Shenzhen Yong*,[2] Shenzhen Intermediate People's Court held that a clause referring to "CIETAC Shenzhen branch" actually referred to SCIA.

In *Jiangxi LDK v. Suzhou CSI*,[3] the clause under examination attributed jurisdiction to "CIETAC Shanghai". According to the Suzhou Intermediate People's Court, after the concerned arbitration institution changed its name from "CIETAC Shanghai" to "SHIAC", it was no longer to be considered the institution agreed upon by the parties before the split. In *Risen Energy v. Jiangxi LDK*,[4] Ningbo Intermediate People's Court refused to enforce an award rendered by the newly independent CIETAC Shanghai based on the same reasoning. Significantly, in both cases the High People's Courts of Jiangsu and Zhejiang Provinces ordered the Intermediate People's Courts to review their decision in these cases.

In *Jiangxi LDK v. Zhejiang Kingdom*,[5] the Taizhou (Zhejiang) Intermediate People's Court held that CIETAC Shanghai (then SHIAC) had jurisdiction in a case in which the arbitration clause designated "CIETAC Shanghai branch".

Finally, in September 2013, the Supreme People's Court intervened in the matter, issuing a document bearing the title *Notice on Certain Issues Relating to*

[1]See, for example, TAO Jingzhou, M. ZHONG, "Picking the Right Arbitration Institution in China", in *China Law & Practice*, September/October 2014, 28–30; J. D'AGOSTINO, J. BOOTH, T. WU, "The Aftermath of the CIETAC Split: two years on, lower courts take clashing views on arbitration agreements and awards– but higher courts strive for consistency", published May 2, 2014 in *Kluwer Arbitration Blog*: http://kluwerarbitrationblog.com/blog/2014/05/02/the-aftermath-of-the-cietac-split-two-years-on-lower-courts-take-clashing-views-on-arbitration-agreements-and-awards-but-higher-courts-strive-for-consistency/.

[2]*Hong Kong Jia Development Co. v. Shenzhen Yong Co.*, [2012] Shen Zhong Fa She Wai Zhong Zi No. 226, Shenzhen Intermediate People's Court, November 20, 2012.

[3]*Jiangxi LDK Solar Hi-tech v. Suzhou CSI Technology*, [2013] Su Zhong Shang Zhong Shen Zi No. 0004, Suzhou Intermediate People's Court, May 7, 2013.

[4]*Risen Energy v. Jiangxi LDK Solar Hi-tech*, [2013] Zhe Yong Zhi Cai Zi No. 1, Ningbo Intermediate People's Court, May 22, 2013; *Risen Energy v Jiangxi LDK Solar Hi-tech*, [2013] Zhe Yong Jian Zi No. 1, Ningbo Intermediate People's Court, July 25, 2013.

[5]*Jiangxi LDK Solar Hi-tech v. Zhejiang Kingdom Solar Energy Technic*, [2013] Zhe Tai Zhi Cai Zi No.2, Taizhou (Zhejiang) Intermediate People's Court, July 29, 2013.

Correct Handling of Judicial Review of Arbitration Matters. The *Notice* established a particular report system: whenever a case features issues related to the CIETAC split, the court has to report it, level by level, up to the Supreme People's Court. This provision resembles the general *Report System* established by the SPC (see § 5.4), the notable difference being that, while in the latter an obligation to report only exists if the involved court intends to deny enforcement, here the obligation exists regardless of the predicted outcome of the case.

Towards the end of 2014, CIETAC made an attempt to clarify the issue—and to claim jurisdiction over all the cases involving ambiguous arbitration clauses—in the drafting of its new Arbitration Rules, which entered into force on January 1, 2015. Under Article 2(6) of the new Rules, "[…] *Where the parties have agreed to arbitration by a sub-commission/arbitration center, the arbitration court of the sub-commission/arbitration center agreed upon by the parties shall accept the arbitration application and administer the case. Where the sub-commission/arbitration center agreed upon by the parties does not exist or its authorization has been terminated, or where the agreement is ambiguous* [the reference is to SHIAC and SCIA], *the Arbitration Court shall accept the arbitration application and administer the case. In the event of any dispute, a decision shall be made by CIETAC*".

However, Chinese courts have not backed up CIETAC's approach; on the contrary, they have confirmed the legality and the jurisdictional power of the institutions stemming from the split. In 2014, the Shanghai No. 2 Intermediate People's Court, in *Ni Laibao and Liu Donglian v. Soudal Investments Ltd.*, decided that SHIAC has jurisdiction when the arbitration clause designates the CIETAC Shanghai sub-commission.[6] At the beginning of 2015, the Shenzhen Intermediate People's Court gave a substantially similar ruling[7]; a number of rulings rendered in the same period by the same courts are in line with the cited ones.

This makes it quite sure that, as of May 2015, Shanghai and Shenzhen courts will consistently consider SHIAC and SCIA to have jurisdiction where an arbitration clause mentions "CIETAC Shanghai/Shenzhen". This conclusion should not be automatically extended to all other courts in China, given that the courts of Shanghai and Shenzhen have traditionally been friendlier than other courts towards the arbitration institutions seated in their respective territories. There are grounds to believe that the Supreme Court would confirm the view expressed by the Shanghai and Shenzhen courts.[8] However, Chinese courts will not be under an obligation to

[6] *Ni Laibao and Liu Donglian v. Soudal Investments Ltd.*, [2012] Hu Er Zhong Min Ren (Zhong Xie) Zi No. 5, Shanghai No. 2 Intermediate People's Court, December 31, 2014. The judgment was greeted with satisfaction by SHIAC: see http://www.cietac-sh.org/Announcement.aspx?nid=845.

[7] [2013] Shen Zhong Fa She Wai Zhong Zi No. 133, Shenzhen Intermediate People's Court, January 6, 2015.

[8] Supreme People's Court, *Reply to the Request for Instructions of Guangdong Province High People's Court on the Case of Zhaoqing United Nations Metal Products Factory Co., Ltd. Requesting not to Enforce Award No. D19 (2013) of the South China International Economic and Trade Arbitration Commission*, [2014] Min Si Ta Zi No. 52.

follow the view of the Supreme Court until it is endorsed in a legally binding document (namely, an *Interpretation*).

In any event, the parties to any arbitration agreement "flawed" as a result of the CIETAC split are strongly advised to renegotiate such an agreement as soon as possible, before any dispute arises.

Chapter 7
Sample Arbitration Proceedings

7.1 Commencing Arbitration Proceedings in China: Filing a Notice of Arbitration

I. Heading

In the Matter of an Arbitration under the SHIAC Administered Arbitration Rules

Case No. SHIAC/111111

Between:

"A" Co., Ltd.

Claimant

And

"B" Co., Ltd.

Respondent

Notice of Arbitration

Jun. 13, 2015

By and on behalf of the Claimant

[NAME]

[CLAIMANT'S ELECTED DOMICILE]

G. Pisacane et al., *Arbitration in China*,
China Law, Tax & Accounting, DOI 10.1007/978-981-10-0684-5_7

II. Indication of Parties and Counsel
    Claimant
    Respondent
III. Indication of the contract out of which or in relation to which the dispute has arisen
IV. Indication of the dispute, general nature of the claim and amount involved
V. Indication of the arbitration agreement
VI. Demand for Arbitration
VII. Indication of the number of Arbitrators and appointment of Arbitrator
VIII. Indication of remedies sought
IX. Service Confirmation

7.2 Jurisdiction Challenge by the Respondent

I. Heading

In the Matter of an Arbitration under the SHIAC Administered Arbitration Rules

Case No. SHIAC/111111

Between:

"A" Co., Ltd.

Claimant

And

"B" Co., Ltd.

Respondent

Notice of Arbitration

Jul. 10, 2015

By and on behalf of the Respondent

[NAME]

[RESPONDENT'S ELECTED DOMICILE]

II. Indication of case and Parties
III. Challenge to the jurisdiction of the arbitration institution and related grounds
IV. Request not to include the Applicant in the arbitration proceedings as a Respondent

7.3 Reply by the Respondent to the Notice of Arbitration

I. The Respondent's reply to the Claimant's claims (Notice of arbitration)
II. Appointment of Respondent's Arbitrator
III. Service Confirmation

7.4 Tribunal Order for Direction No. 1

I. The Claimant shall produce a reply to the Respondent's objection to jurisdiction within ** days of receipt of this order and serviced paperwork.
II. The Respondent shall produce a response to the reply of the Claimant on jurisdiction within ** days of receipt of this order.
III. The Tribunal will make a decision on the matter of jurisdiction within ** days after both Parties submit their responses.

7.5 Tribunal Order for Direction No. 2

I. The Claimant shall produce its statement of claims within **days of the date of this order.
II. The Respondent shall produce its statement of defence and counterclaims (if any) within ** days from the receipt of the statement of claim.
III. The Claimant shall, if so requested, produce its reply and defence to any counterclaims within ** days from the receipt of statement of defence and counterclaims.
IV. The Respondent shall, if so requested, produce its reply to the Claimant's reply to counterclaim within ** days from the receipt of the reply.
V. Either Party can petition to have more time if conditions request so.
VI. Both Parties are to select their arbitrators within ** day of receipt of this order.
VII. Both Parties are to discuss and agree to select a presiding arbitrator within ** day of the receipt of the order. If the Parties cannot reach an agreement on the third presiding arbitrator, the secretariat of the arbitration institution will appoint one for the case as presiding arbitrator within ** days of the order.

7.6 Tribunal Order for Direction No. 3—Producing Documents

I. The Parties shall deliver Request to produce Documents.
II. The Parties shall deliver Objection to Requests to Produce Documents.
III. The Tribunal rules on the request to produce evidence.
IV. The Parties shall produce documents per Tribunal ruling.
V. The Parties shall deliver factual witness statements, and confirm the number of experts who will testify before the Tribunal.
VI. Expert witness statement.
VII. Pre-hearing directions telephone conference shall be held.

7.7 Tribunal Order for Direction No. 4—Hearing Notice

I. 3-day hearing at SHIAC venue, with opening statement, exchange of evidences, expert witness testifying, finding of facts, debate sessions.

7.8 Tribunal Order for Direction No. 5—Final Award (Quantum of Costs)

I. The proceedings.
II. Confirmed facts of the dispute.
III. The tribunal's opinion.
IV. Dispositive part—Final Decision.

7.9 Applying Enforcement of Arbitration Tribunal's Final Award

I. Filing at local Chinese court.
II. Enforcing the award by the court.

Chapter 8
Arbitration in China—Questions and Answers

The following common practical questions[1] have been selected as representative questions concerning arbitration in China. They are carefully devised to elaborate on the most important aspects of the arbitration process in China.

1. **How is arbitration different from litigation in China**?

Arbitration is generally more flexible and efficient than litigation in China. Petitioning Parties expect a quicker and more definitive result from the arbitration tribunal. Given litigation in Chinese courts requires more stringent procedures and formal compliance with documents and evidences, arbitration would serve disputing parties more efficiently. In addition, arbitration proceedings are conducted in private, rather than in court, and are heard by an arbitrator rather than a judge. Arbitration proceedings are is less formal, and there are no restrictions on who may represent the parties in an arbitration. Foreign counsels and lawyers qualify to represent parties in the arbitration in China. See Sect. 1.1.

2. **What are the main advantages of arbitration in China**?

As stated above, in addition to more efficiency, the parties can select a panel of arbitrators, which may have more expertise in the relevant field and may be from the same country speaking the same language as the parties, and to hold the arbitration in a neutral venue. Arbitration is conducted in private and the whole process is more confidential. Furthermore, an arbitration award can be enforced more conveniently

[1]Some of the questions listed in this Part are drawn from the lists of general questions that CIETAC and SHIAC publish in order to illustrate their respective institutional arbitration rules. Common questions published by the Hong Kong International Arbitration Committee (HKIAC) have also been used. The authors made some modifications to those questions, so as to make them fit better the specific purposes of this book.

The remaining questions have been originally devised by the authors based on many years of professional experience in the dispute resolution field in China.

G. Pisacane et al., *Arbitration in China*,
China Law, Tax & Accounting, DOI 10.1007/978-981-10-0684-5_8

and legally in the New York convention Contracting States, while a Chinese judgement is more difficult to enforce abroad. See Sect. 1.1.

3. **Why is arbitration more favourable to foreign entities in disputes involving mainland Chinese parties**?

Arbitration is particularly suitable for international disputes involving mainland Chinese parties because Chinese courts will enforce an arbitration award more easily than a foreign judgement. See Sect. 1.1.

4. **What are the potential disadvantages of arbitration in China**?

As arbitration is based on the consent of the parties, arbitrators generally have no power to make orders affecting non-parties to the arbitration agreement. See Sect. 2.4. Compared to Chinese courts, they generally do not have the power to compel witnesses to testify or produce documents, to require third parties to participate in arbitration proceedings, or to make awards requiring a third party to do (or to refrain from doing) something. An arbitration panel cannot issue restraining orders or injunctive relief. See Sect. 4.6.

5. **Does China allow ad hoc arbitration**?

Currently, Chinese arbitration law only permits institutional arbitration that is to be administered by an arbitration institution, such as CIETAC, or SHIAC, etc. These arbitrations must be conducted according to the rules effective at the time. Ad hoc arbitrations arranged solely between the arbitrators and the parties, are technically illegal and the award cannot be enforced. See Sects. 2.2.1 (c) and 5.2.4.

6. **Is arbitration less expensive than litigation**?

The cost of arbitration may depend greatly on the fees charged by the selected arbitration institution, how many arbitrators are appointed, which arbitrators are selected, and the fees charged by the arbitrators and the representative counsels. Because of its flexibility and informality, arbitration is generally cheaper than court proceedings. However if the parties take a strongly adversarial stand, the proceedings can be as expensive and lengthy as litigation. See Sect. 4.18, *as well as the Arbitration Rules of each institution reproduced in Appendix II.*

7. **Is arbitration faster than litigation**?

Generally, due to its flexibility and informality, it is possible to conduct the procedure in a faster fashion. In addition, the parties' right to appeal arbitration awards is limited and restricted only to certain instances. This most times makes the process quicker. However, there is no default or summary judgement even in simple cases where the facts support a prima facie determination. Arbitration proceedings always require holding a hearing.

8. **Are arbitral awards appealable**?

Generally the answer is no. Arbitration awards are final and not subject to higher level review on the merits of the case. Under Chinese law, an arbitration award may be appealed only in limited circumstances, mostly on the grounds of procedural error or misconduct or serious defects in the proceedings.

9. **Why arbitrate in China**?

Doing business inevitably entails the possibility of having a dispute. Choosing arbitration ensures that parties can take advantage of the benefits of arbitration. In addition, China has a strong, arbitration-friendly legal system with a good history of arbitration. One has access to a large pool of arbitrators, many of whom are international. Lawyers and other professionals are mostly familiar with the arbitration process. See Sect. 1.1.

10. **Must the parties retain Chinese legal counsel in a Chinese arbitration**?

No. The parties can appoint locally qualified advisors, foreign legal advisors or non-legal professionals to represent them in arbitration proceedings. Chinese laws do not restrict legal representation for arbitration. See Sect. 4.5.

11. **What rules govern arbitration proceedings in China**?

Chinese arbitration law provides a basic, general legal framework for arbitration. The detailed procedure is governed by the rules of the arbitration institution (such as CIETAC or SHIAC Arbitration Rules) in force at the time when a dispute is arbitrated. Where the arbitration rules are not clear, an arbitral tribunal may have discretion to adopt appropriate rules or laws to ensure arbitration is carried out in a fair, efficient and equitable way. See Sect. 1.2.

12. **Must the parties have an arbitration agreement**?

Yes. As arbitration is a consensual process, parties must have agreed to submit their disputes to the jurisdiction of arbitration. In addition, they can specify more details in their agreement, such as the applicable rules and substantive law, the language chosen, the number of arbitrators and how they are to be appointed, etc. See Sect. 2.1; *for the model arbitration clauses provided by the main arbitration institutions, see Appendix III.*

13. **What effect does an arbitration agreement have**?

An effective arbitration agreement would exclude the Chinese court's jurisdiction, as well as provide the basis for an arbitration institution's jurisdiction. The institution will only accept "a request for arbitration" where a valid arbitration agreement exists. See Sect. 2.1.

14. **What happens if a party attempts to litigate a dispute which is covered by an arbitration agreement**?

If a party commences court proceedings in a dispute which is covered by an arbitration agreement, the court should stay its proceedings and decline to hear the dispute. See Chap. 3.

15. **Do arbitration agreements have to be in writing**?

Generally, yes. The agreement must be made in writing or evidenced in writing in order to constitute a basis for arbitral jurisdiction. Otherwise, parties can orally attest or prove to the arbitration institution that an effective arbitration agreement exists between them. See Sect. 2.2.3.

16. **How many arbitrators are needed for an arbitration**?

An arbitral tribunal will usually consist of either one or three arbitrators. The number of arbitrators is generally agreed upon in the arbitration clause, or may be agreed by the parties after a dispute has arisen. If there is no consent or agreement as to the number that will form the tribunal, the institution secretariat will decide on it. See Sects. 2.5 and 4.7.

17. **How to dccide whether one arbitrator or three arbitrators is more appropriate**?

There can be several factors to consider. One arbitrator is less expensive, while a three-arbitrator tribunal is more able to deal with complex or technical disputes. In cases where parties come from jurisdictions with separate legal systems and cultures, a panel of arbitrators from an international background can help bridge different legal systems and commercial customs. See Sects. 2.5 and 4.7.

18. **What language should be chosen to conduct the arbitration proceedings**?

Generally, the Parties are free to select a language they both agree on. However in reality language should be determined keeping in mind not only the parties' convenience, but also the nature and substance of the disputes (contracts, documents, evidence and proceedings), as well as the convenience of potential arbitrators. The parties do not want to limit their choice of arbitrators due to language restrictions. If the parties do not specify which language, the default language for arbitration will be Chinese. See Sect. 2.9.

19. **What happens if the parties agree to conduct the arbitration in two languages**?

The parties oftentimes agree to conduct arbitration in two languages, such as Chinese and English. This requires every document to be presented in both languages and oral submissions and evidence to be translated at the hearing. The requirement to produce such translations can add significantly to the cost and length of the proceedings. See Sect. 2.9.

20. **Does the arbitration tribunal apply Chinese law or the governing law of the contract**?

Generally, the arbitral tribunal will apply the governing law of the contract to determine the substantive issues regarding a contractual claim. See Sect. 2.7. On the other hand, procedural rules are governed by the applicable arbitration rules or Chinese laws. See Sect. 4.1.

21. **How to commence arbitration**?

Routinely, arbitration is commenced when the claimant serves the respondent a notice requesting that the dispute be referred to arbitration. The claimant can file an arbitration claim or petition the arbitration institution to issue a notice to the respondent. The notice issued by the arbitration institution formally starts the procedure. The format of a notice should be determined by the specific requirements under the applicable procedural rules. See Sect. 4.2.

22. **Are there time limits for commencing arbitration**?

Yes. In the same way as it happens for litigation before a Chinese court, the time limits to submit a dispute to arbitration are the same.

23. **How are the arbitrators appointed**?

A single arbitrator is usually appointed by agreement of the parties or by the arbitration institution. In the case of three-arbitrator tribunal, each party will have the right to appoint one arbitrator, and the third arbitrator will be appointed as a neutral and presiding arbitrator. In the event the appointment of an arbitrator cannot be agreed upon by the parties, the arbitration institution will make the final appointment. See Sect. 4.7.

24. **Who can be appointed as arbitrator**?

The parties may, in writing, spell out the detailed criteria for appointing arbitrators (professional expertise, language requirement, nationality, etc.). Arbitration institutions publish lists of arbitrators from which the parties can choose. Overall, the arbitration institution will help the parties make the decision, and in any case may preside over the selection and appointment process. See Sects. 2.5 and 4.7.

25. **Is neutrality and independence required for the selected arbitrators**?

Yes. All arbitrators are required to be neutral and independent, regardless of how they are appointed. Once selected, they are not allowed to discuss privately or secretly with the parties as to the merit of the case. See Sect. 2.5. In addition, they must disclose any background information that may indicate a of conflict of interest. See Sect. 4.8.

26. **Can either party raise objections to the appointment of an arbitrator**?

Yes, given different reasons that may cause the loss or justifiable doubt on the neutrality or independence of the arbitrator, either party may object to their appointment. However, to succeed in the objection, parties usually must have solid evidence to prove a conflict of interest. See Sect. 4.8. In certain instances, it may be grounds for setting aside of the award. See Sects. 5.1.1 and 5.2.1.

27. **What would be the next step after the arbitration tribunal has been formed**?

The next step taken by the arbitral tribunal will usually be to solicit preliminary notes from the parties to establish a schedule for arbitration proceedings and to consider any other preliminary matters.

28. **Can parties challenge the tribunal's jurisdiction**?

Yes, but the time to raise the challenge is usually before the parties submit their statement of defense. Grounds for challenge usually involve the absence or the invalidity of the arbitration clause, both of which exclude the jurisdiction of an arbitration institution. The secretariat of the arbitration institution would first consider the challenge. If the secretariat cannot decide on the matter, the decision is commonly referred to the arbitral tribunal once it has been formed. See Chap. 3.

29. **What powers does an arbitrator have**?

An arbitrator has a wide range of powers in the arbitration proceedings. Such powers are generally regulated in the Arbitration Rules of the relevant institution. These powers include, but are not limited to, deciding on procedural and substantive issues pertaining to the arbitration; ordering the discovery of documents; directing the manner in which evidence is to be produced; issuing tribunal orders and notices, etc. See Chap. 4.

30. **How do parties formally file a case or respond to the filing of a case**?

Parties can formally file a "Statement of Claim" or "Defense Statement" at the beginning of the process. Such document should indicate the main dispute, the supporting facts and evidences, etc., so as to clearly illustrate each party's position, claims and grounds. Arbitration pleas shall sometimes include a counter-claim and a reply to a counter-claim or a statement of defense against a counter-claim. See Sect. 4.4.

31. **Can the arbitral tribunal continue hearings and decide a case if the respondent fails to respond**?

Yes. Regardless of whether or not the respondent replies to the statement of claim, the tribunal can still hear the case according to the institution's arbitration rules based on what has been submitted, and sometimes even in the absence of one of the parties. See Sect. 4.12.

32. **Do the parties have the power to examine, inspect and challenge each other's documents and evidence**?

Yes. The process of discovery is intended to allow the parties to examine the disputed matter thoroughly, argue and rebut each other's claims. This can only be done if the parties are fully aware of each piece of evidence and have a change to express their opinion on them. See Sect. 4.11.

33. **Can a witness be cross-examined**?

Yes. Witness statements, expert statements or evaluation reports must be exchanged before the hearing. If either party requests that a witness be present at the arbitration hearing to question him, the tribunal must order them to be cross-examined by the other party's advocate, who will try to highlight inconsistencies or weaknesses in their statement. The party calling the witness may exercise its right to re-examine the witness, trying to clarify any matters raised in the preceding cross-examination.

34. **Can expert witnesses be used in arbitration**?

Yes. As happens in litigation, expert witnesses can be used in arbitration. Either party or the arbitral tribunal can appoint an expert to be present at hearings. See Sect. 4.11.

35. **In what sequence does an arbitral tribunal decide matters in a case**?

Generally an arbitral tribunal will decide on jurisdiction first, then splitting the merit into the two phases of determining liability and quantifying damages. In the "liability phase", the arbitral tribunal will decide the parties' responsibilities; in the second phase of quantifying liability, the tribunal will assess damages. This is to make arbitration proceedings more efficient and cost-efficient, due to the fact that the party that is found to be liable will have avoided presenting detailed evidence quantifying its loss that is then found not to be recognized in the first phase of the arbitration.

36. **Can a case be settled or mediated during the course of arbitration**?

Yes. The parties may agree in writing during the course of arbitration that they have reached a settlement. The arbitrator can also mediate the dispute in such a way to fit the needs of the parties. See Sect. 4.16.

37. **Can the arbitral tribunal consolidate two or more arbitration proceedings**?

Yes. The parties may petition the tribunal to join their cases on the grounds that there seems to be a common question of law or fact arising out of the same transaction (or series of transactions). The tribunal and the arbitration institution will coordinate in deciding about the consolidation after a formal consolidation hearing.

38. **What is the time limit for rendering an award**?

Each arbitration institution has its own time limits. Generally, 6 months starting from the formation of the arbitration tribunal. See Sect. 4.14.

39. **Does an arbitral tribunal have the right to award delayed payment or damage interest, loss of expected profit, or punitive damages**?

Yes. An arbitral tribunal can award delayed payment or damage interest, as well as loss of expected profit, based on the merits of a case. On the other hand, an arbitral tribunal can seldom award punitive damages, because in most cases Chinese law does not allow for such remedy.

40. **Does an arbitral tribunal have the power to decide that the costs of arbitration proceedings must be covered by the losing party, such as lawyers' fees, filing fees, and other relevant expenses**?

Yes, arbitral tribunals are more straightforward than courts in allocating arbitration-related expenses based on the degree of responsibility of each party. If one party is completely responsible, it will have to cover all costs related to arbitration (such as professional fees, arbitrators' fees, arbitration fees, etc.). The arbitral tribunal has the power to decide which party shall be liable to pay for arbitration costs, and on what basis. The losing party is usually ordered to pay the winning party's costs. See Sect. 4.18.2.

41. **How is an arbitration award enforced in China**?

An arbitral award legally made in China can be enforced by the competent Chinese court. The winning party needs to go through the court process to complete the execution. See Sect. 5.2.

42. **Is an arbitration award final, and on what grounds can it be challenged**?

Generally, an award is final and is not subject to appeal on its merits. An award can be set aside on the following grounds: lack of jurisdiction, improper constitution of the tribunal, or arbitration procedure violating the rules of the relevant institution or the parties' mutual agreement. Petitions to set aside an award must be filed with a court. See Sect. 5.1.

43. **What is the New York Convention**?

The term "New York Convention" refers to the *United Nations Convention on the Recognition and Enforcement of Foreign Arbitral Awards*, signed in New York in 1958, providing the foundations for cross-border enforcement of arbitral awards. As of today, over 130 countries altogether, included China have joined the Convention, undertaking to recognize and to enforce foreign awards. See Sect. 5.2.3.

44. **Does the New York Convention apply to China**?

Yes. The Chinese Government has signed the Convention. Under the New York Convention, foreign awards can be enforced in the same manner as domestic awards. See Sect. 5.2.3.

45. **Under what circumstances can a foreign award be denied enforcement**?

In almost the same way as domestic awards, the grounds to deny enforcement of a foreign award are limited to lack of jurisdiction, improper composition of the arbitral tribunal, serious procedural irregularity or violation of China's public policy. Misunderstandings of fact or misapplication law do not constitute valid grounds for refusal of enforcement. See Sect. 5.2.3.

46. **Are Chinese arbitral awards enforceable in the New York Convention countries**?

Yes, absolutely.

47. **Are arbitration proceedings confidential? Are there any exceptions**?

Arbitration proceedings in China are strictly confidential. Anything relating to the arbitration and the award made in the process is confidential. The arbitral tribunal's decision-making process must be kept confidential as well. This is one of the advantages of arbitration compared to litigation. However, if the parties want to submit proceeding documents and information to a governmental agency, to a court for enforcement, or to professionals and advisors for review, then an exception to confidentiality should be made.

48. **Is the award published**?

No. The publication of awards goes against the rule of confidentiality.

49. **How many cases are arbitrated by arbitration institutions in China**?

Thousands of cases are arbitrated in China every year, CIETAC alone administered 1968 cases in 2015. Arbitration is a very popular and effective way to settle disputes.

50. **What would be the fee schedule for arbitration in China**?

Arbitration fees vary for each arbitration institution. Generally, filing fees are higher than those of Chinese courts. See Sect. 4.18.1, *as well as the Arbitration Rules reproduced in Appendix II.*

Appendix I
Arbitration Rules

CIETAC Arbitration Rules[1]

China International Economic and Trade Arbitration Commission (CIETAC) Arbitration Rules

Revised and adopted by the China Council for the Promotion of International Trade/China Chamber of International Commerce on November 4, 2014. Effective as of January 1, 2015.

Chapter I General Provisions

Article 1 The Arbitration Commission

1. The China International Economic and Trade Arbitration Commission ("CIETAC"), originally named the Foreign Trade Arbitration Commission of the China Council for the Promotion of International Trade and later renamed the Foreign Economic and Trade Arbitration Commission of the China Council for the Promotion of International Trade, concurrently uses as its name the "Arbitration Institute of the China Chamber of International Commerce".
2. Where an arbitration agreement provides for arbitration by the China Council for the Promotion of International Trade/China Chamber of International Commerce, or by the Arbitration Commission or the Arbitration Institute of the China Council for the Promotion of International Trade/China Chamber of International Commerce, or refers to CIETAC's previous names, it shall be deemed that the parties have agreed to arbitration by CIETAC.

[1]http://www.cietac.org/index.cms.

G. Pisacane et al., *Arbitration in China*,
China Law, Tax & Accounting, DOI 10.1007/978-981-10-0684-5

Article 2 Structure and Duties

1. The Chairman of CIETAC shall perform the functions and duties vested in him/her by these Rules while a Vice Chairman may perform the Chairman's functions and duties with the Chairman's authorization.
2. CIETAC has an Arbitration Court (the "Arbitration Court"), which performs its functions in accordance with these Rules under the direction of the authorized Vice Chairman and the President of the Arbitration Court.
3. CIETAC is based in Beijing. It has sub-commissions or arbitration centers (Appendix I). The sub-commissions/arbitration centers are CIETAC's branches, which accept arbitration applications and administer arbitration cases with CIETAC's authorization.
4. A sub-commission/arbitration center has an arbitration court, which performs the functions of the Arbitration Court in accordance with these Rules under the direction of the president of the arbitration court of the sub-commission/arbitration center.
5. Where a case is administered by a sub-commission/arbitration center, the functions and duties vested in the President of the Arbitration Court under these Rules may, by his/her authorization, be performed by the president of the arbitration court of the relevant sub-commission/arbitration center.
6. The parties may agree to submit their disputes to CIETAC or a sub-commission/arbitration center of CIETAC for arbitration. Where the parties have agreed to arbitration by CIETAC, the Arbitration Court shall accept the arbitration application and administer the case. Where the parties have agreed to arbitration by a sub-commission/arbitration center, the arbitration court of the sub-commission/arbitration center agreed upon by the parties shall accept the arbitration application and administer the case. Where the sub-commission/arbitration center agreed upon by the parties does not exist or its authorization has been terminated, or where the agreement is ambiguous, the Arbitration Court shall accept the arbitration application and administer the case. In the event of any dispute, a decision shall be made by CIETAC.

Article 3 Jurisdiction

1. CIETAC accepts cases involving economic, trade and other disputes of a contractual or non-contractual nature, based on an agreement of the parties.
2. The cases referred to in the preceding paragraph include:

    (a) international or foreign-related disputes;
    (b) disputes related to the Hong Kong Special Administrative Region, the Macao Special Administrative Region and the Taiwan region; and
    (c) domestic disputes.

Article 4 Scope of Application

1. These Rules uniformly apply to CIETAC and its sub-commissions/arbitration centers.
2. Where the parties have agreed to refer their dispute to CIETAC for arbitration, they shall be deemed to have agreed to arbitration in accordance with these Rules.
3. Where the parties agree to refer their dispute to CIETAC for arbitration but have agreed on a modification of these Rules or have agreed on the application of other arbitration rules, the parties' agreement shall prevail unless such agreement is inoperative or in conflict with a mandatory provision of the law applicable to the arbitral proceedings. Where the parties have agreed on the application of other arbitration rules, CIETAC shall perform the relevant administrative duties.
4. Where the parties agree to refer their dispute to arbitration under these Rules without providing the name of the arbitration institution, they shall be deemed to have agreed to refer the dispute to arbitration by CIETAC.
5. Where the parties agree to refer their dispute to arbitration under CIETAC's customized arbitration rules for a specific trade or profession, the parties' agreement shall prevail. However, if the dispute falls outside the scope of the specific rules, these Rules shall apply.

Article 5 Arbitration Agreement

1. An arbitration agreement means an arbitration clause in a contract or any other form of a written agreement concluded between the parties providing for the settlement of disputes by arbitration.
2. The arbitration agreement shall be in writing. An arbitration agreement is in writing if it is contained in the tangible form of a document such as a contract, letter, telegram, telex, fax, electronic data interchange, or email. An arbitration agreement shall be deemed to exist where its existence is asserted by one party and not denied by the other during the exchange of the Request for Arbitration and the Statement of Defense.
3. Where the law applicable to an arbitration agreement has different provisions as to the form and validity of the arbitration agreement, those provisions shall prevail.
4. An arbitration clause contained in a contract shall be treated as a clause independent and separate from all other clauses of the contract, and an arbitration agreement attached to a contract shall also be treated as independent and separate from all other clauses of the contract. The validity of an arbitration clause or an arbitration agreement shall not be affected by any modification, cancellation, termination, transfer, expiry, invalidity, ineffectiveness, rescission or non-existence of the contract.

Article 6 Objection to Arbitration Agreement and/or Jurisdiction

1. CIETAC has the power to determine the existence and validity of an arbitration agreement and its jurisdiction over an arbitration case. CIETAC may, where necessary, delegate such power to the arbitral tribunal.
2. Where CIETAC is satisfied by prima facie evidence that a valid arbitration agreement exists, it may make a decision based on such evidence that it has jurisdiction over the arbitration case, and the arbitration shall proceed. Such a decision shall not prevent CIETAC from making a new decision on jurisdiction based on facts and/or evidence found by the arbitral tribunal during the arbitral proceedings that are inconsistent with the prima facie evidence.
3. Where CIETAC has delegated the power to determine jurisdiction to the arbitral tribunal, the arbitral tribunal may either make a separate decision on jurisdiction during the arbitral proceedings or incorporate the decision in the final arbitral award.
4. Any objection to an arbitration agreement and/or the jurisdiction over an arbitration case shall be raised in writing before the first oral hearing held by the arbitral tribunal. Where a case is to be decided on the basis of documents only, such an objection shall be raised before the submission of the first substantive defense.
5. The arbitration shall proceed notwithstanding an objection to the arbitration agreement and/or jurisdiction over the arbitration case.
6. The aforesaid objections to and/or decisions on jurisdiction by CIETAC shall include objections to and/or decisions on a party's standing to participate in the arbitration.
7. CIETAC or its authorized arbitral tribunal shall decide to dismiss the case upon finding that CIETAC has no jurisdiction over an arbitration case. Where a case is to be dismissed before the formation of the arbitral tribunal, the decision shall be made by the President of the Arbitration Court. Where the case is to be dismissed after the formation of the arbitral tribunal, the decision shall be made by the arbitral tribunal.

Article 7 Place of Arbitration

1. Where the parties have agreed on the place of arbitration, the parties' agreement shall prevail.
2. Where the parties have not agreed on the place of arbitration or their agreement is ambiguous, the place of arbitration shall be the domicile of CIETAC or its sub-commission/arbitration center administering the case. CIETAC may also determine the place of arbitration to be another location having regard to the circumstances of the case.
3. The arbitral award shall be deemed as having been made at the place of arbitration.

Article 8 Service of Documents and Periods of Time

1. All documents, notices and written materials in relation to the arbitration may be delivered in person or sent by registered mail or express mail, fax, or by any other means considered proper by the Arbitration Court or the arbitral tribunal.
2. The arbitration documents referred to in the preceding Paragraph 1 shall be sent to the address provided by the party itself or by its representative(s), or to an address agreed by the parties. Where a party or its representative(s) has not provided an address or the parties have not agreed on an address, the arbitration documents shall be sent to such party's address as provided by the other party or its representative(s).
3. Any arbitration correspondence to a party or its representative(s) shall be deemed to have been properly served on the party if delivered to the addressee or sent to the addressee's place of business, place of registration, domicile, habitual residence or mailing address, or where, after reasonable inquiries by the other party, none of the aforesaid addresses can be found, the arbitration correspondence is sent by the Arbitration Court to the addressee's last known place of business, place of registration, domicile, habitual residence or mailing address by registered or express mail, or by any other means that can provide a record of the attempt at delivery, including but not limited to service by public notary, entrustment or retention.
4. The periods of time specified in these Rules shall begin on the day following the day when the party receives or should have received the arbitration correspondence, notices or written materials sent by the Arbitration Court.

Article 9 Good Faith

Arbitration participants shall proceed with the arbitration in good faith.

Article 10 Waiver of Right to Object

A party shall be deemed to have waived its right to object where it knows or should have known that any provision of, or requirement under, these Rules has not been complied with and yet participates in or proceeds with the arbitral proceedings without promptly and explicitly submitting its objection in writing to such non-compliance.

Chapter II Arbitral Proceedings

Section 1 Request for Arbitration, Defense and Counterclaim

Article 11 Commencement of Arbitration

The arbitral proceedings shall commence on the day on which the Arbitration Court receives a Request for Arbitration.

Article 12 Application for Arbitration

A party applying for arbitration under these Rules shall:

1. Submit a Request for Arbitration in writing signed and/or sealed by the Claimant or its authorized representative(s), which shall, inter alia, include:
   (a) the names and addresses of the Claimant and the Respondent, including the zip code, telephone, fax, email, or any other means of electronic telecommunications;
   (b) a reference to the arbitration agreement that is invoked;
   (c) a statement of the facts of the case and the main issues in dispute;
   (d) the claim of the Claimant; and
   (e) the facts and grounds on which the claim is based.
2. Attach to the Request for Arbitration the relevant documentary and other evidence on which the Claimant's claim is based.
3. Pay the arbitration fee in advance to CIETAC in accordance with its Arbitration Fee Schedule.

Article 13 Acceptance of a Case

1. Upon the written application of a party, CIETAC shall accept a case in accordance with an arbitration agreement concluded between the parties either before or after the occurrence of the dispute, in which it is provided that disputes are to be referred to arbitration by CIETAC.
2. Upon receipt of a Request for Arbitration and its attachments, where after examination the Arbitration Court finds the formalities required for arbitration application to be complete, it shall send a Notice of Arbitration to both parties together with one copy each of these Rules and CIETAC's Panel of Arbitrators. The Request for Arbitration and its attachments submitted by the Claimant shall be sent to the Respondent under the same cover.
3. Where after examination the Arbitration Court finds the formalities required for the arbitration application to be incomplete, it may request the Claimant to complete them within a specified time period. The Claimant shall be deemed not to have submitted a Request for Arbitration if it fails to complete the required formalities within the specified time period. In such a case, the Claimant's Request for Arbitration and its attachments shall not be kept on file by the Arbitration Court.
4. After CIETAC accepts a case, the Arbitration Court shall designate a case manager to assist with the procedural administration of the case.

Article 14 Multiple Contracts

The Claimant may initiate a single arbitration concerning disputes arising out of or in connection with multiple contracts, provided that:

(a) such contracts consist of a principal contract and its ancillary contract(s), or such contracts involve the same parties as well as legal relationships of the same nature;
(b) the disputes arise out of the same transaction or the same series of transactions; and
(c) the arbitration agreements in such contracts are identical or compatible.

Article 15 Statement of Defense

1. The Respondent shall file a Statement of Defense in writing within forty-five (45) days from the date of its receipt of the Notice of Arbitration. If the Respondent has justified reasons to request an extension of the time period, the arbitral tribunal shall decide whether to grant an extension. Where the arbitral tribunal has not yet been formed, the decision on whether to grant the extension of the time period shall be made by the Arbitration Court.
2. The Statement of Defense shall be signed and/or sealed by the Respondent or its authorized representative(s), and shall, inter alia, include the following contents and attachments:

    (a) the name and address of the Respondent, including the zip code, telephone, fax, email, or any other means of electronic telecommunications;
    (b) the defense to the Request for Arbitration setting forth the facts and grounds on which the defense is based; and
    (c) the relevant documentary and other evidence on which the defense is based.

3. The arbitral tribunal has the power to decide whether to accept a Statement of Defense submitted after the expiration of the above time period.
4. Failure by the Respondent to file a Statement of Defense shall not affect the conduct of the arbitral proceedings.

Article 16 Counterclaim

1. The Respondent shall file a counterclaim, if any, in writing within forty-five (45) days from the date of its receipt of the Notice of Arbitration. If the Respondent has justified reasons to request an extension of the time period, the arbitral tribunal shall decide whether to grant an extension. Where the arbitral tribunal has not yet been formed, the decision on whether to grant the extension of the time period shall be made by the Arbitration Court.
2. When filing the counterclaim, the Respondent shall specify the counterclaim in its Statement of Counterclaim and state the facts and grounds on which the counterclaim is based with the relevant documentary and other evidence attached thereto.

3. When filing the counterclaim, the Respondent shall pay an arbitration fee in advance in accordance with the Arbitration Fee Schedule of CIETAC within a specified time period, failing which the Respondent shall be deemed not to have filed any counterclaim.
4. Where the formalities required for filing a counterclaim are found to be complete, the Arbitration Court shall send a Notice of Acceptance of Counterclaim to the parties. The Claimant shall submit its Statement of Defense in writing within thirty (30) days from the date of its receipt of the Notice. If the Claimant has justified reasons to request an extension of the time period, the arbitral tribunal shall decide whether to grant such an extension. Where the arbitral tribunal has not yet been formed, the decision on whether to grant the extension of the time period shall be made by the Arbitration Court.
5. The arbitral tribunal has the power to decide whether to accept a counterclaim or a Statement of Defense submitted after the expiration of the above time period.
6. Failure of the Claimant to file a Statement of Defense to the Respondent's counterclaim shall not affect the conduct of the arbitral proceedings.

Article 17 Amendment to Claim or Counterclaim

The Claimant may apply to amend its claim and the Respondent may apply to amend its counterclaim. However, the arbitral tribunal may refuse any such amendment if it considers that the amendment is too late and may delay the arbitral proceedings.

Article 18 Joinder of Additional Parties

1. During the arbitral proceedings, a party wishing to join an additional party to the arbitration may file the Request for Joinder with CIETAC, based on the arbitration agreement invoked in the arbitration that prima facie binds the additional party. Where the Request for Joinder is filed after the formation of the arbitral tribunal, a decision shall be made by CIETAC after the arbitral tribunal hears from all parties including the additional party if the arbitral tribunal considers the joinder necessary.

   The date on which the Arbitration Court receives the Request for Joinder shall be deemed to be the date of the commencement of arbitration against the additional party.
2. The Request for Joinder shall contain the case number of the existing arbitration; the name, address and other means of communication of each of the parties, including the additional party; the arbitration agreement invoked to join the additional party as well as the facts and grounds the request relies upon; and the claim.

   The relevant documentary and other evidence on which the request is based shall be attached to the Request for Joinder.
3. Where any party objects to the arbitration agreement and/or jurisdiction over the arbitration with respect to the joinder proceedings, CIETAC has the power to decide on its jurisdiction based on the arbitration agreement and relevant evidence.

4. After the joinder proceedings commence, the conduct of the arbitral proceedings shall be decided by the Arbitration Court if the arbitral tribunal is not formed, or shall be decided by the arbitral tribunal if it has been formed.
5. Where the joinder takes place prior to the formation of the arbitral tribunal, the relevant provisions on party's nominating or entrusting of the Chairman of CIETAC to appoint arbitrator under these Rules shall apply to the additional party. The arbitral tribunal shall be formed in accordance with Article 29 of these Rules.
   Where the joinder takes place after the formation of the arbitral tribunal, the arbitral tribunal shall hear from the additional party of its comments on the past arbitral proceedings including the formation of the arbitral tribunal. If the additional party requests to nominate or entrust the Chairman of CIETAC to appoint an arbitrator, both parties shall nominate or entrust the Chairman of CIETAC to appoint arbitrators again. The arbitral tribunal shall be formed in accordance with Article 29 of these Rules.
6. The relevant provisions on the submission of the Statement of Defense and the Statement of Counterclaim under these Rules shall apply to the additional party. The time period for the additional party to submit its Statement of Defense and Statement of Counterclaim shall start counting from the date of its receipt of the Notice of Joinder.
7. CIETAC shall have the power to decide not to join an additional party where the additional party is prima facie not bound by the arbitration agreement invoked in the arbitration, or where any other circumstance exists that makes the joinder inappropriate.

Article 19 Consolidation of Arbitrations

1. At the request of a party, CIETAC may consolidate two or more arbitrations pending under these Rules into a single arbitration if:

   (a) all of the claims in the arbitrations are made under the same arbitration agreement;
   (b) the claims in the arbitrations are made under multiple arbitration agreements that are identical or compatible and the arbitrations involve the same parties as well as legal relationships of the same nature;
   (c) the claims in the arbitrations are made under multiple arbitration agreements that are identical or compatible and the multiple contracts involved consist of a principle contract and its ancillary contract(s); or
   (d) all the parties to the arbitrations have agreed to consolidation.

2. In deciding whether to consolidate the arbitrations in accordance with the preceding Paragraph 1, CIETAC shall take into account the opinions of all parties and other relevant factors such as the correlation between the arbitrations concerned, including the nomination and appointment of arbitrators in the separate arbitrations.

3. Unless otherwise agreed by all the parties, the arbitrations shall be consolidated into the arbitration that was first commenced.
4. After the consolidation of arbitrations, the conduct of the arbitral proceedings shall be decided by the Arbitration Court if the arbitral tribunal is not formed, or shall be decided by the arbitral tribunal if it has been formed.

Article 20 Submission and Exchange of Arbitration Documents

1. All arbitration documents from the parties shall be submitted to the Arbitration Court.
2. All arbitration documents to be exchanged during the arbitral proceedings shall be exchanged among the arbitral tribunal and the parties by the Arbitration Court unless otherwise agreed by the parties and with the consent of the arbitral tribunal or otherwise decided by the arbitral tribunal.

Article 21 Copies of Arbitration Documents

When submitting the Request for Arbitration, the Statement of Defense, the Statement of Counterclaim, evidence, and other arbitration documents, the parties shall make their submissions in quintuplicate. Where there are multiple parties, additional copies shall be provided accordingly. Where the party applies for preservation of property or protection of evidence, it shall also provide additional copies accordingly. Where the arbitral tribunal is composed of a sole arbitrator, the number of copies submitted may be reduced by two.

Article 22 Representation

A party may be represented by its authorized Chinese and/or foreign representative (s) in handling matters relating to the arbitration. In such a case, a Power of Attorney shall be forwarded to the Arbitration Court by the party or its authorized representative(s).

Article 23 Conservatory and Interim Measures

1. Where a party applies for conservatory measures pursuant to the laws of the People's Republic of China, CIETAC shall forward the party's application to the competent court designated by that party in accordance with the law.
2. In accordance with the applicable law or the agreement of the parties, a party may apply to the Arbitration Court for emergency relief pursuant to the CIETAC Emergency Arbitrator Procedures (Appendix III). The emergency arbitrator may decide to order or award necessary or appropriate emergency measures. The decision of the emergency arbitrator shall be binding upon both parties.
3. At the request of a party, the arbitral tribunal may decide to order or award any interim measure it deems necessary or proper in accordance with the applicable law or the agreement of the parties and may require the requesting party to provide appropriate security in connection with the measure.

Section 2 Arbitrators and the Arbitral Tribunal

Article 24 Duties of Arbitrator

An arbitrator shall not represent either party, and shall be and remain independent of the parties and treat them equally.

Article 25 Number of Arbitrators

1. The arbitral tribunal shall be composed of one or three arbitrators.
2. Unless otherwise agreed by the parties or provided by these Rules, the arbitral tribunal shall be composed of three arbitrators.

Article 26 Nomination or Appointment of Arbitrator

1. CIETAC maintains a Panel of Arbitrators which uniformly applies to itself and all its sub-commissions/arbitration centers. The parties shall nominate arbitrators from the Panel of Arbitrators provided by CIETAC.
2. Where the parties have agreed to nominate arbitrators from outside CIETAC's Panel of Arbitrators, an arbitrator so nominated by the parties or nominated according to the agreement of the parties may act as arbitrator subject to the confirmation by the Chairman of CIETAC.

Article 27 Three-Arbitrator Tribunal

1. Within fifteen (15) days from the date of receipt of the Notice of Arbitration, the Claimant and the Respondent shall each nominate, or entrust the Chairman of CIETAC to appoint, an arbitrator, failing which the arbitrator shall be appointed by the Chairman of CIETAC.
2. Within fifteen (15) days from the date of the Respondent's receipt of the Notice of Arbitration, the parties shall jointly nominate, or entrust the Chairman of CIETAC to appoint, the third arbitrator, who shall act as the presiding arbitrator.
3. The parties may each recommend one to five arbitrators as candidates for the presiding arbitrator and shall each submit a list of recommended candidates within the time period specified in the preceding Paragraph 2. Where there is only one common candidate on the lists, such candidate shall be the presiding arbitrator jointly nominated by the parties. Where there is more than one common candidate on the lists, the Chairman of CIETAC shall choose the presiding arbitrator from among the common candidates having regard to the circumstances of the case, and he/she shall act as the presiding arbitrator jointly nominated by the parties. Where there is no common candidate on the lists, the presiding arbitrator shall be appointed by the Chairman of CIETAC.
4. Where the parties have failed to jointly nominate the presiding arbitrator according to the above provisions, the presiding arbitrator shall be appointed by the Chairman of CIETAC.

Article 28 Sole-Arbitrator Tribunal

Where the arbitral tribunal is composed of one arbitrator, the sole arbitrator shall be nominated pursuant to the procedures stipulated in Paragraphs 2, 3 and 4 of Article 27 of these Rules.

Article 29 Multiple-Party Tribunal

1. Where there are two or more Claimants and/or Respondents in an arbitration case, the Claimant side and/or the Respondent side, following discussion, shall each jointly nominate or jointly entrust the Chairman of CIETAC to appoint one arbitrator.
2. The presiding arbitrator or the sole arbitrator shall be nominated in accordance with the procedures stipulated in Paragraphs 2, 3 and 4 of Article 27 of these Rules. When making such nomination pursuant to Paragraph 3 of Article 27 of these Rules, the Claimant side and/or the Respondent side, following discussion, shall each submit a list of their jointly agreed candidates.
3. Where either the Claimant side or the Respondent side fails to jointly nominate or jointly entrust the Chairman of CIETAC to appoint one arbitrator within fifteen (15) days from the date of its receipt of the Notice of Arbitration, the Chairman of CIETAC shall appoint all three members of the arbitral tribunal and designate one of them to act as the presiding arbitrator.

Article 30 Considerations in Appointing Arbitrators

When appointing arbitrators pursuant to these Rules, the Chairman of CIETAC shall take into consideration the law applicable to the dispute, the place of arbitration, the language of arbitration, the nationalities of the parties, and any other factor(s) the Chairman considers relevant.

Article 31 Disclosure

1. An arbitrator nominated by the parties or appointed by the Chairman of CIETAC shall sign a Declaration and disclose any facts or circumstances likely to give rise to justifiable doubts as to his/her impartiality or independence.
2. If circumstances that need to be disclosed arise during the arbitral proceedings, the arbitrator shall promptly disclose such circumstances in writing.
3. The Declaration and/or the disclosure of the arbitrator shall be submitted to the Arbitration Court to be forwarded to the parties.

Article 32 Challenge to Arbitrator

1. Upon receipt of the Declaration and/or the written disclosure of an arbitrator, a party wishing to challenge the arbitrator on the grounds of the disclosed facts or circumstances shall forward the challenge in writing within ten (10) days from the date of such receipt. If a party fails to file a challenge within the above time period, it may not subsequently challenge the arbitrator on the basis of the matters disclosed by the arbitrator.

2. A party having justifiable doubts as to the impartiality or independence of an arbitrator may challenge that arbitrator in writing and shall state the facts and reasons on which the challenge is based with supporting evidence.
3. A party may challenge an arbitrator in writing within fifteen (15) days from the date it receives the Notice of Formation of the Arbitral Tribunal. Where a party becomes aware of a reason for a challenge after such receipt, the party may challenge the arbitrator in writing within fifteen (15) days after such reason has become known to it, but no later than the conclusion of the last oral hearing.
4. The challenge by one party shall be promptly communicated to the other party, the arbitrator being challenged and the other members of the arbitral tribunal.
5. Where an arbitrator is challenged by one party and the other party agrees to the challenge, or the arbitrator being challenged voluntarily withdraws from his/her office, such arbitrator shall no longer be a member of the arbitral tribunal. However, in neither case shall it be implied that the reasons for the challenge are sustained.
6. In circumstances other than those specified in the preceding Paragraph 5, the Chairman of CIETAC shall make a final decision on the challenge with or without stating the reasons.
7. An arbitrator who has been challenged shall continue to serve on the arbitral tribunal until a final decision on the challenge has been made by the Chairman of CIETAC.

Article 33 Replacement of Arbitrator

1. In the event that an arbitrator is prevented de jure or de facto from fulfilling his/her functions, or fails to fulfill his/her functions in accordance with the requirements of these Rules or within the time period specified in these Rules, the Chairman of CIETAC shall have the power to replace the arbitrator. Such arbitrator may also voluntarily withdraw from his/her office.
2. The Chairman of CIETAC shall make a final decision on whether or not an arbitrator should be replaced with or without stating the reasons.
3. In the event that an arbitrator is unable to fulfill his/her functions due to challenge or replacement, a substitute arbitrator shall be nominated or appointed within the time period specified by the Arbitration Court according to the same procedure that applied to the nomination or appointment of the arbitrator being challenged or replaced. If a party fails to nominate or appoint a substitute arbitrator accordingly, the substitute arbitrator shall be appointed by the Chairman of CIETAC.
4. After the replacement of an arbitrator, the arbitral tribunal shall decide whether and to what extent the previous proceedings in the case shall be repeated.

Article 34 Continuation of Arbitration by Majority

After the conclusion of the last oral hearing, if an arbitrator on a three-member tribunal is unable to participate in the deliberations and/or to render the award owing to his/her demise or to his/her removal from CIETAC's Panel of Arbitrators, or for any other reason, the other two arbitrators may request the Chairman of CIETAC to replace that arbitrator pursuant to Article 33 of these Rules. After consulting with the parties and upon the approval of the Chairman of CIETAC, the other two arbitrators may also continue the arbitral proceedings and make decisions, rulings, or render the award. The Arbitration Court shall notify the parties of the above circumstances.

Section 3 Hearing

Article 35 Conduct of Hearing

1. The arbitral tribunal shall examine the case in any way it deems appropriate unless otherwise agreed by the parties. Under all circumstances, the arbitral tribunal shall act impartially and fairly and shall afford a reasonable opportunity to both parties to present their case.
2. The arbitral tribunal shall hold oral hearings when examining the case. However, the arbitral tribunal may examine the case on the basis of documents only if the parties so agree and the arbitral tribunal consents or the arbitral tribunal deems that oral hearings are unnecessary and the parties so agree.
3. Unless otherwise agreed by the parties, the arbitral tribunal may adopt an inquisitorial or adversarial approach in hearing the case having regard to the circumstances of the case.
4. The arbitral tribunal may hold deliberations at any place or in any manner that it considers appropriate.
5. Unless otherwise agreed by the parties, the arbitral tribunal may, if it considers it necessary, issue procedural orders or question lists, produce terms of reference, or hold pre-hearing conferences, etc. With the authorization of the other members of the arbitral tribunal, the presiding arbitrator may decide on the procedural arrangements for the arbitral proceedings at his/her own discretion.

Article 36 Place of Oral Hearing

1. Where the parties have agreed on the place of an oral hearing, the case shall be heard at that agreed place except in the circumstances stipulated in Paragraph 3 of Article 82 of these Rules.
2. Unless otherwise agreed by the parties, the place of oral hearings shall be in Beijing for a case administered by the Arbitration Court or at the domicile of the sub-commission/arbitration center administering the case, or if the arbitral tribunal considers it necessary and with the approval of the President of the Arbitration Court, at another location.

Article 37 Notice of Oral Hearing

1. Where a case is to be examined by way of an oral hearing, the parties shall be notified of the date of the first oral hearing at least twenty (20) days in advance of the oral hearing. A party having justified reasons may request a postponement of the oral hearing. However, the party shall communicate such request in writing to the arbitral tribunal within five (5) days of its receipt of the notice of the oral hearing. The arbitral tribunal shall decide whether or not to postpone the oral hearing.

2. Where a party has justified reasons for its failure to submit a request for a postponement of the oral hearing in accordance with the preceding Paragraph 1, the arbitral tribunal shall decide whether or not to accept the request.
3. A notice of a subsequent oral hearing, a notice of a postponed oral hearing, as well as a request for postponement of such an oral hearing, shall not be subject to the time periods specified in the preceding Paragraph 1.

Article 38 Confidentiality

1. Hearings shall be held in camera. Where both parties request an open hearing, the arbitral tribunal shall make a decision.
2. For cases heard in camera, the parties and their representatives, the arbitrators, the witnesses, the interpreters, the experts consulted by the arbitral tribunal, the appraisers appointed by the arbitral tribunal and other relevant persons shall not disclose to any outsider any substantive or procedural matters relating to the case.

Article 39 Default

1. If the Claimant fails to appear at an oral hearing without showing sufficient cause, or withdraws from an on-going oral hearing without the permission of the arbitral tribunal, the Claimant may be deemed to have withdrawn its application for arbitration. In such a case, if the Respondent has filed a counterclaim, the arbitral tribunal shall proceed with the hearing of the counterclaim and make a default award.
2. If the Respondent fails to appear at an oral hearing without showing sufficient cause, or withdraws from an on-going oral hearing without the permission of the arbitral tribunal, the arbitral tribunal may proceed with the arbitration and make a default award. In such a case, if the Respondent has filed a counterclaim, the Respondent may be deemed to have withdrawn its counterclaim.

Article 40 Record of Oral Hearing

1. The arbitral tribunal may arrange for a written and/or an audio-visual record to be made of an oral hearing. The arbitral tribunal may, if it considers it necessary, take minutes of the oral hearing and request the parties and/or their representatives, witnesses and/or other persons involved to sign and/or affix their seals to the written record or the minutes.
2. The written record, the minutes and the audio-visual record of an oral hearing shall be available for use and reference by the arbitral tribunal.
3. At the request of a party, the Arbitration Court may, having regard to the specific circumstances of the arbitration, decide to engage a stenographer to make a stenographic record of an oral hearing, the cost of which shall be advanced by the parties.

Article 41 Evidence

1. Each party shall bear the burden of proving the facts on which it relies to support its claim, defense or counterclaim and provide the basis for its opinions, arguments and counter-arguments.
2. The arbitral tribunal may specify a time period for the parties to produce evidence and the parties shall produce evidence within the specified time period. The arbitral tribunal may refuse to admit any evidence produced after that time period. If a party experiences difficulties in producing evidence within the specified time period, it may apply for an extension before the end of the period. The arbitral tribunal shall decide whether or not to extend the time period.
3. If a party bearing the burden of proof fails to produce evidence within the specified time period, or if the produced evidence is not sufficient to support its claim or counterclaim, it shall bear the consequences thereof.

Article 42 Examination of Evidence

1. Where a case is examined by way of an oral hearing, the evidence shall be produced at the oral hearing and may be examined by the parties.
2. Where a case is to be decided on the basis of documents only, or where the evidence is submitted after the hearing and both parties have agreed to examine the evidence by means of writing, the parties may examine the evidence in writing. In such circumstances, the parties shall submit their written opinions on the evidence within the time period specified by the arbitral tribunal.

Article 43 Investigation and Evidence Collection by the Arbitral Tribunal

1. The arbitral tribunal may undertake investigation and collect evidence as it considers necessary.
2. When investigating and collecting evidence, the arbitral tribunal may notify the parties to be present. In the event that one or both parties fail to be present after being notified, the investigation and collection of evidence shall proceed without being affected.
3. Evidence collected by the arbitral tribunal through its investigation shall be forwarded to the parties for their comments.

Article 44 Expert's Report and Appraiser's Report

1. The arbitral tribunal may consult experts or appoint appraisers for clarification on specific issues of the case. Such an expert or appraiser may be a Chinese or foreign institution or natural person.
2. The arbitral tribunal has the power to request the parties, and the parties are also obliged, to deliver or produce to the expert or appraiser any relevant materials, documents, property, or physical objects for examination, inspection or appraisal by the expert or appraiser.

3. Copies of the expert's report and the appraiser's report shall be forwarded to the parties for their comments. At the request of either party and with the approval of the arbitral tribunal, the expert or appraiser shall participate in an oral hearing and give explanations on the report when the arbitral tribunal considers it necessary.

Article 45 Suspension of the Arbitral Proceedings

1. Where the parties jointly or separately request a suspension of the arbitral proceedings, or under circumstances where such suspension is necessary, the arbitral proceedings may be suspended.
2. The arbitral proceedings shall resume as soon as the reason for the suspension disappears or the suspension period ends.
3. The arbitral tribunal shall decide whether to suspend or resume the arbitral proceedings. Where the arbitral tribunal has not yet been formed, the decision shall be made by the President of the Arbitration Court.

Article 46 Withdrawal and Dismissal

1. A party may withdraw its claim or counterclaim in its entirety. In the event that the Claimant withdraws its claim in its entirety, the arbitral tribunal may proceed with its examination of the counterclaim and render an arbitral award thereon. In the event that the Respondent withdraws its counterclaim in its entirety, the arbitral tribunal may proceed with the examination of the claim and render an arbitral award thereon.
2. A party may be deemed to have withdrawn its claim or counterclaim if the arbitral proceedings cannot proceed for reasons attributable to that party.
3. A case may be dismissed if the claim and counterclaim have been withdrawn in their entirety. Where a case is to be dismissed prior to the formation of the arbitral tribunal, the President of the Arbitration Court shall make a decision on the dismissal. Where a case is to be dismissed after the formation of the arbitral tribunal, the arbitral tribunal shall make the decision.
4. The seal of CIETAC shall be affixed to the Dismissal Decision referred to in the preceding Paragraph 3 and Paragraph 7 of Article 6 of these Rules.

Article 47 Combination of Conciliation with Arbitration

1. Where both parties wish to conciliate, or where one party wishes to conciliate and the other party's consent has been obtained by the arbitral tribunal, the arbitral tribunal may conciliate the dispute during the arbitral proceedings. The parties may also settle their dispute by themselves.
2. With the consents of both parties, the arbitral tribunal may conciliate the case in a manner it considers appropriate.
3. During the process of conciliation, the arbitral tribunal shall terminate the conciliation proceedings if either party so requests or if the arbitral tribunal considers that further conciliation efforts will be futile.
4. The parties shall sign a settlement agreement where they have reached settlement through conciliation by the arbitral tribunal or by themselves.

5. Where the parties have reached a settlement agreement through conciliation by the arbitral tribunal or by themselves, they may withdraw their claim or counterclaim, or request the arbitral tribunal to render an arbitral award or a conciliation statement in accordance with the terms of the settlement agreement.
6. Where the parties request for a conciliation statement, the conciliation statement shall clearly set forth the claims of the parties and the terms of the settlement agreement. It shall be signed by the arbitrators, sealed by CIETAC, and served upon both parties.
7. Where conciliation is not successful, the arbitral tribunal shall resume the arbitral proceedings and render an arbitral award.
8. Where the parties wish to conciliate their dispute but do not wish to have conciliation conducted by the arbitral tribunal, CIETAC may, with the consents of both parties, assist the parties to conciliate the dispute in a manner and procedure it considers appropriate.
9. Where conciliation is not successful, neither party may invoke any opinion, view or statement, and any proposal or proposition expressing acceptance or opposition by either party or by the arbitral tribunal in the process of conciliation as grounds for any claim, defense or counterclaim in the subsequent arbitral proceedings, judicial proceedings, or any other proceedings.
10. Where the parties have reached a settlement agreement by themselves through negotiation or conciliation before the commencement of an arbitration, either party may, based on an arbitration agreement concluded between them that provides for arbitration by CIETAC and the settlement agreement, request CIETAC to constitute an arbitral tribunal to render an arbitral award in accordance with the terms of the settlement agreement. Unless otherwise agreed by the parties, the Chairman of CIETAC shall appoint a sole arbitrator to form such an arbitral tribunal, which shall examine the case in a procedure it considers appropriate and render an award in due course. The specific procedure and time period for rendering the award shall not be subject to other provisions of these Rules.

Chapter III Arbitral Award

Article 48 Time Period for Rendering Award

1. The arbitral tribunal shall render an arbitral award within six (6) months from the date on which the arbitral tribunal is formed.
2. Upon the request of the arbitral tribunal, the President of the Arbitration Court may extend the time period if he/she considers it truly necessary and the reasons for the extension truly justified.
3. Any suspension period shall be excluded when calculating the time period in the preceding Paragraph 1.

Article 49 Making of Award

1. The arbitral tribunal shall independently and impartially render a fair and reasonable arbitral award based on the facts of the case and the terms of the contract, in accordance with the law, and with reference to international practices.
2. Where the parties have agreed on the law applicable to the merits of their dispute, the parties' agreement shall prevail. In the absence of such an agreement or where such agreement is in conflict with a mandatory provision of the law, the arbitral tribunal shall determine the law applicable to the merits of the dispute.
3. The arbitral tribunal shall state in the award the claims, the facts of the dispute, the reasons on which the award is based, the result of the award, the allocation of the arbitration costs, and the date on which and the place at which the award is made. The facts of the dispute and the reasons on which the award is based may not be stated in the award if the parties have so agreed, or if the award is made in accordance with the terms of a settlement agreement between the parties. The arbitral tribunal has the power to fix in the award the specific time period for the parties to perform the award and the liabilities for failure to do so within the specified time period.
4. The seal of CIETAC shall be affixed to the arbitral award.
5. Where a case is examined by an arbitral tribunal composed of three arbitrators, the award shall be rendered by all three arbitrators or a majority of the arbitrators. A written dissenting opinion shall be kept with the file and may be appended to the award. Such dissenting opinion shall not form a part of the award.
6. Where the arbitral tribunal cannot reach a majority opinion, the arbitral award shall be rendered in accordance with the presiding arbitrator's opinion. The written opinions of the other arbitrators shall be kept with the file and may be appended to the award. Such written opinions shall not form a part of the award.
7. Unless the arbitral award is made in accordance with the opinion of the presiding arbitrator or the sole arbitrator and signed by the same, the arbitral award shall be signed by a majority of the arbitrators. An arbitrator who has a dissenting opinion may or may not sign his/her name on the award.
8. The date on which the award is made shall be the date on which the award comes into legal effect.
9. The arbitral award is final and binding upon both parties. Neither party may bring a lawsuit before a court or make a request to any other organization for revision of the award.

Article 50 Partial Award

1. Where the arbitral tribunal considers it necessary, or where a party so requests and the arbitral tribunal agrees, the arbitral tribunal may first render a partial award on any part of the claim before rendering the final award. A partial award is final and binding upon both parties.

2. Failure of either party to perform a partial award shall neither affect the arbitral proceedings nor prevent the arbitral tribunal from making the final award.

Article 51 Scrutiny of Draft Award

The arbitral tribunal shall submit its draft award to CIETAC for scrutiny before signing the award. CIETAC may bring to the attention of the arbitral tribunal issues addressed in the award on the condition that the arbitral tribunal's independence in rendering the award is not affected.

Article 52 Allocation of Fees

1. The arbitral tribunal has the power to determine in the arbitral award the arbitration fees and other expenses to be paid by the parties to CIETAC.
2. The arbitral tribunal has the power to decide in the arbitral award, having regard to the circumstances of the case, that the losing party shall compensate the winning party for the expenses reasonably incurred by it in pursuing the case. In deciding whether or not the winning party's expenses incurred in pursuing the case are reasonable, the arbitral tribunal shall take into consideration various factors such as the outcome and complexity of the case, the workload of the winning party and/or its representative(s), the amount in dispute, etc.

Article 53 Correction of Award

1. Within a reasonable time after the award is made, the arbitral tribunal may, on its own initiative, make corrections in writing of any clerical, typographical or calculation errors, or any errors of a similar nature contained in the award.
2. Within thirty (30) days from its receipt of the arbitral award, either party may request the arbitral tribunal in writing for a correction of any clerical, typographical or calculation errors, or any errors of a similar nature contained in the award. If such an error does exist in the award, the arbitral tribunal shall make the correction in writing within thirty (30) days of its receipt of the written request for the correction.
3. The above written correction shall form a part of the arbitral award and shall be subject to the provisions in Paragraphs 4–9 of Article 49 of these Rules.

Article 54 Additional Award

1. Where any matter which should have been decided by the arbitral tribunal was omitted from the arbitral award, the arbitral tribunal may, on its own initiative, make an additional award within a reasonable time after the award is made.
2. Either party may, within thirty (30) days from its receipt of the arbitral award, request the arbitral tribunal in writing for an additional award on any claim or counterclaim which was advanced in the arbitral proceedings but was omitted from the award. If such an omission does exist, the arbitral tribunal shall make an additional award within thirty (30) days of its receipt of the written request.
3. Such additional award shall form a part of the arbitral award and shall be subject to the provisions in Paragraphs 4–9 of Article 49 of these Rules.

Article 55 Performance of Award

1. The parties shall perform the arbitral award within the time period specified in the award. If no time period is specified in the award, the parties shall perform the award immediately.
2. Where one party fails to perform the award, the other party may apply to a competent court for enforcement of the award in accordance with the law.

Chapter IV Summary Procedure

Article 56 Application

1. The Summary Procedure shall apply to any case where the amount in dispute does not exceed RMB 5,000,000 unless otherwise agreed by the parties; or where the amount in dispute exceeds RMB 5,000,000, yet one party applies for arbitration under the Summary Procedure and the other party agrees in writing; or where both parties have agreed to apply the Summary Procedure.
2. Where there is no monetary claim or the amount in dispute is not clear, CIETAC shall determine whether or not to apply the Summary Procedure after full consideration of relevant factors, including but not limited to the complexity of the case and the interests involved.

Article 57 Notice of Arbitration

Where after examination the Claimant's arbitration application is accepted for arbitration under the Summary Procedure, the Arbitration Court shall send a Notice of Arbitration to both parties.

Article 58 Formation of the Arbitral Tribunal

Unless otherwise agreed by the parties, a sole-arbitrator tribunal shall be formed in accordance with Article 28 of these Rules to hear a case under the Summary Procedure.

Article 59 Defense and Counterclaim

1. The Respondent shall submit its Statement of Defense, evidence and other supporting documents within twenty (20) days of its receipt of the Notice of Arbitration. Counterclaim, if any, shall also be filed with evidence and supporting documents within such time period.
2. The Claimant shall file its Statement of Defense to the Respondent's counterclaim within twenty (20) days of its receipt of the counterclaim and its attachments.
3. If a party has justified reasons to request an extension of the time period, the arbitral tribunal shall decide whether to grant such extension. Where the arbitral tribunal has not yet been formed, such decision shall be made by the Arbitration Court.

Article 60 Conduct of Hearing

The arbitral tribunal may examine the case in the manner it considers appropriate. The arbitral tribunal may decide whether to examine the case solely on the basis of the written materials and evidence submitted by the parties or to hold an oral hearing after hearing from the parties of their opinions.

Article 61 Notice of Oral Hearing

1. For a case examined by way of an oral hearing, after the arbitral tribunal has fixed a date for the first oral hearing, the parties shall be notified of the date at least fifteen (15) days in advance of the oral hearing. A party having justified reasons may request a postponement of the oral hearing. However, the party shall communicate such request in writing to the arbitral tribunal within three (3) days of its receipt of the notice of the oral hearing. The arbitral tribunal shall decide whether or not to postpone the oral hearing.
2. If a party has justified reasons for failure to submit a request for a postponement of the oral hearing in accordance with the preceding Paragraph 1, the arbitral tribunal shall decide whether to accept such a request.
3. A notice of a subsequent oral hearing, a notice of a postponed oral hearing, as well as a request for postponement of such oral hearing, shall not be subject to the time periods specified in the preceding Paragraph 1.

Article 62 Time Period for Rendering Award

1. The arbitral tribunal shall render an arbitral award within three (3) months from the date on which the arbitral tribunal is formed.
2. Upon the request of the arbitral tribunal, the President of the Arbitration Court may extend the time period if he/she considers it truly necessary and the reasons for the extension truly justified.
3. Any suspension period shall be excluded when calculating the time period in the preceding Paragraph 1.

Article 63 Change of Procedure

The Summary Procedure shall not be affected by any amendment to the claim or by the filing of a counterclaim. Where the amount in dispute of the amended claim or that of the counterclaim exceeds RMB 5,000,000, the Summary Procedure shall continue to apply unless the parties agree or the arbitral tribunal decides that a change to the general procedure is necessary.

Article 64 Context Reference

The relevant provisions in the other chapters of these Rules shall apply to matters not covered in this chapter.

Chapter V Special Provisions for Domestic Arbitration

Article 65 Application

1. The provisions of this chapter shall apply to domestic arbitration cases.
2. The provisions of the Summary Procedure in Chapter IV shall apply if a domestic arbitration case falls within the scope of Article 56 of these Rules.

Article 66 Acceptance of a Case

1. Upon receipt of a Request for Arbitration, where the Arbitration Court finds the Request to meet the requirements specified in Article 12 of these Rules, the Arbitration Court shall notify the parties accordingly within five (5) days from its receipt of the Request. Where a Request for Arbitration is found not to be in conformity with the requirements, the Arbitration Court shall notify the party in writing of its refusal of acceptance with reasons stated.
2. Upon receipt of a Request for Arbitration, where after examination, the Arbitration Court finds the Request not to be in conformity with the formality requirements specified in Article 12 of these Rules, it may request the Claimant to comply with the requirements within a specified time period.

Article 67 Formation of the Arbitral Tribunal

The arbitral tribunal shall be formed in accordance with the provisions of Articles 25, 26, 27, 28, 29, 30 of these Rules.

Article 68 Defense and Counterclaim

1. Within twenty (20) days from the date of its receipt of the Notice of Arbitration, the Respondent shall submit its Statement of Defense, evidence and other supporting documents. Counterclaim, if any, shall also be filed with evidence and other supporting documents within the time period.
2. The Claimant shall file its Statement of Defense to the Respondent's counterclaim within twenty (20) days from the date of its receipt of the counterclaim and its attachments.
3. If a party has justified reasons to request an extension of the time period, the arbitral tribunal shall decide whether to grant such extension. Where the arbitral tribunal has not yet been formed, such decision shall be made by the Arbitration Court.

Article 69 Notice of Oral Hearing

1. For a case examined by way of an oral hearing, after the arbitral tribunal has fixed a date for the first oral hearing, the parties shall be notified of the date at least fifteen (15) days in advance of the oral hearing. A party having justified reason may request a postponement of the oral hearing. However, the party shall communicate such request in writing to the arbitral tribunal within three (3) days of its receipt of the notice of the oral hearing. The arbitral tribunal shall decide whether or not to postpone the oral hearing.

2. If a party has justified reasons for failure to submit a request for a postponement of the oral hearing in accordance with the preceding Paragraph 1, the arbitral tribunal shall decide whether to accept such a request.
3. A notice of a subsequent oral hearing, a notice of a postponed oral hearing, as well as a request for postponement of such oral hearing, shall not be subject to the time periods specified in the preceding Paragraph 1.

Article 70 Record of Oral Hearing

1. The arbitral tribunal shall make a written record of the oral hearing. Any party or participant in the arbitration may apply for a correction upon finding any omission or mistake in the record regarding its own statements. If the application is refused by the arbitral tribunal, it shall nevertheless be recorded and kept with the file.
2. The written record shall be signed or sealed by the arbitrator(s), the recorder, the parties, and any other participant in the arbitration.

Article 71 Time Period for Rendering Award

1. The arbitral tribunal shall render an arbitral award within four (4) months from the date on which the arbitral tribunal is formed.
2. Upon the request of the arbitral tribunal, the President of the Arbitration Court may extend the time period if he/she considers it truly necessary and the reasons for the extension truly justified.
3. Any suspension period shall be excluded when calculating the time period in the preceding Paragraph 1.

Article 72 Context Reference

The relevant provisions in the other chapters of these Rules, with the exception of Chapter VI, shall apply to matters not covered in this chapter.

Chapter VI Special Provisions for Hong Kong Arbitration

Article 73 Application

1. CIETAC has established the CIETAC Hong Kong Arbitration Center in the Hong Kong Special Administrative Region. The provisions of this chapter shall apply to arbitration cases accepted and administered by the CIETAC Hong Kong Arbitration Center.
2. Where the parties have agreed to submit their disputes to the CIETAC Hong Kong Arbitration Center for arbitration or to CIETAC for arbitration in Hong Kong, the CIETAC Hong Kong Arbitration Center shall accept the arbitration application and administer the case.

Article 74 Place of Arbitration and Law Applicable to the Arbitral Proceedings

Unless otherwise agreed by the parties, for an arbitration administered by the CIETAC Hong Kong Arbitration Center, the place of arbitration shall be Hong

Kong, the law applicable to the arbitral proceedings shall be the arbitration law of Hong Kong, and the arbitral award shall be a Hong Kong award.

Article 75 Decision on Jurisdiction

Any objection to an arbitration agreement and/or the jurisdiction over an arbitration case shall be raised in writing no later than the submission of the first substantive defense.

The arbitral tribunal shall have the power to determine the existence and validity of the arbitration agreement and its jurisdiction over the arbitration case.

Article 76 Nomination or Appointment of Arbitrator

The CIETAC Panel of Arbitrators in effect shall be recommended in arbitration cases administered by the CIETAC Hong Kong Arbitration Center. The parties may nominate arbitrators from outside the CIETAC's Panel of Arbitrators. An arbitrator so nominated shall be subject to the confirmation of the Chairman of CIETAC.

Article 77 Interim Measures and Emergency Relief

1. Unless otherwise agreed by the parties, the arbitral tribunal has the power to order appropriate interim measures at the request of a party.
2. Where the arbitral tribunal has not yet been formed, a party may apply for emergency relief pursuant to the CIETAC Emergency Arbitrator Procedures (Appendix III).

Article 78 Seal on Award

The seal of the CIETAC Hong Kong Arbitration Center shall be affixed to the arbitral award.

Article 79 Arbitration Fees

The CIETAC Arbitration Fee Schedule III (Appendix II) shall apply to the arbitration cases accepted and administered in accordance with this chapter.

Article 80 Context Reference

The relevant provisions in the other chapters of these Rules, with the exception of Chapter V, shall apply to matters not covered in this chapter.

Chapter VII Supplementary Provisions

Article 81 Language

1. Where the parties have agreed on the language of arbitration, their agreement shall prevail. In the absence of such agreement, the language of arbitration to be used in the proceedings shall be Chinese. CIETAC may also designate another language as the language of arbitration having regard to the circumstances of the case.

2. If a party or its representative(s) or witness(es) requires interpretation at an oral hearing, an interpreter may be provided either by the Arbitration Court or by the party.
3. The arbitral tribunal or the Arbitration Court may, if it considers it necessary, require the parties to submit a corresponding translation of their documents and evidence into Chinese or other languages.

Article 82 Arbitration Fees and Costs

1. Apart from the arbitration fees charged in accordance with its Arbitration Fee Schedule, CIETAC may charge the parties for any other additional and reasonable actual costs, including but not limited to arbitrators' special remuneration, their travel and accommodation expenses incurred in dealing with the case, engagement fees of stenographers, as well as the costs and expenses of experts, appraisers or interpreters appointed by the arbitral tribunal. The Arbitration Court shall, after hearing from the arbitrator and the party concerned, determine the arbitrator's special remuneration with reference to the standards of arbitrators' fees and expenses set forth in the CIETAC Arbitration Fee Schedule III (Appendix II).
2. Where a party has nominated an arbitrator but fails to advance a deposit for such actual costs as the special remuneration, travel and accommodation expenses of the nominated arbitrator within the time period specified by CIETAC, the party shall be deemed not to have nominated the arbitrator.
3. Where the parties have agreed to hold an oral hearing at a place other than the domicile of CIETAC or its relevant sub-commission/arbitration center, they shall advance a deposit for the actual costs such as travel and accommodation expenses incurred thereby. In the event that the parties fail to do so within the time period specified by CIETAC, the oral hearing shall be held at the domicile of CIETAC or its relevant sub-commission/arbitration center.
4. Where the parties have agreed to use two or more than two languages as the languages of arbitration, or where the parties have agreed on a three-arbitrator tribunal in a case where the Summary Procedure shall apply in accordance with Article 56 of these Rules, CIETAC may charge the parties for any additional and reasonable costs.

Article 83 Interpretation

1. The headings of the articles in these Rules shall not be construed as interpretations of the contents of the provisions contained therein.
2. These Rules shall be interpreted by CIETAC.

Article 84 Coming into Force

These Rules shall be effective as of January 1, 2015. For cases administered by CIETAC or its sub-commissions/arbitration centers before these Rules come into force, the Arbitration Rules effective at the time of acceptance shall apply, or where both parties agree, these Rules shall apply.

Appendix I: Directory of China International Economic and Trade Arbitration Commission and Its Sub-commissions/Arbitration Centers

China International Economic and Trade Arbitration Commission (CIETAC)
Add: 6/F, CCOIC Building, No. 2 Huapichang Hutong,
Xicheng District, Beijing, 10035, P.R. China
Tel: 86 10 82217788
Fax: 86 10 82217766/64643500
E-mail: info@cietac.org
Website: http://www.cietac.org

CIETAC South China Sub-Commission[2]
Add: 14A01, Anlian Plaza, No. 4018, Jintian Road, Futian District, Shenzhen 518026, Guangdong Province, P.R.China
Tel: 86 755 82796739
Fax: 86 755 23964130
E-mail: infosz@cietac.org
Website: http://www.cietac.org

CIETAC Shanghai Sub-Commission[3]
Add: 18/F, Tomson Commercial Building, 710 Dongfang Road,
Pudong New Area, Shanghai 200122, P.R.China
Tel: 86 21 60137688
Fax: 86 21 60137689
E-Mail: infosh@cietac.org
Website: http://www.cietac.org

CIETAC Tianjin International Economic and Financial Arbitration Center (Tianjin Sub-commission)
Add: 4/F, E2-ABC, Financial Street, No. 20 Guangchangdong Road,
Tianjin Economic-Technological Development Zone,
Tianjin 300457, P.R.China
Tel: 86 22 66285688
Fax: 86 22 66285678
Email: tianjin@cietac.org
Website: http://www.cietac-tj.org

CIETAC Southwest Sub-Commission
Add: 1/F, Bld B, Caifu 3, Caifu Garden, Cai fu Zhongxin, Yubei, Chongqing 401121, China
Tel: 86 23 86871307
Fax: 86 23 86871190

[2]Now an independent arbitral institution with the acronym SCIA.
[3]Now an independent arbitral institution with the acronym SHIAC.

Email: cietac-sw@cietac.org
Website: http://www.cietac-sw.org

CIETAC Hong Kong Arbitration Center
Add: Unit 4705, 47th Floor, Far East Finance Center, No.16 Harcourt Road, Hong Kong.
Tel: 852 25298066
Fax: 852 25298266
Email: hk@cietac.org
Website: http://www.cietachk.org

Appendix II: China International Economic and Trade Arbitration Commission Arbitration Fee Schedule I

(This fee schedule applies to arbitration cases accepted under Item (a) and (b), Paragraph 2 of Article 3 of the Arbitration Rules)

Amount in dispute (RMB)	Arbitration fee (RMB)
Up to 1,000,000	4 % of the amount, minimum 10,000
From 1,000,001 to 2,000,000	40,000 + 3.5 % of the amount over 1,000,000
From 2,000,001 to 5,000,000	75,000 + 2.5 % of the amount over 2,000,000
From 5,000,001 to 10,000,000	150,000 + 1.5 % of the amount over 5,000,000
From 10,000,001 to 50,000,000	225,000 + 1 % of the amount over 10,000,000
From 50,000,001 to 100,000,000	625,000 + 0.5 % of the amount over 50,000,000
From 100,000,001 to 500,000,000	875,000 + 0.48 % of the amount over 100,000,000
From 500,000,001 to 1,000,000,000	2,795,000 + 0.47 % of the amount over 500,000,000
From 1,000,000,001 to 2,000,000,000	5,145,000 + 0.46 % of the amount over 1,000,000,000
Over 2,000,000,001	9,745,000 + 0.45 % of the amount over 2,000,000,000, maximum 15,000,000

When a case is accepted, an additional amount of RMB 10,000 shall be charged as the registration fee, which shall include the expenses for examining the application for arbitration, initiating the arbitral proceedings, computerizing management and filing documents.

The amount in dispute referred to in this Schedule shall be based on the sum of money claimed by the Claimant. If the amount claimed is different from the actual amount in dispute, the actual amount in dispute shall be the basis for calculation.

Where the amount in dispute is not ascertained at the time of applying for arbitration, or where special circumstances exist, the amount of the arbitration fee shall be determined by CIETAC.

Where the arbitration fee is to be charged in a foreign currency, the amount in the foreign currency shall be equivalent to the corresponding amount in RMB as specified in this Schedule.

Apart from charging the arbitration fee according to this Schedule, CIETAC may also collect other additional and reasonable actual expenses pursuant to the relevant provisions of the Arbitration Rules.

China International Economic and Trade Arbitration Commission Arbitration Fee Schedule II

(This fee schedule applies to arbitration cases accepted under Item (c), Paragraph 2 of Article 3 of the Arbitration Rules)

I. Registration Fee

Amount in dispute (RMB)	Registration fee (RMB)
Up to 1000	Minimum 100
From 1001 to 50,000	100 + 5 % of the amount over 1000
From 50,001 to 100,000	2550 + 4 % of the amount over 50,000
From 100,001 to 200,000	4550 + 3 % of the amount over 100,000
From 200,001 to 500,000	7550 + 2 % of the amount over 200,000
From 500,001 to 1,000,000	13,550 + 1 % of the amount over 500,000
Over 1,000,001	18,550 + 0.5 % of the amount over 1,000,000

II. Handling Fee

Amount in dispute (RMB)	Handling fee (RMB)
Up to 200,000	Minimum 6000
From 200,001 to 500,000	6000 + 2 % of the amount over 200,000
From 500,001 to 1,000,000	12,000 + 1.5 % of the amount over 500,000
From 1,000,001 to 2,000,000	19,500 + 0.5 % of the amount over 1,000,000
From 2,000,001 to 5,000,000	24,500 + 0.45 % of the amount over 2,000,000
From 5,000,001 to 10,000,000	38,000 + 0.4 % of the amount over 5,000,000
From 10,000,001 to 20,000,000	58,000 + 0.3 % of the amount over 10,000,000
From 20,000,001 to 40,000,000	88,000 + 0.2 % of the amount over 20,000,000
From 40,000,001 to 100,000,000	128,000 + 0.15 % of the amount over 40,000,000
From 100,000,001 to 500,000,000	218,000 + 0.13 % of the amount over 100,000,000
Over 500,000,001	738,000 + 0.12 % of the amount over 500,000,000

The amount in dispute referred to in this Schedule shall be based on the sum of money claimed by the Claimant. If the amount claimed is different from the actual amount in dispute, the actual amount in dispute shall be the basis for calculation.

Where the amount in dispute is not ascertained at the time of applying for arbitration, or where special circumstances exist, the amount of the arbitration fee deposit shall be determined by CIETAC in consideration of the specific rights and interests involved in the dispute.

Apart from charging the arbitration fee according to this Schedule, CIETAC may also collect other additional and reasonable actual expenses pursuant to the relevant provisions of the Arbitration Rules.

China International Economic and Trade Arbitration Commission Arbitration Fee Schedule III

(This fee schedule applies to arbitration cases administered by the CIETAC Hong Kong Arbitration Center under Chapter VI of the Arbitration Rules)

I. Registration Fee

When submitting a Request for Arbitration to the CIETAC Hong Kong Arbitration Center, the Claimant shall pay a registration fee of HKD 8000, which shall include the expenses for examining the application for arbitration, initiating the arbitral proceedings, computerizing management, filing documents and labor costs. The registration fee is not refundable.

II. Administrative Fee

1. Administrative Fee Table

Amount in dispute (HKD)	Administrative fee (HKD)
Up to 500,000	16,000
From 500,001 to 1,000,000	16,000 + 0.78 % of the amount over 500,000
From 1,000,001 to 5,000,000	19,900 + 0.65 % of the amount over 1,000,000
From 5,000,001 to 10,000,000	45,900 + 0.38 % of the amount over 5,000,000
From 10,000,001 to 20,000,000	64,900 + 0.22 % of the amount over 10,000,000
From 20,000,001 to 40,000,000	86,900 + 0.15 % of the amount over 20,000,000
From 40,000,001 to 80,000,000	116,900 + 0.08 % of the amount over 40,000,000
From 80,000,001 to 200,000,000	148,900 + 0.052 % of the amount over 80,000,000
From 200,000,001 to 400,000,000	211,300 + 0.04 % of the amount over 200,000,000
Over 400,000,001	291,300

2. The administrative fee includes the remuneration of the case manager and the costs of using oral hearing rooms of CIETAC and/or its sub-commissions/ arbitration centers.
3. Claims and counterclaims are aggregated for the determination of the amount in dispute. Where the amount in dispute is not ascertained at the time of applying for arbitration, or where special circumstances exist, the amount of the administrative fee shall be determined by CIETAC taking into account the circumstances of the case.
4. Apart from charging the administrative fee according to this Table, the CIETAC Hong Kong Arbitration Center may also collect other additional and reasonable actual expenses pursuant to the relevant provisions of the

Arbitration Rules, including but not limited to translation fees, written record fees, and the costs of using oral hearing rooms other than those of CIETAC and/or its sub-commissions/arbitration centers.

5. Where the registration fee and the administrative fee are to be charged in a currency other than HKD, the CIETAC Hong Kong Arbitration Center shall charge an amount of the foreign currency equivalent to the corresponding amount in HKD as specified in this table.

III. Arbitrator's Fees and Expenses

A. Arbitrator's Fees (Based o and Expenses n the Amount in Dispute)

1. Arbitrator's Fees Table

Amount in dispute (HKD)	Arbitrator's fees (HKD, per arbitrator)	
	Minimum	Maximum
Up to 500,000	15,000	60,000
From 500,001 to 1,000,000	15,000 + 2.30 % of the amount over 500,000	60,000 + 8.50 % of the amount over 500,000
From 1,000,001 to 5,000,000	26,500 + 0.80 % of the amount over 1,000,000	102,500 + 4.3 % of the amount over 1,000,000
From 5,000,001 to 10,000,000	58,500 + 0.60 % of the amount over 5,000,000	274,500 + 2.30 % of the amount over 5,000,000
From 10,000,001 to 20,000,000	88,500 + 0.35 % of the amount over 10,000,000	389,500 + 1.00 % of the amount over 10,000,000
From 20,000,001 to 40,000,000	123,500 + 0.20 % of the amount over 20,000,000	489,500 + 0.65 % of the amount over 20,000,000
From 40,000,001 to 80,000.000	163,500 + 0.07 % of the amount over 40,000,000	619,500 + 0.35 % of the amount over 40,000,000
From 80,000,001 to 200,000,000	191,500 + 0.05 % of the amount over 80,000,000	759,500 + 0.25 % of the amount over 80,000,000
From 200,000,001 to 400,000,000	251,500 + 0.03 % of the amount over 200,000,000	1,059,500 + 0.15 % of the amount over 200,000,000
From 400,000,001 to 600,000,000	311,500 + 0.02 % of the amount over 400,000,000	1,359,500 + 0.12 % of the amount over 400,000,000
From 600,000,001 to 750,000,000	351,500 + 0.01 % of the amount over 600,000,000	1,599,500 + 0.10 % of the amount over 600,000,000
Over 750,000,001	366,500 + 0.008 % of the amount over 750,000,000	1,749,500 + 0.06 % of the amount over 750,000,000

2. Unless otherwise stipulated in this Schedule, the arbitrator's fees shall be determined by CIETAC in accordance with the above table taking into account the circumstances of the case. The arbitrator's expenses shall include all reasonable actual expenses incurred from the arbitrator's arbitration activities.
3. The arbitrator's fees may exceed the corresponding maximum amount listed in the table provided that the parties so agree in writing or CIETAC so determines under exceptional circumstances.

4. The parties shall advance the payment of the arbitrator's fees and expenses determined by CIETAC to the CIETAC Hong Kong Arbitration Center. Subject to the approval of the CIETAC Hong Kong Arbitration Center, the parties may pay the arbitrator's fees and expenses in installments. The parties shall be jointly and severally liable for the payment of the arbitrator's fees and expenses.
5. Claims and counterclaims are aggregated for the determination of the amount in dispute. Where the amount in dispute is not ascertainable, or where special circumstances exist, the amount of the arbitrator's fees shall be determined by CIETAC taking into account the circumstances of the case.

B. Arbitrator's Fees and Expenses (Based on an Hourly Rate)

1. Where the parties have agreed in writing that the arbitrator's fees and expenses are to be based on an hourly rate, their agreement shall prevail. The arbitrator is entitled to fees based on an hourly rate for all the reasonable efforts devoted in the arbitration. The arbitrator's expenses shall include all reasonable actual expenses incurred from the arbitrator's arbitration activities.
2. Where a party applies for the Emergency Arbitrator Procedures, the emergency arbitrator's fees shall be based on an hourly rate.
3. The hourly rate for each co-arbitrator shall be the rate agreed upon by that co-arbitrator and the nominating party. The hourly rate for a sole or presiding arbitrator shall be the rate agreed upon by that arbitrator and both parties. Where the hourly rate cannot be agreed upon, or the arbitrator is appointed by the Chairman of CIETAC, the hourly rate of the arbitrator shall be determined by CIETAC. The hourly rate for the emergency arbitrator shall be determined by CIETAC.
4. An agreed or determined hourly rate shall not exceed the maximum rate fixed by CIETAC as provided on the website of the CIETAC Hong Kong Arbitration Center on the date of the submission of the Request for Arbitration. The arbitrator's fees may exceed the fixed maximum rate provided that the parties so agree in writing or CIETAC so determines under exceptional circumstances.
5. The parties shall advance the payment of the arbitrator's fees and expenses to the CIETAC Hong Kong Arbitration Center, which amount shall be fixed by the latter. The parties shall be jointly and severally liable for the payment of the arbitrator's fees and expenses.

C. Miscellaneous

1. In accordance with the decision of the arbitral tribunal, the CIETAC Hong Kong Arbitration Center shall have a lien over the award rendered by the tribunal so as to secure the payment of the outstanding fees for the arbitrators and all the expenses due. After all such fees and expenses have been paid in full jointly or by one of the parties, the CIETAC Hong Kong Arbitration Center shall release such award to the parties according to the decision of the arbitral tribunal.

2. Where the arbitrator's fees and expenses are to be charged in a currency other than HKD, the CIETAC Hong Kong Arbitration Center shall charge an amount of the foreign currency equivalent to the corresponding amount in HKD as specified in this Schedule.

Appendix III: China International Economic and Trade Arbitration Commission Emergency Arbitrator Procedures

Article 1 Application for the Emergency Arbitrator Procedures

1. A party requiring emergency relief may apply for the Emergency Arbitrator Procedures based upon the applicable law or the agreement of the parties.
2. The party applying for the Emergency Arbitrator Procedures (the "Applicant") shall submit its Application for the Emergency Arbitrator Procedures to the Arbitration Court or the arbitration court of the relevant sub-commission/ arbitration center of CIETAC administering the case prior to the formation of the arbitral tribunal.
3. The Application for the Emergency Arbitrator Procedures shall include the following information:

   (a) the names and other basic information of the parties involved in the Application;
   (b) a description of the underlying dispute giving rise to the Application and the reasons why emergency relief is required;
   (c) a statement of the emergency measures sought and the reasons why the applicant is entitled to such emergency relief;
   (d) other necessary information required to apply for the emergency relief; and
   (e) comments on the applicable law and the language of the Emergency Arbitrator Procedures.

   When submitting its Application, the Applicant shall attach the relevant documentary and other evidence on which the Application is based, including but not limited to the arbitration agreement and any other agreements giving rise to the underlying dispute.
   The Application, evidence and other documents shall be submitted in triplicate. Where there are multiple parties, additional copies shall be provided accordingly.
4. The Applicant shall advance the costs for the Emergency Arbitrator Procedures.
5. Where the parties have agreed on the language of arbitration, such language shall be the language of the Emergency Arbitrator Procedures. In the absence of such agreement, the language of the Procedures shall be determined by the Arbitration Court.

Article 2 Acceptance of Application and Appointment of the Emergency Arbitrator

1. After a preliminary review on the basis of the Application, the arbitration agreement and relevant evidence submitted by the Applicant, the Arbitration Court shall decide whether the Emergency Arbitrator Procedures shall apply. If the Arbitration Court decides to apply the Emergency Arbitrator Procedures, the President of the Arbitration Court shall appoint an emergency arbitrator within one (1) day from his/her receipt of both the Application and the advance payment of the costs for the Emergency Arbitrator Procedures.
2. Once the emergency arbitrator has been appointed by the President of the Arbitration Court, the Arbitration Court shall promptly transmit the Notice of Acceptance and the Applicant's application file to the appointed emergency arbitrator and the party against whom the emergency measures are sought, meanwhile copying the Notice of Acceptance to each of the other parties to the arbitration and the Chairman of CIETAC.

Article 3 Disclosure and Challenge of the Emergency Arbitrator

1. An emergency arbitrator shall not represent either party, and shall be and remain independent of the parties and treat them equally.
2. Upon acceptance of the appointment, an emergency arbitrator shall sign a Declaration and disclose to the Arbitration Court any facts or circumstances likely to give rise to justifiable doubts as to his/her impartiality or independence. If circumstances that need to be disclosed arise during the Emergency Arbitrator Procedures, the emergency arbitrator shall promptly disclose such circumstances in writing.
3. The Declaration and/or the disclosure of the emergency arbitrator shall be communicated to the parties by the Arbitration Court.
4. Upon receipt of the Declaration and/or the written disclosure of an emergency arbitrator, a party wishing to challenge the arbitrator on the grounds of the facts or circumstances disclosed by the emergency arbitrator shall forward the challenge in writing within two (2) days from the date of such receipt. If a party fails to file a challenge within the above time period, it may not subsequently challenge the emergency arbitrator on the basis of the matters disclosed by the emergency arbitrator.
5. A party which has justifiable doubts as to the impartiality or independence of the appointed emergency arbitrator may challenge that emergency arbitrator in writing and shall state the facts and reasons on which the challenge is based with supporting evidence.
6. A party may challenge an emergency arbitrator in writing within two (2) days from the date of its receipt of the Notice of Acceptance. Where a party becomes aware of a reason for a challenge after such receipt, the party may challenge the emergency arbitrator in writing within two (2) days after such reason has become known, but no later than the formation of the arbitral tribunal.

7. The President of the Arbitration Court shall make a final decision on the challenge of the emergency arbitrator. If the challenge is accepted, the President of the Arbitration Court shall reappoint an emergency arbitrator within one (1) day from the date of the decision confirming the challenge, and copy the decision to the Chairman of CIETAC. The emergency arbitrator who has been challenged shall continue to perform his/her functions until a final decision on the challenge has been made.
   The disclosure and challenge proceedings shall apply equally to the reappointed emergency arbitrator.
8. Unless otherwise agreed by the parties, the emergency arbitrator shall not accept nomination or appointment to act as a member of the arbitral tribunal in any arbitration relating to the underlying dispute.

Article 4 Place of the Emergency Arbitrator Proceedings

Unless otherwise agreed by the parties, the place of the emergency arbitrator proceedings shall be the place of arbitration, which is determined in accordance with Article 7 of the Arbitration Rules.

Article 5 The Emergency Arbitrator Proceedings

1. The emergency arbitrator shall establish a procedural timetable for the emergency arbitrator proceedings within a time as short as possible, best within two (2) days from his/her acceptance of the appointment. The emergency arbitrator shall conduct the proceedings in the manner the emergency arbitrator considers to be appropriate, taking into account the nature and the urgency of the emergency relief, and shall ensure that each party has a reasonable opportunity to present its case.
2. The emergency arbitrator may order the provision of appropriate security by the party seeking the emergency relief as the precondition of taking emergency measures.
3. The power of the emergency arbitrator and the emergency arbitrator proceedings shall cease on the date of the formation of the arbitral tribunal.
4. The emergency arbitrator proceedings shall not affect the right of the parties to seek interim measures from a competent court pursuant to the applicable law.

Article 6 Decision of the Emergency Arbitrator

1. The emergency arbitrator has the power to make a decision to order or award necessary emergency relief, and shall make every reasonable effort to ensure that the decision is valid.
2. The decision of the emergency arbitrator shall be made within fifteen (15) days from the date of that arbitrator's acceptance of the appointment. The President of the Arbitration Court may extend the time period upon the request of the emergency arbitrator only if the President of the Arbitration Court considers it reasonable.

3. The decision of the emergency arbitrator shall state the reasons for taking the emergency measures, be signed by the emergency arbitrator and stamped with the seal of the Arbitration Court or the arbitration court of its relevant sub-commission/arbitration center.
4. The decision of the emergency arbitrator shall be binding upon both parties. A party may seek enforcement of the decision from a competent court pursuant to the relevant law provisions of the enforcing state or region. Upon a reasoned request of a party, the emergency arbitrator or the arbitral tribunal to be formed may modify, suspend or terminate the decision.
5. The emergency arbitrator may decide to dismiss the application of the Applicant and terminate the emergency arbitrator proceedings, if that arbitrator considers that circumstances exist where emergency measures are unnecessary or unable to be taken for various reasons.
6. The decision of the emergency arbitrator shall cease to be binding:

   (a) if the emergency arbitrator or the arbitral tribunal terminates the decision of the emergency arbitrator;
   (b) if the President of the Arbitration Court decides to accept a challenge against the emergency arbitrator;
   (c) upon the rendering of a final award by the arbitral tribunal, unless the arbitral tribunal decides that the decision of the emergency arbitrator shall continue to be effective;
   (d) upon the Applicant's withdrawal of all claims before the rendering of a final award;
   (e) if the arbitral tribunal is not formed within ninety (90) days from the date of the decision of the emergency arbitrator. This period of time may be extended by agreement of the parties or by the Arbitration Court under circumstances it considers appropriate; or
   (f) if the arbitration proceedings have been suspended for sixty (60) consecutive days after the formation of the arbitral tribunal.

Article 7 Costs of the Emergency Arbitrator Proceedings

1. The Applicant shall advance an amount of RMB 30,000 as the costs of the emergency arbitrator proceedings, consisting of the remuneration of the emergency arbitrator and the administrative fee of CIETAC. The Arbitration Court may require the Applicant to advance any other additional and reasonable actual costs.
   A party applying to the CIETAC Hong Kong Arbitration Center for emergency relief shall advance the costs of the emergency arbitrator proceedings in accordance with the CIETAC Arbitration Fee Schedule III (Appendix II).
2. The emergency arbitrator shall determine in its decision in what proportion the costs of the emergency arbitrator proceedings shall be borne by the parties, subject to the power of the arbitral tribunal to finally determine the allocation of such costs at the request of a party.

3. The Arbitration Court may fix the amount of the costs of the emergency arbitrator proceedings refundable to the Applicant if such proceedings terminate before the emergency arbitrator has made a decision.

Article 8 Miscellaneous

These rules for the Emergency Arbitrator Procedures shall be interpreted by CIETAC.

SHIAC Arbitration Rules[4]

Shanghai International Economic and Trade Arbitration Commission (Shanghai International Arbitration Center) Arbitration Rules

Adopted at the Fifth Meeting of the Second Session of the Shanghai International Economic and Trade Arbitration Commission (Shanghai International Arbitration Center), effective as from January 1, 2015

Chapter I General Provisions

Article 1 These Rules

These Rules are formulated in accordance with the Arbitration Law of the People's Republic of China and relevant provisions of other applicable laws.

Article 2 Institution and Functions

1. Shanghai International Economic and Trade Arbitration Commission (also "Shanghai International Arbitration Center," formerly the "China International Economic and Trade Arbitration Commission Shanghai Commission/Sub-Commission," hereinafter referred to as "SHIAC") is an arbitration institution which resolves contractual disputes and other disputes over rights and interests in property between natural persons, legal persons and other economic organizations with equal status.

[4]http://www.shiac.org/upload/day_141230/SHIAC_ARBITRATION_RULES_2015_141222.pdf.

2. SHIAC has established the China (Shanghai) Pilot Free Trade Zone Court of Arbitration in China (Shanghai) Pilot Free Trade Zone, to provide arbitration services including consulting, case filing and hearings.
3. SHIAC has established the Shanghai International Aviation Court of Arbitration, to provide arbitration services including consulting, case filing and hearings.
4. Where an arbitration agreement provides for arbitration by the Shanghai International Economic and Trade Arbitration Commission, Shanghai International Arbitration Center, or by the China International Economic and Trade Arbitration Commission Shanghai Commission/Shanghai Sub-Commission, the parties shall be deemed to have agreed that arbitration shall be administered by SHIAC. Where an arbitration agreement provides for arbitration by the Arbitration Commission or the Court of Arbitration of the China Council for the Promotion of International Trade Shanghai Sub-Council/Chamber of International Commerce Shanghai, or by the Shanghai Foreign Economic and Trade Arbitration Commission, or by the China (Shanghai) Pilot Free Trade Zone Court of Arbitration, or by the Shanghai International Aviation Court of Arbitration, or designates an institution that can reasonably be inferred to be SHIAC, the parties shall be deemed to have agreed that arbitration shall be administered by SHIAC.
5. SHIAC formulated The China (Shanghai) Pilot Free Trade Zone Arbitration Rules for the purpose of resolving disputes in connection with the China (Shanghai) Pilot Free Trade Zone.
6. SHIAC shall perform the functions that should be performed by an arbitration institution referred to in other arbitration rules which are applicable upon parties' agreement.
7. Where the parties agree to arbitrate under the Arbitration Rules of the United Nations Commission on International Trade Law (here in after the "UNCITRAL Arbitration Rules") or other arbitration rules, SHIAC shall be the appointing authority and shall perform other relevant administrative functions in accordance with the provisions of the UNCITRAL Arbitration Rules or the agreement of the parities.
8. The Chairman of SHIAC shall perform the functions and duties vested in him/her by these Rules while a Vice-Chairman may perform the Chairman's functions and duties with the Chairman's authorization.
9. SHIAC has a Secretariat, which handles its day-to-day work under the direction of the Secretary General, and performs the functions and duties vested by these Rules.
10. SHIAC is domiciled in Shanghai, China.
11. SHIAC shall establish a Panel of Arbitrators.
12. SHIAC shall establish a Panel of Mediators in respect of "Mediation by Mediator" under The China (Shanghai) Pilot Free Trade Zone Arbitration Rules.

Article 3 Scope of Application

1. These Rules shall apply where parties have agreed to refer their disputes to SHIAC.
2. Where the parties have agreed to refer their disputes to SHIAC for arbitration under other arbitration rules, or agreed on any modification of these Rules, the parties' agreement shall prevail except where such an agreement is inoperative or in conflict with a mandatory provision of the law of the place of arbitration.
3. Where parties agree to refer their disputes to arbitration under these Rules without designating an arbitration institution, they shall be deemed to have agreed to refer their disputes to SHIAC for arbitration under these Rules.
4. The China (Shanghai) Pilot Free Trade Zone Arbitration Rules shall apply where parties have agreed to refer their disputes to SHIAC and the parties or the subject matter to a dispute or the legal facts that lead to the establishment, change or termination of civil and commercial relationship are connected with the China (Shanghai) Pilot Free Trade Zone, unless otherwise agreed to by the parties with respect to arbitration rules.
5. The China (Shanghai) Pilot Free Trade Zone Arbitration Rules shall apply where parties have agreed to refer their disputes to SHIAC for arbitration and have agreed to apply The China (Shanghai) Pilot Free Trade Zone Arbitration Rules for arbitration.
6. The China (Shanghai) Pilot Free Trade Zone Arbitration Rules shall apply where parties have agreed to refer their disputes to SHIAC and arbitration is to be conducted at the China (Shanghai) Pilot Free Trade Zone Court of Arbitration, or have agreed to refer their disputes to the China (Shanghai) Pilot Free Trade Zone Court of Arbitration or have designated an institution that can reasonably be inferred to be the China (Shanghai) Pilot Free Trade Zone Court of Arbitration; the China (Shanghai) Pilot Free Trade Zone Arbitration Rules shall also apply where parties have agreed to refer their disputes to SHIAC and arbitration is to be conducted at the Shanghai International Aviation Court of Arbitration, or have agreed to refer their disputes to the Shanghai International Aviation Court of Arbitration or have designated an institution that can reasonably be inferred to be the Shanghai International Aviation Court of Arbitration, unless otherwise agreed to by the parties with respect to arbitration rules.
7. Where parties agree to refer their disputes to arbitration under The China (Shanghai) Pilot Free Trade Zone Arbitration Rules without designating an arbitration institution, they shall be deemed to have agreed to refer their disputes to SHIAC for arbitration under The China (Shanghai) Pilot Free Trade Zone Arbitration Rules.
8. SHIAC has the discretion to decide on an objection to the application of these Rules by a party.

Article 4 Jurisdiction

SHIAC accepts cases involving:

1. international or foreign-related disputes;
2. disputes relating to the Hong Kong Special Administrative Region, the Macao Special Administrative Region or the Taiwan region; and
3. domestic disputes.

Article 5 Arbitration Agreement

1. SHIAC shall, upon the written application of a party, accept a case in accordance with the arbitration agreement concluded between the parties, either before or after the occurrence of the dispute, in which it is provided that a dispute is to be referred to SHIAC for arbitration.
2. An arbitration agreement means an arbitration clause in a contract concluded between the parties or any other form of written agreement providing for the settlement of disputes by arbitration.
3. An arbitration agreement shall be in writing. An arbitration agreement is in writing if it is contained in a tangible form of a document such as, but not limited to, a contract, letter, telegram, telex, facsimile, EDI, or email. An arbitration agreement shall be deemed to exist where its existence is asserted by one party and not denied by the other during the exchange of the Request for Arbitration and the Statement of Defense.
4. Where there are different provisions on the form and validity of an arbitration agreement in the laws applicable to an arbitration agreement, such provisions shall prevail.
5. An arbitration clause contained in a contract shall be treated as a clause independent of and separate from all other clauses of the contract, and an arbitration agreement attached to a contract shall also be treated as independent of and separate from all other clauses of the contract. The validity of an arbitration clause or an arbitration agreement shall not be affected by any modification, rescission, termination, transfer, expiration, invalidity, ineffectiveness, revocation or non-existence of the contract.

Article 6 Objection to Arbitration Agreement and/or Jurisdiction

1. SHIAC has the discretion to decide on the existence and validity of an arbitration agreement and its jurisdiction over an arbitration case. SHIAC may, if necessary, delegate such power to the tribunal, and the tribunal, according to such delegation, may either render a separate decision on jurisdiction during the arbitration proceedings, or incorporate the decision in the award.
2. Where SHIAC is satisfied with *prima facie* evidence that an arbitration agreement providing for arbitration by SHIAC and binding on the parties exists, it may decide based on such evidence that it has jurisdiction over the arbitration case, and arbitration shall proceed. Where, after SHIAC renders such a decision, the tribunal finds the facts and/or evidence inconsistent with the *prima facie*

evidence during the arbitration proceedings, SHIAC may delegate the tribunal to render a new decision on jurisdiction.

3. An objection to an arbitration agreement and/or jurisdiction over an arbitration case shall be made in writing before the first hearing is held by the tribunal. Where a case is to be decided solely on documentary evidence, such an objection shall be made before the time when the substantive defense is first submitted.
4. Arbitration shall proceed notwithstanding an objection to the arbitration agreement and/or jurisdiction over the arbitration case.
5. The aforesaid objections to and/or decisions on jurisdiction by SHIAC shall include objections to and/or decisions on a party's standing to participate in arbitration.

Article 7 Place of Arbitration

1. Where the parties have agreed on the place of arbitration in writing, the parties' agreement shall prevail.
2. Where the parties have not agreed on the place of arbitration, the place of arbitration shall be the domicile of SHIAC.
3. An award shall be deemed as being rendered at the place of arbitration.

Article 8 *Bona Fides*

The parties shall proceed with the arbitration in a *bona fides* manner.

Article 9 Waiver of Right to Object

A party shall be deemed to have waived its right to object where it knows or should have known that any provision of, or requirement under, these Rules or arbitration agreements has not been complied with and yet participates in or proceeds with the arbitration proceedings without promptly and explicitly submitting its objection in writing to such non-compliance.

Chapter II Arbitral Proceedings

Section 1 Request for Arbitration and Counterclaim

Article 10 Commencement of Arbitration

The arbitration proceedings shall commence on the date on which SHIAC receives the Request for Arbitration by SHIAC.

Article 11 Application for Arbitration

A party applying for arbitration under these Rules shall:

1. Submit a Request for Arbitration in writing signed by and/or sealed by the Claimant and/or its authorized representative(s), which shall, inter alia, include:
   (a) the names and domiciles of the Claimant and the Respondent, including the post code, telephone, telex, fax and telegraph numbers, email addresses or any other means of electronic telecommunications;

(b) a reference to the arbitration agreement that is invoked;
(c) the claims of the Claimant; and
(d) the facts and grounds on which the claims are based.

2. Attach to the Request for Arbitration the evidence which supports the Claimant's claims, documents certifying the party's identity and other relevant documentary evidence.
3. Pay the arbitration fees in advance to SHIAC according to the Schedules of Arbitration Fees attached with these Rules.

Article 12 Acceptance

1. Upon receipt of the Request for Arbitration and its attachments, SHIAC may request the Claimant to complete if it finds, after examination, the formalities required for the application for arbitration to be incomplete. Where the party fails to complete the formalities as required, the party is deemed to have not submitted the Request for Arbitration.
2. Where the formalities of Application for Arbitration are found to be complete, the Secretariat shall send a Notice of Acceptance to the Claimant together with the Arbitration Rules, the Panel of Arbitrators and the Schedules of Arbitration Fees within five (5) days. The Secretariat shall send to the Respondent, within five (5) days after the Notice of Acceptance is sent, the Notice of Arbitration together with the Request for Arbitration and its attachments, the Arbitration Rules, the Panel of Arbitrators and the Schedules of Arbitration Fees.
3. SHIAC shall, after accepting a case, designate one or two staff members of the Secretariat to assist the tribunal in the procedural administration of the case.

Article 13 Defense

1. Within forty five (45) days from the date of receipt of the Notice of Arbitration, the Respondent shall submit a Statement of Defense in writing to the Secretariat. For such cases involving disputes referred to in Article 4.3 of these Rules, the corresponding period shall be twenty (20) days.
2. If the Respondent does have justifiable reasons to request an extension of the time limit for submitting the Statement of Defense, the tribunal shall, at its discretion, decide whether or not to grant such request. If the tribunal has not been constituted, the Secretariat shall render a decision.
3. The Statement of Defense shall be signed by and/or sealed by the Respondent and/or its authorized representative(s), and shall, inter alia, include:

   (a) the name and domicile of the Respondent, including the post code, telephone, telex, fax and telegraph numbers, Email addresses or any other means of electronic telecommunications; and
   (b) the defense to the Request for Arbitration setting forth the facts and grounds on which the defense is based.

4. When submitting the Statement of Defense, the Respondent shall attach thereto the evidence on which the Defense is based, documents certifying the party's identity and other relevant evidence.
5. The tribunal has the discretion to decide whether to accept a Statement of Defense submitted after the expiration of the aforesaid time limit.
6. Failure of the Respondent to submit a Statement of Defense shall not affect the conduct of the arbitration proceedings.

Article 14 Counterclaim and Defense

1. Within forty-five (45) days from the date of receipt of the Notice of Arbitration, the Respondent shall file with the Secretariat its counterclaim in writing, if any. For cases involving disputes referred to in Article 4.3 of these Rules, the corresponding period shall be twenty (20) days.
2. If the Respondent does have justifiable reasons to request an extension of the time limit for submitting the counterclaim, the tribunal shall, at its discretion, decide whether to grant such request. If the tribunal has not been constituted, the Secretariat shall make the decision.
3. The tribunal has the discretion to decide whether to accept a counterclaim submitted after the expiration of the aforesaid time limit.
4. When submitting a counterclaim, the Respondent shall specify in writing in its Statement of Counterclaim and state the facts and grounds upon which its counterclaim is based, together with relevant evidence attached thereto.
5. When submitting a counterclaim, the Respondent shall pay the arbitration fees in advance according to the Schedules of Arbitration Fees attached with these Rules within a specified period of time, failing which the Respondent shall be deemed not to have submitted any counterclaim.
6. Where the formalities required for filing a counterclaim are found to be complete, SHIAC shall send the Statement of Counterclaim and its attachments to the Claimant. The Claimant shall, within thirty (30) days from the date of receipt of the Statement of Counterclaim and the attachment, submit in writing its Statement of Defense to the Respondent's counterclaim. For such cases involving disputes as referred to in Article 4.3 of these Rules, the corresponding period shall be twenty (20) days. If the Claimant does have justifiable reasons to request an extension of the time limit for filing the Statement of Defense, the tribunal shall, at its discretion, decide whether to extend it or not. If the tribunal has not been constituted, the Secretariat shall make the decision.
7. The tribunal has the discretion to decide whether to accept a Statement of Defense to the Respondent's counterclaim submitted after expiration of the aforesaid time limit.
8. Failure of the Claimant to submit a Statement of Defense to the Respondent's counterclaim shall not affect the conduct of arbitration proceedings.

Article 15 Amendment to Claim or Counterclaim

The Claimant may amend its claim and the Respondent may amend its counterclaim. However, the tribunal has the power to refuse any such amendment if it considers that the amendment is so late that it may affect the arbitration proceedings.

Article 16 Copies of Submissions

When submitting the Request for Arbitration, the Statement of Defense, the Statement of Counterclaim, evidence and other documents, the parties shall make the submissions in quintuplicate. Where there are more than two parties, additional copies shall be provided accordingly. Where the tribunal is composed of a sole arbitrator, the number of copies submitted may be reduced by two. Where a party applies for preservation measures, that party shall submit additional copies accordingly.

Article 17 Representation

1. A party may be represented by one (1) to five (5) authorized Chinese and/or foreign representative(s) to handle matters relating to arbitration. In such a case, a Power of Attorney shall be submitted.
2. If a party intends to be represented by more than five (5) authorized representatives, a written application stating the reasons is required. The tribunal has the discretion to decide whether or not to grant such application in accordance with circumstances of the arbitration. Where the request is made before the tribunal is constituted, the Secretariat shall make the decision.

Article 18 Preservation Measures

1. When any party applies for the preservation of property, SHIAC shall forward the party's application for a ruling to the competent court at the place where the domicile of the party against whom the preservation of property is sought is located or where the property of the said party is located.
2. When any party applies for the preservation of evidence, SHIAC shall forward the party's application for a ruling to the competent court at the place where the evidence of the said party is located.

Section 2 Tribunal

Article 19 Duties of Arbitrator(s)

An arbitrator shall not represent either party, and shall remain independent of the parties and treat them equally.

Article 20 Number of Arbitrator(s)

1. The tribunal shall be composed of one or three arbitrators.
2. Unless otherwise agreed to by the parties or provided by these Rules, the tribunal shall be composed of three arbitrators.

Article 21 Appointment of Arbitrator(s)

1. Parties may appoint arbitrators from the Panel of Arbitrators.
2. Where the parties have agreed to appoint arbitrators from outside of the Panel of Arbitrators, the arbitrator(s) so appointed by the parties or nominated according to the agreement of the parties may act as co-arbitrator, presiding arbitrator or sole arbitrator after the appointment has been confirmed by the Chairman of SHIAC in accordance with the law.

Article 22 Three-arbitrator Tribunal

1. Within fifteen (15) days upon the receipt of the Notice of Acceptance/Notice of Arbitration, both parties shall respectively appoint or entrust the Chairman of SHIAC to appoint one arbitrator. Where a party fails to appoint or entrust the Chairman of SHIAC to appoint an arbitrator within the specified period of time, the Chairman of SHIAC shall appoint the arbitrator. If a party requests to extend the time limit of appointing an arbitrator, it shall submit a written application to SHIAC within the time limit in this Article. The Secretariat shall decide whether to accept such a request.
2. Within fifteen (15) days from the date of the Respondent's receipt of the Notice of Arbitration, the third arbitrator shall be jointly appointed from the Panel of Arbitrators by the parties or by the Chairman of SHIAC upon the parties' joint authorization. The third arbitrator shall act as the presiding arbitrator of the tribunal.
3. Both parties may respectively recommend one (1) to three (3) arbitrators as candidates for the presiding arbitrator and shall submit the list of recommended candidates to the Secretariat within the period of time specified in Article 22.2. Where there is only one common candidate in the lists, such a candidate shall act as the presiding arbitrator jointly appointed by the parties. Where there are more than one (1) common candidate on the lists, the Chairman of SHIAC shall choose a presiding arbitrator from among the common candidates based on the specific nature and circumstances of the case, who shall act as the presiding arbitrator jointly appointed by the parties. Where there is no common candidate in the lists, the Chairman of SHIAC shall appoint the presiding arbitrator from out of the lists of recommended candidates.
4. Where the parties have failed to jointly appoint the presiding arbitrator according to the above provisions, the presiding arbitrator shall be appointed by the Chairman of SHIAC.
5. The parties shall bear the expenses for travel and accommodation, arbitrators' special remuneration and other necessary costs incurred by the arbitrators for hearing a case. If either party fails to make the payment for such expenses in advance as a deposit within the specified period of time, such an arbitrator appointed by the party shall be deemed to have not been appointed by that party, and such agreement as in connection with the appointment of arbitrators by the parties will be deemed inoperative. Under such circumstances, the Chairman of

SHIAC shall appoint/re-appoint an arbitrator pursuant to the provisions in these Rules.

6. Where an appointed arbitrator refuses to accept the appointment, or is incapable of participating in the hearing of the case due to his/her health or other reasons which may affect the normal performance of his/her duties as arbitrator, the party shall appoint another arbitrator within ten (10) days upon the date of receipt of the notice to appoint another arbitrator by that party. Where the party fails to appoint another arbitrator according this Article, the Chairman of SHIAC shall appoint the arbitrator.

Article 23 Sole-arbitrator Tribunal

Where the tribunal is composed of one arbitrator, the sole arbitrator shall be appointed pursuant to the procedures stipulated in Article 22.2, Article 22.3, Article 22.4 and Article 22.5.

Article 24 Tribunal in Multiple Parties' Arbitration

1. Where there are two (2) or more Claimants and/or Respondents in an arbitration case, the Claimants and/or the Respondents each shall, through consultation, jointly appoint or jointly entrust the Chairman of this Commission to appoint one arbitrator from the Panel of Arbitrators.
2. Where the Claimants and/or the Respondents fail to jointly appoint or jointly entrust the Chairman of SHIAC to appoint one arbitrator within fifteen (15) days from the date of receipt of the Notice of Acceptance/Notice of Arbitration, the arbitrator shall be appointed by the Chairman of SHIAC.
3. The presiding arbitrator or sole arbitrator shall be appointed in accordance with the procedure stipulated in Article 22.2, Article 22.3, Article 22.4 and Article 22.5 of these Rules. When appointing the presiding arbitrator or the sole arbitrator pursuant to Article 22.3, the Claimants and/or the Respondents shall, through consultation, submit a list of their jointly agreed candidates to the Secretariat of SHIAC.

Article 25 Disclosure

1. The arbitrator(s) shall sign a Declaration and disclose to SHIAC in writing any facts or circumstances which may give a rise to justifiable doubts as to his/her impartiality or independence.
2. If circumstances that need to be disclosed arise during the arbitration proceedings, the relevant arbitrator shall promptly disclose such circumstances in writing to SHIAC.
3. The arbitrator shall submit the Declaration and/or the disclosure to the Secretariat. The Secretariat shall forward the arbitrator's submissions to the parties.

Article 26 Challenge to Arbitrator(s)

1. Upon receipt of the Declaration and/or written disclosure of an arbitrator communicated by the Secretariat, a party who intends to challenge the arbitrator

on the grounds of the facts or circumstances disclosed by the arbitrator shall forward the challenge in writing to SHIAC within ten (10) days upon the date of such receipt. If a party fails to raise a challenge within the aforesaid time limit, it shall not challenge an arbitrator later on the basis of facts disclosed by the arbitrator.

2. A party who has justifiable doubts as to the impartiality or independence of arbitrator(s) may make a request in writing to SHIAC for that arbitrator's withdrawal. In the request, the facts and reasons on which the request is based shall be stated with supporting evidence. The aforesaid challenge of arbitrator shall be made in writing within fifteen (15) days upon the date of receipt of the Notice of the Constitution of the Tribunal. Where a party becomes aware of the facts and reasons for a challenge after that time, the party may challenge the arbitrator in writing within fifteen (15) days after such facts and reasons become known to the party, but no later than the conclusion of the last hearing.
3. The Secretariat shall communicate the challenge promptly to the other party, the arbitrator being challenged and the other members of the tribunal, who subsequently may all provide their comments on such challenge.
4. Where an arbitrator is challenged by one party and the other party agrees to the challenge, or the arbitrator being challenged withdraws from his/her office, such arbitrator shall no longer act as an arbitrator. Neither circumstance shall imply that the challenge made by the party is sustainable.
5. In circumstances other than those specified in Article 26.4, the Chairman of SHIAC shall render a decision on the challenge with or without stating the reasons thereof.
6. An arbitrator who has been challenged shall continue to perform his/her functions as arbitrator until a decision on the challenge has been made by the Chairman of SHIAC.

Article 27 Replacement of Arbitrator(s)

1. In the event that an arbitrator is prevented *de jure* or *de facto* from performing his/her functions, or he/she fails to perform his/her functions in accordance with the requirements in these Rules or within the period of time specified in these Rules, the Chairman of SHIAC has the discretion to decide whether to replace such arbitrator. Such arbitrator may also withdraw from his/her office.
2. In the event that an arbitrator is unable to perform his/her functions owing to his/her health reasons, removal from the Panel of Arbitrators, withdrawal, resignation or any other reasons, a substitute arbitrator shall be appointed according to Article 22.6.
3. After the replacement of the arbitrator(s), the tribunal shall decide whether to resume the proceedings that have been wholly or partially conducted.
4. The Chairman of SHIAC shall make the decision on whether or not an arbitrator should be replaced with or without stating the reasons therefor.

Article 28 Remaining Arbitrators to Continue Arbitration

In the event that, after the conclusion of the last hearing, an arbitrator in a three-arbitrator tribunal is unable to participate in the deliberation and/or render the award owing to his/her health reasons, or removal from the Panel of Arbitrators, the remaining arbitrators may request the Chairman of SHIAC to replace the arbitrator pursuant to Article 27. After consulting with the parties and upon the approval of the Chairman of SHIAC, the remaining arbitrators may continue the arbitration proceedings and make decisions or render the award. The Secretariat shall notify the parties of the matters above.

Section 3 Hearings

Article 29 Conduct of Hearing

1. The tribunal shall examine the case in any manner that it deems appropriate unless otherwise agreed to by the parties. Under any circumstance, the tribunal shall act impartially and fairly and shall provide reasonable opportunities to all parties for them to present and argue their cases.
2. The tribunal shall hold hearings when examining the case. However, hearings may be omitted and the case shall be examined on the basis of documents only if the parties so request or agree to and the tribunal also deems that hearings are unnecessary.
3. The tribunal may hold the deliberations at any place or in any manner that it deems appropriate.
4. Unless otherwise agreed to by the parties, the tribunal may, if it considers necessary, issue procedural directions and lists of questions, hold pre-hearing meetings and preliminary hearings, and produce terms of reference, and may also make an arrangement for the exchange and/or examination of evidence.

Article 30 Consolidation of Arbitrations

1. The tribunal may, on the application of any party and with the consent of all other parties concerned, order the consolidation of related arbitrations or arbitrations involving same or same sort of subject matter.
2. Unless otherwise agreed to by the parties, cases shall be consolidated into the case that has commenced first. Unless the parties otherwise jointly request for a single award, the tribunal shall render separate awards on the consolidated cases.
3. This Article shall not apply to cases where the arbitrators of the tribunals are different.

Article 31 Joinder of Third Parties

The Claimant and the Respondent may request a third party to be joined in arbitration with its consent by a joint written application. A third party may also apply in writing to become a party in arbitration with the written consent of both parties. The tribunal shall decide on the joinder of a third party, or, if the tribunal has not been constituted, the Secretariat shall make such decision.

Article 32 Notice of Hearing

1. The date of the first hearing shall be fixed by the tribunal and notified to the parties by the Secretariat at least twenty (20) days in advance of the date of hearing. For cases involving disputes referred to in Article 4.3 of these Rules, parties shall be notified by the Secretariat at least fifteen (15) days in advance of the date of hearing.
2. A party with justifiable reasons may request a postponement of the hearing. However, such request must be communicated to the tribunal in writing at least seven (7) days in advance of the date of hearing. The tribunal shall decide whether to postpone the hearing or not.
3. If a party having justifiable reasons fails to request a postponement of the hearing within the time limit in Article 32.2, the tribunal shall decide whether to accept such request or not.
4. A notice of hearing subsequent to the first hearing and a notice of a postponed hearing shall not be subject to the time limit in Article 32.1.

Article 33 Place of Hearing

1. Where the parties have agreed on the place of hearing, the case shall be heard at that agreed place except for circumstances stipulated in Article 63.2 of these Rules.
2. Unless otherwise agreed to by the parties, a case accepted by SHIAC shall be heard in Shanghai, or if the tribunal considers it necessary, at other places with the approval of the Secretary General of SHIAC.

Article 34 Confidentiality

1. Hearings shall be held in camera. Where both parties request an open hearing, the tribunal shall make such decision.
2. For cases heard in camera, the parties, their representatives, witnesses, interpreters, arbitrators, experts, appraisers and the relevant staff-members of the Secretariat shall not disclose to any outsiders any substantive or procedural matters of the case.

Article 35 Default

1. If the Claimant fails to appear at a hearing without showing justifiable reasons for such failure, or withdraws from an on-going hearing without the permission of the tribunal, the Claimant may be deemed to have withdrawn its Request for Arbitration. In such a case, if the Respondent has filed a counterclaim, the tribunal shall proceed with the hearing of the counterclaim and render a default award.
2. If the Respondent fails to appear at a hearing without showing justifiable reasons for such failure, or withdraws from an on-going hearing without the permission of the tribunal, the tribunal may proceed with arbitration and render a default award. In such a case, if the Respondent has filed a counterclaim, the Respondent may be deemed to have withdrawn its counterclaim.

Article 36 Record of Hearing

1. During the hearing, excluding that for mediation, the tribunal shall make written record of the hearing, and may arrange a stenographic and/or audio-visual record of the hearing.
2. The written record and the stenographic and/or audio-visual record of the hearing shall be available for the use and reference by the tribunal.
3. Any party or participant in arbitration may apply for a rectification of any omission or error in the minutes of its own statement. If the request for rectification is refused by the tribunal, the application shall nevertheless be recorded into the file.
4. The written record shall be signed or sealed by the arbitrator(s), the recorder, the parties, and other participants in arbitration, if any.

Article 37 Evidence

1. Each party is under the burden of proving the facts on which its claim, defense or counterclaim is based.
2. The tribunal may specify a period of time for the parties to submit evidence and the parties shall produce evidence within the specified period of time. The tribunal may refuse to admit any evidence produced beyond the period. If a party has difficulties in submitting evidence within the specified period of time, it may apply for an extension before the expiration of the period. The tribunal shall decide whether or not to extend the period of time.
3. Parties that bear the burden of proof shall bear the consequences for their failure to produce evidence within the specified period of time, or for the produced evidence is insufficient to support its claim or counterclaim.
4. Where the parties have agreed on matters or rules relating to evidence, the parties' agreement shall prevail except where such agreement is inoperative.

Article 38 Investigation by Tribunal

1. The tribunal may, on its own initiative, undertake investigations and collect evidence as it considers necessary.
2. When investigating and collecting evidence by itself, the tribunal shall promptly notify the parties to be present at such investigation if it considers it necessary. In the event that one or both parties fail to be present, the investigation and collection shall proceed without being affected.
3. The tribunal shall, through the Secretariat, transmit the evidence collected by itself to the parties and provide them with an opportunity to comment.

Article 39 Expert Opinion and Appraiser Report

1. The parties may request for consultation or appraisal on specific issues of a case. The tribunal has the discretion to decide whether to grant the aforesaid request. The tribunal may consult or appoint expert(s) and/or appraiser(s) for clarification on specific issues of a case as it considers necessary. Such expert(s) or appraiser (s) may either be a Chinese or foreign organization or natural person.

2. Such an expert or appraiser may be appointed jointly by the parties, who may make the joint appointment with reference to Article 22.2 and Article 22.3. If the parties fail to reach an agreement on the appointment, the tribunal shall make the appointment.
3. The parties shall pay in advance the consultation/appraisal fees according to the percentage agreed to or specified by the tribunal. Where the parties fail to pay such fees in advance within the specified period of time, the tribunal has the discretion to decide not to conduct the relevant consultation or appraisal.
4. The tribunal has the discretion to request the parties to deliver or produce to the expert or appraiser relevant materials, documents, or properties and goods for examination, inspection and/or appraisal. The parties are obliged to comply with such request.
5. The expert opinion and/or the appraiser report shall be transmitted to the parties by the Secretariat. The parties shall be given an opportunity to respond. At the request of either party and with the approval of the tribunal, the expert or the appraiser may be heard at a hearing where, if considered necessary and appropriate by the tribunal, he/she may give explanations on their reports.

Article 40 Examination of Evidence

1. Unless otherwise agreed to by the parties, all evidence submitted by a party shall be filed with the Secretariat for transmission to the other party and the tribunal.
2. Unless otherwise agreed to by the parties, where a case is examined by way of hearing, the evidence shall be exhibited at the hearing and examined by the parties.
3. In the event that evidence is submitted after the hearing and the tribunal decides to admit the evidence without holding further hearings, the tribunal may request the parties to submit their opinions thereon in writing within a specified period of time.

Article 41 Combination of Arbitration with Mediation

1. Where the parties have reached a settlement agreement by themselves through negotiation or mediation without involving SHIAC, the parties may, based on an arbitration agreement concluded between them that provides for arbitration by SHIAC and the settlement agreement, request SHIAC to constitute a tribunal to render the award on the basis of the terms of the settlement agreement. Unless otherwise agreed to by the parties, the Chairman of SHIAC shall appoint a sole arbitrator to constitute such tribunal, which shall examine the case using the procedures it considers appropriate and render the award. The specific procedures and the time limit for rendering the award shall not be subject to other Articles in these Rules.
2. Where both parties have the desire for mediation or one party so desires and the other party agrees when approached by the tribunal, the tribunal may mediate the case during the course of the arbitration proceedings.
3. The tribunal may mediate the case in the manner it considers appropriate.

4. The tribunal shall terminate mediation and continue the arbitration proceedings, until rendering the award, if either party requests such termination or if the tribunal believes that further efforts to mediate will be futile.
5. A settlement agreement reached between the parties in mediation by the tribunal but without the involvement of the tribunal shall be deemed as one reached through the mediation by the tribunal.
6. Where settlement is reached through mediation by the tribunal, the parties shall sign a written settlement agreement. The parties may withdraw their requests for arbitration or counterclaims, or request the tribunal to render the award on the basis of the terms of the settlement agreement.
7. Where mediation fails, the tribunal shall proceed with arbitration and render an arbitral award.
8. Where mediation fails, any opinion, view or statement, and any proposal or proposition expressing acceptance or opposition, by either party or by the mediator or by the tribunal in the process of mediation shall not be invoked as grounds for any claim, defense or counterclaim in the subsequent arbitration proceedings, judicial proceedings or any other proceedings.

Article 42 Suspension of Proceedings

1. The arbitration proceedings may be suspended when the parties so request, or if other circumstances occur during the proceedings which make such suspension necessary.
2. The decision to suspend the arbitration proceedings shall be made by the tribunal, or it shall be made by the Secretary General of SHIAC in the event that the tribunal is not constituted.

Article 43 Withdrawal and Dismissal

1. A party may submit a request to withdraw its claim or counterclaim in its entirety. In the event that the Claimant withdraws its claim in its entirety, the tribunal shall proceed with its examination of the counterclaim and render the award thereon. In the event that the Respondent withdraws its counterclaim in its entirety, the tribunal shall proceed with the examination of the claim and render the award thereon.
2. Where a case is to be dismissed before the constitution of the tribunal, the decision shall be made by the Secretary General of SHIAC. Where the case is to be dismissed after the constitution of the tribunal, the decision shall be made by the tribunal.

Chapter III The Award

Article 44 Time Limit for Rendering Award

1. For cases involving disputes referred to in Article 4.1 and Article 4.2 of these Rules, the tribunal shall render the award within six (6) months upon the date the tribunal is constituted.

2. For cases involving disputes referred to in Article 4.3 of these Rules, the tribunal shall render the award within four (4) months upon the date the tribunal is constituted.
3. Upon the request of the tribunal, the Secretary General of SHIAC may extend aforesaid time limit if he/she considers it necessary with justifiable reasons.
4. The following periods of time shall not be counted within the aforesaid time limit:

   (a) the period of time during which a consultation or appraisal is conducted, as provided in Article 39 of these Rules; and
   (b) the period of time during which any arbitration proceedings is suspended in accordance with laws and/or these Rules.

Article 45 Rendering Award

1. The tribunal shall fairly and reasonably render the award on the basis of facts and in accordance with laws.
2. The tribunal shall state in the award the claims, the facts of the dispute, the reasons on which the award is based, the result of the award, the allocation of the arbitration costs and the date on which and the place at which the award is rendered. The facts of the dispute and the reasons on which the award is based may not be stated in the award if the parties have agreed so, or if the award is rendered in accordance with the terms of a settlement agreement between the parties. The tribunal has the discretion to determine in the award the specific period of time for the parties to execute the award and the liabilities to be borne by a party failing to execute the award within the specified time limit.
3. SHIAC shall affix its seal to an award rendered in an arbitration which is agreed to be submitted to SHIAC or to the China (Shanghai) Pilot Free Trade Zone Court of Arbitration, or to SHIAC and arbitration is conducted in the China (Shanghai) Pilot Free Trade Zone Court of Arbitration, or to the Shanghai International Aviation Court of Arbitration, or to SHIAC and arbitration is conducted in the Shanghai International Aviation Court of Arbitration.
4. Where a case is examined by a three-arbitrator tribunal, the award shall be rendered by all three arbitrators or a majority of the arbitrators. A written dissenting opinion shall be docketed into the file and may be attached to the award, but it shall not constitute a part of the award.
5. Where the tribunal cannot reach a majority opinion, the award shall be rendered in accordance with the presiding arbitrator's opinion. The written opinion of other arbitrators shall be docketed into the file and may be attached to the award, but it shall not constitute a part of the award.
6. Unless the award is rendered with the opinion of the presiding arbitrator or the sole arbitrator, the award shall be signed by a majority of arbitrators. An arbitrator who has a dissenting opinion may or may not sign his/her name on the award.
7. The date on which the award is rendered shall be the date on which the award becomes legally effective.

8. The award is final and binding upon both parties. Neither party may bring a suit before a court or make a request to any other organization for revising the award.

Article 46 Partial Award

A partial award may be rendered by the tribunal during arbitration but before the final award is rendered if it considers it necessary, or if the parties so request and the tribunal accepts. Failure to perform the partial award by any one of the parties will neither affect the continuation of the arbitration proceedings nor prevent the tribunal from rendering the final award.

Article 47 Allocation of Costs

1. The tribunal has the discretion to determine in the award the arbitration fees and other expenses to be paid by the parties to SHIAC.
2. The tribunal has the discretion to decide in the award, according to the specific circumstances of the case, that the losing party shall compensate the winning party for the expenses reasonably incurred by it in pursuing its case. The tribunal shall consider the factors such as the outcome and complexity of the case, the workload of the winning party and/or its representative(s), and the amount in dispute, etc.

Article 48 Scrutiny of Draft Award

The tribunal shall submit its award draft to SHIAC for scrutiny before signing the award. SHIAC may remind the tribunal of issues in the award on condition that the tribunal's independence in rendering the award is not affected.

Article 49 Rectification of Award

Within thirty (30) days upon its receipt of the award, either party may request in writing for rectification of any clerical, typographical, or calculation error or errors of a similar nature contained in the award; if such errors do exist in the award, the tribunal shall make a rectification in writing within thirty (30) days upon the receipt of the written request for the rectification. The tribunal may rectify such errors in writing on its own initiative within a reasonable time after the award is rendered. Such rectification in writing shall constitute a part of the award.

Article 50 Supplementary Award

Within thirty (30) days upon the receipt of the award, either party may request the tribunal in writing for a supplementary award which was advanced in the arbitration proceedings but was omitted from the award. If such omission does exist, the tribunal shall render a supplementary award within thirty (30) days upon the date of receipt of the written request. The tribunal may also render a supplementary award on its own initiative within a reasonable period of time after the award is rendered. Such supplementary award shall constitute a part of the award previously rendered.

Article 51 Execution of Award

1. The parties must execute the award within the period of time specified in the award. If no time limit is specified in the award, the parties shall execute the award immediately.
2. Where one party fails to execute the award, the other party may apply to a competent court for enforcement of the award pursuant to laws.

Chapter IV Summary Procedures

Article 52 Application of Summary Procedures

1. Unless otherwise agreed to by the parties, the Summary Procedures shall apply to any case where the amount in dispute does not exceed RMB 1,000,000, or to any case where the amount in dispute exceeds RMB 1,000,000 where one party applies for arbitration under these Summary Procedures and the other party agrees in writing.
2. Where no monetary claim is specified or the amount in dispute is not clear, SHIAC shall determine whether or not to apply the Summary Procedures after a full consideration of such factors as the complexity of the case and the interests involved, etc.

Article 53 Constitution of Tribunal

A sole-arbitrator tribunal shall be constituted in accordance with Article 23 under the Summary Procedures.

Article 54 Defense and Counterclaim

1. Within twenty (20) days upon the receipt of the Notice of Arbitration, the Respondent shall submit its Defense and relevant evidence, documents certifying the party's identity and other supporting documents to the Secretariat; counterclaims, if any, from the Respondent shall also be filed with supporting evidence within the aforesaid period of time.
2. Within twenty (20) days upon the receipt of the counterclaim and its attachments, the Claimant shall submit its Statement of Defense to the Respondent's counterclaim.
3. If the party does have justifiable reasons to request for an extension of the aforesaid time period, the tribunal shall decide whether to extend the time limit or not; and such decision shall be made by the Secretariat in the event that the tribunal has not been constituted.

Article 55 Conduct of Hearing

The tribunal may hear the case in the manner it considers appropriate. The tribunal may in its full discretion decide to hold hearings or examine the case only on the basis of the written materials and evidence submitted by the parties.

Article 56 Notice of Hearing

1. For a case examined by way of a hearing, the Secretariat shall, after the tribunal has fixed a date for the hearing, notify the parties of the date at least ten (10) days in advance of the date of hearing. A party having justifiable reasons may request the tribunal for a postponement of the hearing. However, such request must be submitted to the tribunal at least five (5) days in advance of the date of hearing. The tribunal shall decide whether to postpone the hearing or not.
2. If the party does have justifiable reasons for failure to request for a postponement of the hearing within the time limit provided in Article 56.1, the tribunal will decide whether to accept its request for postponement or not.
3. A notice of the subsequent hearing and a notice of a postponed hearing shall not be subject to the time limit provided in Article 56.1.

Article 57 Time Limit for Rendering Award

1. The tribunal shall render the award within three (3) months upon the date the tribunal is constituted.
2. Upon the request of the tribunal, the Secretary General of SHIAC may extend the time limit if he/she considers it necessary with justifiable reasons.

Article 58 Change of Procedures

1. The application of the Summary Procedures shall not be affected by any amendment to the claim, or by the filing of or any amendment to a counterclaim.
2. Where the amount in dispute of the amended claim or filing of or amendment of counterclaim exceeds RMB 1,000,000, the procedures of the case shall be changed from the Summary Procedures to the procedures provided for in Chapters II and III of these Rules unless the parties have agreed to the continuous application of the Summary Procedures.

Article 59 Application of Other Articles in These Rules

As to matters not covered in this chapter, the relevant Articles in the other chapters of these Rules shall apply.

Chapter V Supplementary Provisions

Article 60 Language

1. Where the parties have agreed on the language for arbitration, their agreement shall prevail. Absent such an agreement, the Chinese language shall be the working language of arbitration. The tribunal may, based on the mutual agreement of parties, decide to use other languages as the working language for arbitration, taking the working language of arbitration agreement, the language of the contract and other factors in arbitration into account.
2. At a hearing, a party or its representative(s) or witness(es) may employ interpreter(s) if it/they requires, or may ask the Secretariat to employ the interpreter (s) on their behalf.

3. The tribunal and/or the Secretariat may, if it considers necessary, request the parties to submit a corresponding version of the documents and evidence by the parties in Chinese or in other languages.

Article 61 Service

1. Unless otherwise agreed to by the parties, documents, notices and written materials in relation to arbitration may be sent to the parties and/or their representatives in person, or by registered mail or express mail, facsimile, telex, cable, or by any other means considered appropriate by the Secretariat.
2. Documents, notices and written materials in relation to arbitration to a party and/or its representative(s) shall be deemed to have been properly served on the party if delivered to the parties in person or delivered at its place of business, registration, domicile, habitual residence or mailing address, or where, after reasonable inquiries by the other party, none of the aforesaid addresses can be found, the written correspondence is sent by the Secretariat to its last known place of business, domicile, habitual residence or mailing address by registered mail or by any other means that provides a record of the attempt of delivery.

Article 62 Calculation of Time Limit

1. A time limit specified in or fixed in accordance with these Rules shall commence to run on the day after the date on which such period commences. The day from which a time limit commences shall not be counted as within such time limit.
2. If the day after the date on which the time limit falls on a public holiday or non-business day at the place of the addressee, then the time limit shall commence from the first subsequent business day. The public holiday and the non-business day occurring within such period shall be included in calculating the period of time. If the expiration date of a time limit falls on a public holiday or a nonbusiness day, then the period of time shall expire on the first subsequent business day.

Article 63 Arbitration Fees and Actual Expenses

1. Apart from charging arbitration fees to the parties according to the Schedules of Arbitration Fees, SHIAC may collect from the parties other additional, reasonable and actual expenses including arbitrators' special remuneration and their travel and accommodation expenses incurred when hearing a case, as well as the costs and expenses for experts, appraisers and interpreters appointed by the tribunal, etc.
2. Where the parties have agreed to hold a hearing at a place other than SHIAC's domicile, extra expenses including travel and accommodation expenses incurred

thereby shall be paid in advance as a deposit by the parties. In the event that the parties fail to do so, the hearing shall be held at the domicile of SHIAC.

Article 64 Interpretation of These Rules

1. SHIAC reserves the right to interpret these Rules.
2. The headings of Articles in these Rules shall not serve as interpretations of the contents of the Articles contained herein.
3. Unless stated otherwise, other documents issued by SHIAC shall not constitute a part of these Rules.

Article 65 Official Versions of These Rules

All the versions of these Rules as published by SHIAC in Chinese, English and other languages are the official versions. In the event of any discrepancies among different versions, the Chinese version shall prevail.

Article 66 Coming into Force

These Rules shall be effective as from January 1, 2015. For cases accepted by SHIAC before these Rules become effective, the Arbitration Rules effective at the time of acceptance shall apply.

Shanghai International Economic and Trade Arbitration Commission (Shanghai International Arbitration Center) Schedules of Arbitration Fees

The Shanghai International Economic and Trade Arbitration Commission (Shanghai International Arbitration Center) Arbitration Rules applies in these disputes

Article 1—Provisions as to Fees and Costs of Arbitration for International and Foreign-related Cases and Arbitration Cases related to the Hong Kong Special Administrative Region, the Macau Special Administrative Region and the Taiwan Region

Amount of claim (RMB Yuan)	Amount of fee (RMB Yuan)
1,000,000 or less	3.5 % of the claimed amount, minimum 10,000
1,000,001–5,000,000	35,000 plus 2.5 % of the amount above 1,000,000
5,000,001–10,000,000	135,000 plus 1.5 % of the amount above 5,000,000
10,000,001–50,000,000	210,000 plus 1 % of the amount above 10,000,000
50,000,000 or more	610,000 plus 0.5 % of the amount above 50,000,000

Each case, when being accepted, shall be charged an additional amount of RMB 10,000 Yuan as a Registration Fee which includes the expenses for examining the application for arbitration, initiating the arbitral proceedings, computerizing management and filing the documents.

Where the amount of the claim is not ascertained at the time when application for arbitration is handed in, or there exists special circumstances, the amount of arbitration fee shall be determined by the Secretariat of this Commission.

If the arbitration fee is charged in foreign currency, an amount of foreign currency equivalent to the corresponding RMB value specified in this schedule shall be paid.

Apart from charging arbitration fee according to this Arbitration Fee Schedule, this Commission may collect other extra, reasonable and actual expenses pursuant to the relevant provisions of the Arbitration Rules.

Article 2—Provisions as to Fees and Costs of Arbitration for Chinese Mainland Arbitration Cases

Registration Fee

Amount of claim (RMB Yuan)	Amount of fee (RMB Yuan)
1,000 or less	Minimum 100
1001–50,000	100 plus 5 % of the amount above 1000
50,001–100,000	2550 plus 4 % of the amount above 50,000
100,001–200,000	4550 plus 3 % of the amount above 100,000
200,001–500,000	7550 plus 2 % of the amount above 200,000
500,001–1,000,000	13,550 plus 1 % of the amount above 500,000
1,000,001 or more	18,550 plus 0.5 % of the amount above 1,000,000

Handling Fee

Amount of claim (RMB Yuan)	Amount of fee (RMB Yuan)
200,000 or less	5000
200,001–500,000	5000 plus 2 % of the amount above 200,000
500, 001–1,000,000	11,000 plus 1.5 % of the amount above 500,000
1,000,001–3,000,000	18,500 plus 0.5 % of the amount above 1,000,000
3,000,001–6,000,000	28,500 plus 0.45 % of the amount above 3,000,000
6,000,001–10,000,000	42,000 plus 0.4 % of the amount above 6,000,000
10,000,001–20,000,000	58,000 plus 0.3 % of the amount above 10,000,000
20,000,001–40,000,000	88,000 plus 0.2 % of the amount above 20,000,000
40,000,001 or more	128,000 plus 0.15 % of the amount above 40,000,000

The Amount of Claim referred to in this schedule shall be based on the sum of money claimed by the Claimant. If the amount claimed is different from the actual amount in dispute, the actual amount in dispute shall be the basis for calculation.

Where the amount of claim is not ascertained at the time when application for arbitration is handed in, or there exists special circumstances, the amount of arbitration fee deposit shall be determined by the Secretariat of this Commission in consideration of the specific rights and interests involved in the disputes.

Apart from charging arbitration fee according to this Arbitration Fee Schedule, this Commission may collect other extra, reasonable and actual expenses pursuant to the relevant provisions of the Arbitration Rules.

China (Shanghai) Pilot Free Trade Zone Arbitration Rules applies in these disputes

Article 1—Provisions as to Fees and Costs of Arbitration for International and Foreign-related Cases and Arbitration Cases related to the Hong Kong Special Administrative Region, the Macau Special Administrative Region and the Taiwan Region

(This Schedule of Arbitration Fees applies to the arbitration cases accepted under Article 4.1, Article 4.2 of these Rules, and is effective as from May 1, 2014)

Amount of claim (RMB Yuan)	Amount of fee (RMB Yuan)
1,000,000 or less	3.5 % of the claimed amount, minimum 10,000
1,000,001–5,000,000	35,000 plus 2.5 % of the amount above 1,000,000
5,000,001–10,000,000	135,000 plus 1.5 % of the amount above 5,000,000
10,000,001–50,000,000	210,000 plus 1 % of the amount above 10,000,000
50,000,000 or more	610,000 plus 0.5 % of the amount above 50,000,000

Each case, when being accepted, shall be charged an additional amount of RMB 10,000 as a Registration Fee which includes the expenses for examining the application for arbitration, initiating the arbitral proceedings, computerizing management and filing the documents.

Where the amount of the claim is not ascertained at the time when application for arbitration is handed in, or there exists special circumstances, the amount of arbitration fee shall be determined by the Secretariat.

If the arbitration fee is charged in foreign currency, an amount of foreign currency equivalent to the corresponding RMB value specified in this Schedule shall be paid.

Apart from charging arbitration fee according to this Schedule, SHIAC may collect other extra, reasonable and actual expenses pursuant to the relevant provisions of these Rules.

Article 2—Provisions as to Fees and Costs of Arbitration for Chinese Mainland Arbitration Cases

(This Schedule of Arbitration Fees applies to the arbitration cases accepted under Article 4.3 of these Rules, and is effective as from May 1, 2014.)

In accordance with the Notice of the Measures for the Charging of Arbitration Fee by the Arbitration Commissions with the reference number of Guo Ban Fa No. 44/1995 issued by the General Office of the State Council, the arbitration fee for cases accepted by SHIAC under Article 4.3 of these Rules are charged in the following way:

I. Registration Fee

Amount of claim (RMB Yuan)	Amount of fee (RMB Yuan)
100,000 or less	100
100,001–200,000	4550 plus 3 % of the amount above 100,000
200,001–500,000	7550 plus 2 % of the amount above 200,000
500,001–1,000,000	13,550 plus 1 % of the amount above 500,000
1,000,001 or more	18,550 plus 0.5 % of the amount above 1,000,000

II. Handling Fee

Amount of claim (RMB Yuan)	Amount of fee (RMB Yuan)
100,000 or less	1250
100,001–200,000	5000
200,001–500,000	5000 plus 2 % of the amount above 200,000
500, 001–1,000,000	11,000 plus 1.5 % of the amount above 500,000
1,000,001–3,000,000	18,500 plus 0.5 % of the amount above 1,000,000
3,000,001–6,000,000	28,500 plus 0.45 % of the amount above 3,000,000
6,000,001–10,000,000	42,000 plus 0.4 % of the amount above 6,000,000
10,000,001–20,000,000	58,000 plus 0.3 % of the amount above 10,000,000
20,000,001–40,000,000	88,000 plus 0.2 % of the amount above 20,000,000
40,000,001 or more	128,000 plus 0.15 % of the amount above 40,000,000

The Amount of Claim referred to in this Schedule shall be based on the sum of money claimed by the Claimant. If the amount claimed is different from the actual amount in dispute, the actual amount in dispute shall be the basis for calculation.

Where the amount of claim is not ascertained at the time when application for arbitration is handed in, or there exists special circumstances, the amount of arbitration fee deposit shall be determined by the Secretariat in consideration of the specific rights and interests involved in the disputes.

Apart from charging arbitration fee according to this Schedule, SHIAC may collect other extra, reasonable and actual expenses pursuant to the relevant provisions of these Rules.

Article 3—The Schedule of Arbitration Fee for Emergency Tribunal

(This Schedule of Arbitration Fee applies to the arbitrations under or involved in Article 21 of these Rules, and is effective as from May 1, 2014.)

The arbitration fee for either party applies for constituting an emergency tribunal to decide interim measure(s), and/or the counterparty applies for interim measure(s) to such emergency tribunal, is charged as follows:

Interim measure(s) claimed	Amount of fee (RMB Yuan)
Apply for one (1) interim measure	10,000
Apply for more than one (1) interim measures	10,000+ (n – 1) * 2000

SHIAC Rules for Arbitration in the Shanghai Pilot Free Trade Zone[5]

The China (Shanghai) Pilot Free Trade Zone Arbitration Rules

[Adopted at the Fifth Meeting of the Second Session of the Shanghai International Economic and Trade Arbitration Commission (Shanghai International Arbitration Center), effective as from January 1, 2015]

Chapter I General Provisions

Article 1 These Rules

These Rules are formulated by the Shanghai International Economic and Trade Arbitration Commission (also "Shanghai International Arbitration Center," formerly the "China International Economic and Trade Arbitration Commission Shanghai Commission/Sub-Commission," hereinafter referred to as "SHIAC") for the purpose of resolving, impartially, professionally and efficiently, contractual disputes and other disputes over rights and interests in property in connection with the China (Shanghai) Pilot Free Trade Zone in accordance with the Arbitration Law of the People's Republic of China and relevant provisions of other applicable laws.

Article 2 Institution and Functions

1. SHIAC is an arbitration institution which resolves contractual disputes and other disputes over rights and interests in property between natural persons, legal persons and other economic organizations with equal status.
2. SHIAC has established the China (Shanghai) Pilot Free Trade Zone Court of Arbitration in China (Shanghai) Pilot Free Trade Zone, to provide arbitration services including consulting, case filing and hearings.
3. Where an arbitration agreement provides for arbitration by the Shanghai International Economic and Trade Arbitration Commission, Shanghai International Arbitration Center, or by the China International Economic and Trade Arbitration Commission Shanghai Commission/Shanghai Sub-Commission, the parties shall be deemed to have agreed that arbitration shall be administered by SHIAC. Where an arbitration agreement provides for

[5]http://www.shiac.org/English/SHIACFTZ_2015_1222_EN.pdf.

arbitration by the Arbitration Commission or the Court of Arbitration of the China Council for the Promotion of International Trade Shanghai Sub-Council/Chamber of International Commerce Shanghai, or by the Shanghai Foreign Economic and Trade Arbitration Commission, or by the China (Shanghai) Pilot Free Trade Zone Court of Arbitration, or designates an institution that can reasonably be inferred to be SHIAC, the parties shall be deemed to have agreed that arbitration shall be administered by SHIAC.

4. SHIAC shall perform the functions that should be performed by an arbitration institution referred to in other arbitration rules which are applicable upon parties' agreement.
5. Where the parties agree to arbitrate under the Arbitration Rules of the United Nations Commission on International Trade Law (hereinafter the "UNCITRAL Arbitration Rules") or other arbitration rules, SHIAC shall be the appointing authority and shall perform other relevant administrative functions in accordance with the provisions of the UNCITRAL Arbitration Rules or the agreement of the parities.
6. The Chairman of SHIAC shall perform the functions and duties vested in him/her by these Rules while a Vice-Chairman may perform the Chairman's functions and duties with the Chairman's authorization.
7. SHIAC has a Secretariat, which handles its day-to-day work under the direction of the Secretary General, and performs the functions and duties vested by these Rules.
8. SHIAC is domiciled in Shanghai, China.
9. SHIAC shall establish a Panel of Arbitrators.
10. SHIAC shall establish a Panel of Mediators in respect of "Mediation by Mediator" under these Rules.

Article 3 Scope of Application

1. These Rules shall apply where parties have agreed to refer their disputes to SHIAC and the parties or the subject matter to a dispute or the legal facts that lead to the establishment, change or termination of civil and commercial relationship are connected with the China (Shanghai) Pilot Free Trade Zone, unless otherwise agreed to by the parties with respect to arbitration rules.
2. These Rules shall apply where parties have agreed to refer their disputes to SHIAC for arbitration and have agreed to apply these Rules for arbitration. Any modification or amendment on these Rules agreed by the parties' shall prevail except where such an agreement is inoperative or in conflict with a mandatory provision of the law of the place of arbitration.
3. These Rules shall apply where parties have agreed to refer their dispute to SHIAC and arbitration is to be conducted at the China (Shanghai) Pilot Free Trade Zone Court of Arbitration, or have agreed to refer their disputes to the China (Shanghai) Pilot Free Trade Zone Court of Arbitration or have designated an institution that can reasonably be inferred to be the China (Shanghai) Pilot Free Trade Zone Court of Arbitration, unless otherwise agreed to by the parties with respect to arbitration rules.

4. These Rules shall apply where These Rules are designated to apply by Arbitration Rules of Shanghai International Economic and Trade Arbitration Commission (Shanghai International Arbitration Center).
5. Where parties agree to refer their disputes to arbitration under these Rules without designating an arbitration institution, they shall be deemed to have agreed to refer their disputes to SHIAC for arbitration.
6. SHIAC has the discretion to decide on an objection to the application of these Rules by a party.

Article 4 Jurisdiction

SHIAC accepts cases involving:

1. international or foreign-related disputes;
2. disputes relating to the Hong Kong Special Administrative Region, the Macao Special Administrative Region or the Taiwan region; and
3. domestic disputes.

Article 5 Arbitration Agreement

1. SHIAC shall, upon the written application of a party, accept a case in accordance with the arbitration agreement concluded between the parties, either before or after the occurrence of the dispute, in which it is provided that a dispute is to be referred to SHIAC for arbitration.
2. An arbitration agreement means an arbitration clause in a contract concluded between the parties or any other form of written agreement providing for the settlement of disputes by arbitration.
3. An arbitration agreement shall be in writing. An arbitration agreement is in writing if it is contained in a tangible form of a document such as, but not limited to, a contract, letter, telegram, telex, facsimile, EDI, or email. An arbitration agreement shall be deemed to exist where its existence is asserted by one party and not denied by the other during the exchange of the Request for Arbitration and the Statement of Defense.
4. Where there are different provisions on the form and validity of an arbitration agreement in the laws applicable to an arbitration agreement, such provisions shall prevail.
5. An arbitration clause contained in a contract shall be treated as a clause independent of and separate from all other clauses of the contract, and an arbitration agreement attached to a contract shall also be treated as independent of and separate from all other clauses of the contract. The validity of an arbitration clause or an arbitration agreement shall not be affected by any modification, rescission, termination, transfer, expiration, invalidity, ineffectiveness, revocation or non-existence of the contract.

Article 6 Objection to Arbitration Agreement and/or Jurisdiction

1. SHIAC has the discretion to decide on the existence and validity of an arbitration agreement and its jurisdiction over an arbitration case. SHIAC may, if necessary, delegate such power to the tribunal, and the tribunal, according to such delegation, may either render a separate decision on jurisdiction during the arbitration proceedings, or incorporate the decision in the award.
2. Where SHIAC is satisfied with prima facie evidence that an arbitration agreement providing for arbitration by SHIAC and binding on the parties exists, it may decide based on such evidence that it has jurisdiction over the arbitration case, and arbitration shall proceed. Where, after SHIAC renders such a decision, the tribunal finds the facts and/or evidence inconsistent with the prima facie evidence during the arbitration proceedings, SHIAC may delegate the tribunal to render a new decision on jurisdiction.
3. An objection to an arbitration agreement and/or jurisdiction over an arbitration case shall be made in writing before the first hearing is held by the tribunal. Where a case is to be decided solely on documentary evidence, such an objection shall be made before the time when the substantive defense is first submitted.
4. Arbitration shall proceed notwithstanding an objection to the arbitration agreement and/or jurisdiction over the arbitration case.
5. The aforesaid objections to and/or decisions on jurisdiction by SHIAC shall include objections to and/or decisions on a party's standing to participate in arbitration.

Article 7 Place of Arbitration

1. Where the parties have agreed on the place of arbitration in writing, the parties' agreement shall prevail.
2. Where the parties have not agreed on the place of arbitration, the place of arbitration shall be the domicile of SHIAC.
3. An award shall be deemed as being rendered at the place of arbitration.

Article 8 *Bona Fides*

The parties shall proceed with the arbitration in a bona fides manner.

Article 9 Waiver of Right to Object

A party shall be deemed to have waived its right to object where it knows or should have known that any provision of, or requirement under, these Rules has not been complied with and yet participates in or proceeds with the arbitration proceedings without promptly and explicitly submitting its objection in writing to such non-compliance.

Chapter II Request for Arbitration and Counterclaim

Article 10 Commencement of Arbitration

The arbitration proceedings shall commence on the date on which SHIAC receives the Request for Arbitration by SHIAC.

Article 11 Application for Arbitration

A party applying for arbitration under these Rules shall:

1. Submit a Request for Arbitration in writing signed by and/or sealed by the Claimant and/or its authorized representative(s), which shall, *inter alia*, include:

   (a) the names and domiciles of the Claimant and the Respondent, including the post code, telephone, telex, fax and telegraph numbers, email addresses or any other means of electronic telecommunications;
   (b) a reference to the arbitration agreement that is invoked;
   (c) the claims of the Claimant; and
   (d) the facts and grounds on which the claims are based.

2. Attach to the Request for Arbitration the evidence which supports the Claimant's claims, documents certifying the party's identity and other relevant documentary evidence.
3. Pay the arbitration fees in advance to SHIAC according to the Schedules of Arbitration Fees.

Article 12 Acceptance

1. Upon receipt of the Request for Arbitration and its attachments, SHIAC may request the Claimant to complete if it finds, after examination, the formalities required for the application for arbitration to be incomplete. Where the party fails to complete the formalities as required, the party is deemed to have not submitted the Request for Arbitration.
2. Where the formalities of Application for Arbitration are found to be complete, the Secretariat shall send a Notice of Acceptance to the Claimant together with the Arbitration Rules, the Panel of Arbitrators and the Schedules of Arbitration Fees within five (5) days. The Secretariat shall send to the Respondent, within five (5) days after the Notice of Acceptance is sent, the Notice of Arbitration together with the Request for Arbitration and its attachments, the Arbitration Rules, the Panel of Arbitrators and the Schedules of Arbitration Fees.
3. SHIAC shall, after accepting a case, designate one or two staff members of the Secretariat to assist the tribunal in the procedural administration of the case.

Article 13 Defense

1. Within forty five (45) days from the date of receipt of the Notice of Arbitration, the Respondent shall submit a Statement of Defense in writing to the Secretariat. For such cases involving disputes referred to in Article 4.3 of these Rules, the corresponding period shall be twenty (20) days.

2. If the Respondent does have justifiable reasons to request an extension of the time limit for submitting the Statement of Defense, the tribunal shall, at its discretion, decide whether or not to grant such request. If the tribunal has not been constituted, the Secretariat shall render a decision.
3. The Statement of Defense shall be signed by and/or sealed by the Respondent and/or its authorized representative(s), and shall, inter alia, include:

   (a) the name and domicile of the Respondent, including the post code, telephone, telex, fax and telegraph numbers, Email addresses or any other means of electronic telecommunications; and
   (b) the defense to the Request for Arbitration setting forth the facts and grounds on which the defense is based.

4. When submitting the Statement of Defense, the Respondent shall attach thereto the evidence on which the Defense is based, documents certifying the party's identity and other relevant evidence.
5. The tribunal has the discretion to decide whether to accept a Statement of Defense submitted after the expiration of the aforesaid time limit.
6. Failure of the Respondent to submit a Statement of Defense shall not affect the conduct of the arbitration proceedings.

Article 14 Counterclaim and Defense

1. Within forty-five (45) days from the date of receipt of the Notice of Arbitration, the Respondent shall file with the Secretariat its counterclaim in writing, if any. For cases involving disputes referred to in Article 4.3 of these Rules, the corresponding period shall be twenty (20) days.
2. If the Respondent does have justifiable reasons to request an extension of the time limit for submitting the counterclaim, the tribunal shall, at its discretion, decide whether to grant such request. If the tribunal has not been constituted, the Secretariat shall make the decision.
3. The tribunal has the discretion to decide whether to accept a counterclaim submitted after the expiration of the aforesaid time limit.
4. When submitting a counterclaim, the Respondent shall specify in writing in its Statement of Counterclaim and state the facts and grounds upon which its counterclaim is based, together with relevant evidence attached thereto.
5. When submitting a counterclaim, the Respondent shall pay the arbitration fees in advance according to the Schedules of Arbitration Fees within a specified period of time, failing which the Respondent shall be deemed not to have submitted any counterclaim.
6. Where the formalities required for filing a counterclaim are found to be complete, SHIAC shall send the Statement of Counterclaim and its attachments to the Claimant. The Claimant shall, within thirty (30) days from the date of receipt of the Statement of Counterclaim and the attachment, submit in writing its Statement of Defense to the Respondent's counterclaim. For such cases involving disputes as referred to in Article 4.3 of these Rules, the corresponding period shall be twenty (20) days. If the Claimant does have justifiable reasons to

request an extension of the time limit for filing the Statement of Defense, the tribunal shall, at its discretion, decide whether to extend it or not. If the tribunal has not been constituted, the Secretariat shall make the decision.

7. The tribunal has the discretion to decide whether to accept a Statement of Defense to the Respondent's counterclaim submitted after expiration of the aforesaid time limit.
8. Failure of the Claimant to submit a Statement of Defense to the Respondent's counterclaim shall not affect the conduct of arbitration proceedings.

Article 15 Amendment to Claim or Counterclaim

The Claimant may amend its claim and the Respondent may amend its counterclaim. However, the tribunal has the power to refuse any such amendment if it considers that the amendment is so late that it may affect the arbitration proceedings.

Article 16 Copies of Submissions

When submitting the Request for Arbitration, the Statement of Defense, the Statement of Counterclaim, evidence and other documents, the parties shall make the submissions in quintuplicate. Where there are more than two parties, additional copies shall be provided accordingly. Where the tribunal is composed of a sole arbitrator, the number of copies submitted may be reduced by two. Where a party applies for interim measures, that party shall submit additional copies accordingly.

Article 17 Representation

1. A party may be represented by one (1) to five (5) authorized Chinese and/or foreign representative(s) to handle matters relating to arbitration. In such a case, a Power of Attorney shall be submitted.
2. If a party intends to be represented by more than five (5) authorized representatives, a written application stating the reasons is required. The tribunal has the discretion to decide whether or not to grant such application in accordance with circumstances of the arbitration. Where the request is made before the tribunal is constituted, the Secretariat shall make the decision.

Chapter III Interim Measures

Article 18 Interim Measures

The parties may apply to SHIAC and/or a competent court for the following interim measure(s) in accordance with the relevant laws of the jurisdiction where the interim measure(s) is sought:

(a) preservation of properties;
(b) preservation of evidence;
(c) requesting and/or prohibiting a party to perform; and
(d) other measure(s) provided by the applicable laws.

Article 19 Pre-arbitration Interim Measures

1. Before filing arbitration application, the applicant for interim measures may directly apply to the competent court for interim measure(s) in accordance with the applicable laws in the jurisdiction where such interim measure(s) is sought, or request assistance from SHIAC in applying to the competent court for interim measure(s).
2. The applicant for interim measure(s) shall provide the following documents if the applicant requests SHIAC to provide assistance:

   (a) an arbitration agreement; and
   (b) an application for interim measures in accordance with Article 20.1.

   Within three (3) days upon the date of receipt of above documents, SHIAC shall transfer the documents to the competent court and notify the applicant if SHIAC finds the assistance sought is feasible.
3. The applicant for interim measure(s) shall apply to SHIAC for arbitration within the mandatory time limit after the court has enforced the interim measure(s) in accordance with the applicable laws in the jurisdiction where the interim measure(s) is sought.

Article 20 Interim Measures in Arbitration

1. Either party applying for interim measure(s) after the case is accepted shall submit a Request for Interim Measure(s) including:

   (a) the names and domiciles of the Claimant and the Respondent;
   (b) the reason(s) for seeking interim measure(s);
   (c) the specific interim measure(s) to be sought;
   (d) the place where the interim measure(s) sought is to be enforced and the court with competent jurisdiction; and
   (e) the relevant laws in the jurisdiction where the interim measure(s) is sought.

2. SHIAC will transfer the application for interim measures, in accordance with the relevant laws in the jurisdiction where the interim measure(s) is sought together with these Rules, to the court with the competent jurisdiction for a ruling, or to the tribunal for a decision, or to the emergency tribunal constituted pursuant to Article 21 of these Rules for a decision.

Article 21 Emergency Tribunal

1. Any party may, who intends to apply for interim measure(s) during the period between the acceptance of a case and the constitution of the tribunal, apply for an emergency tribunal, by submitting a written application and reasons therefor, in accordance with the laws in the jurisdiction where the interim measure(s) is sought. SHIAC shall decide whether to constitute an emergency tribunal.
2. The party shall pay the fees in advance according to the Schedules of Arbitration Fees if SHIAC decides to constitute an emergency tribunal. The Chairman of

SHIAC may appoint an arbitrator from the Panel of Arbitrators to constitute the emergency tribunal within three (3) days upon the completion of formalities. The Secretariat shall inform the parties of the constitution of the emergency tribunal.

3. The arbitrator appointed to constitute the emergency tribunal shall perform his/her disclosure obligation pursuant to Article 31 of these Rules. The parties may, pursuant to Article 32 of these Rules, challenge the arbitrator who constitutes the emergency tribunal.
4. The emergency tribunal shall, pursuant to Article 22 of these Rules, make a decision on the application for interim measure(s).
5. The emergency tribunal shall dissolve on the date when the tribunal is constituted and shall hand over all the materials to the tribunal.
6. Unless otherwise agreed to by the parties, the arbitrator appointed for the emergency tribunal shall not act as an arbitrator in dealing with disputes relating to interim measure(s).
7. The procedures provided in this Article shall not affect the continuation of the arbitration proceedings.
8. Matters not covered in this Article in respect of the arbitrator constituting the emergency tribunal shall take the relevant Articles in Chapter IV of these Rules for reference.

Article 22 Rendering Decision on Interim Measures

1. The emergency tribunal or the tribunal shall, in accordance with the relevant laws in the jurisdiction where the interim measure(s) is sought, render and sign a written decision, in the format as required, with reasons on any application for interim measure(s). Any decision on interim measure(s) rendered and signed by the emergency tribunal or the tribunal shall be sealed by SHIAC.
2. The emergency tribunal or the tribunal may, considering the nature of the interim measure(s) sought, order the provision of appropriate security by the applicant before making a decision.
3. A decision on interim measures in accordance with this Article shall be rendered by the emergency tribunal within twenty (20) days upon its constitution, or by the tribunal within twenty (20) days upon its receipt of the application for interim measure(s). The emergency tribunal or the tribunal shall render a decision on interim measure(s) within ten (10) days upon the date the security is provided pursuant to Article 22.2.

Article 23 Amendment to Decision on Interim Measures

1. Where the opposing party objects to a decision on interim measures, it shall file a written objection with SHIAC within three (3) days upon its receipt of the decision. The emergency tribunal or the tribunal in rendering such decision on interim measure(s) has the discretion to decide whether to accept the objection. If the emergency tribunal in rendering such a decision on interim measure(s) has dissolved, the tribunal that is subsequently constituted shall have the discretion to make such a decision.

2. The emergency tribunal or the tribunal shall, within three (3) days upon its receipt of the objection, decide on whether to maintain, modify, suspend or withdraw the decision on interim measure(s).
3. The emergency tribunal or the tribunal has the discretion to decide whether the decision on interim measure(s) should be modified, suspended or withdrawn. The tribunal has the discretion to decide whether the decision on interim measure(s) rendered by the emergency tribunal should be modified, suspended or withdrawn.
4. Any amendment to a decision on interim measure(s) pursuant to this Article shall be made in writing with supporting reasons by the emergency tribunal or by the tribunal and shall constitute a part of the decision on interim measure(s).
5. The party receiving an amendment to a decision on interim measure(s) shall notify the competent court within five (5) days upon the receipt of such amendment.

Article 24 Compliance with Decision on Interim Measures

The parties shall comply with each decision on interim measure(s) rendered by the emergency tribunal or by the tribunal.

Chapter IV Tribunal

Article 25 Duties of Arbitrator(s)

An arbitrator shall not represent either party, and shall remain independent of the parties and treat them equally.

Article 26 Number of Arbitrator(s)

1. The tribunal shall be composed of one or three arbitrators.
2. Unless otherwise agreed to by the parties or provided by these Rules, the tribunal shall be composed of three arbitrators.

Article 27 Appointment of Arbitrator(s)

1. Parties may appoint arbitrators from the Panel of Arbitrators.
2. Any party may recommend person(s) from outside the Panel of Arbitrators as the arbitrator. Parties may also reach an agreement on jointly recommending a person from outside the Panel of Arbitrators as the presiding/sole arbitrator.

Article 28 Three-arbitrator Tribunal

1. Within fifteen (15) days upon the receipt of the Notice of Acceptance/Notice of Arbitration, both parties shall respectively appoint or entrust the Chairman of SHIAC to appoint one arbitrator. Where a party fails to appoint or entrust the Chairman of SHIAC to appoint an arbitrator within the specified period of time, the Chairman of SHIAC shall appoint the arbitrator. If a party requests to extend the time limit of appointing an arbitrator, it shall submit a written application to SHIAC within the time limit in this Article. The Secretariat shall decide whether to accept such a request.

2. Either party may appoint an arbitrator from the Panel of Arbitrators, and may also respectively recommend one (1) person from outside the Panel of Arbitrators to act as arbitrator. If either party has recommended a person from outside the Panel of Arbitrators to act as arbitrator, the party shall submit the information regarding this person to the Secretariat within the time limit provided in Article 28.1.
   The relevant person may act as an arbitrator only when the Chairman of SHIAC confirms that this is in accordance with laws. If the recommendation is rejected, the party who has recommended such person shall appoint an arbitrator from Panel of Arbitrators or otherwise entrust the Chairman of SHIAC to appoint an arbitrator, within five (5) days upon its receipt of the decision of rejection. The Chairman of SHIAC shall appoint an arbitrator on behalf of the party who failed to appoint one under this Article.
3. Within fifteen (15) days from the date of the Respondent's receipt of the Notice of Arbitration, the third arbitrator shall be jointly appointed from the Panel of Arbitrators by the parties or by the Chairman of SHIAC upon the parties' joint authorization. The third arbitrator shall act as the presiding arbitrator of the tribunal. Where the parties failed to jointly appoint the presiding arbitrator or otherwise entrust the Chairman of SHIAC to appoint the presiding arbitrator according to the aforesaid Articles, the Chairman of SHIAC shall appoint the presiding arbitrator.
4. Both parties may respectively recommend one (1) to three (3) arbitrators as candidates for the presiding arbitrator and shall submit the list of recommended candidates to the Secretariat within the period of time specified in Article 28.3. Where there is only one common candidate in the lists, such a candidate shall act as the presiding arbitrator jointly appointed by the parties. Where there are more than one (1) common candidate on the lists, the Chairman of SHIAC shall choose a presiding arbitrator from among the common candidates based on the specific nature and circumstances of the case, who shall act as the presiding arbitrator jointly appointed by the parties. Where there is no common candidate in the lists, the Chairman of SHIAC shall appoint the presiding arbitrator from out of the lists of recommended candidates.
5. Both parties may reach an agreement on jointly recommending one (1) person not listed in the Panel of Arbitrators as the presiding arbitrator, and shall submit the information of the relevant person to the Secretariat within the time limit in Article 28.3. Such person may only act as the presiding arbitrator only when the Chairman of SHIAC confirms that they may so act under the relevant law. If this recommendation is rejected, both parties shall jointly appoint the presiding arbitrator from the Panel of Arbitrators, or otherwise entrust the Chairman of SHIAC to appoint the presiding arbitrator within five (5) days upon the receipt of the decision on the rejection pursuant to Article 28.3. Where the parties failed to jointly appoint the presiding arbitrator or otherwise entrust the Chairman of SHIAC to appoint the presiding arbitrator according to the aforesaid Articles, the Chairman of SHIAC shall appoint the presiding arbitrator.

6. The parties shall bear the expenses for travel and accommodation, arbitrators' special remuneration and other necessary costs incurred by the arbitrators for hearing a case. If either party fails to make the payment for such expenses in advance as a deposit within the specified period of time, such an arbitrator appointed or recommended by the party shall be deemed to have not been appointed or recommended by that party, and such agreement as in connection with the appointment of arbitrators by the parties will be deemed inoperative. Under such circumstances, the Chairman of SHIAC shall appoint/re-appoint an arbitrator pursuant to Articles in these Rules.
7. Where an appointed arbitrator refuses to accept the appointment, or the person who has been confirmed as arbitrator or presiding arbitrator by the Chairman of SHIAC refuses to act as arbitrator or presiding arbitrator (as the case may be), or any candidate as above-mentioned is incapable of participating in the hearing of the case due to his/her health or other reasons which may affect the normal performance of his/her duties as arbitrator, the party shall appoint another arbitrator within ten (10) days upon the date of receipt of the notice to appoint another arbitrator by that party. Where the party fails to appoint another arbitrator according this Article, the Chairman of SHIAC shall appoint the arbitrator.

Article 29 Sole-arbitrator Tribunal

Where the tribunal is composed of one arbitrator, the sole arbitrator shall be appointed pursuant to the procedures stipulated in Article 28.3, Article 28.4, Article 28.5 and Article 28.6.

Article 30 Tribunal in Multiple Parties' Arbitration

1. Where there are two (2) or more Claimants and/or Respondents in an arbitration case, the Claimants and/or Respondents shall appoint or recommend arbitrator respectively pursuant to Article 28.1 and Article 28.2.
2. The presiding arbitrator or sole arbitrator shall be appointed or recommended pursuant to Article 28.3, Article 28.4, Article 28.5 and Article 28.6.

Article 31 Disclosure

1. The arbitrator(s) shall sign a Declaration and disclose to SHIAC in writing any facts or circumstances which may give a rise to justifiable doubts as to his/her impartiality or independence.
2. If circumstances that need to be disclosed arise during the arbitration proceedings, the relevant arbitrator shall promptly disclose such circumstances in writing to SHIAC.
3. The arbitrator shall submit the Declaration and/or the disclosure to the Secretariat. The Secretariat shall forward the arbitrator's submissions to the parties.

Article 32 Challenge to Arbitrator(s)

1. Upon receipt of the Declaration and/or written disclosure of an arbitrator communicated by the Secretariat, a party who intends to challenge the arbitrator on the grounds of the facts or circumstances disclosed by the arbitrator shall forward the challenge in writing to SHIAC within ten (10) days upon the date of such receipt. Where a party intends to challenge an arbitrator of an emergency tribunal, it shall raise the challenge in writing to SHIAC within five (5) days upon the date of the party's receipt of the written disclosure of the arbitrator. If a party fails to raise a challenge within the aforesaid time limit, it shall not challenge an arbitrator later on the basis of facts disclosed by the arbitrator.
2. A party who has justifiable doubts as to the impartiality or independence of arbitrator(s) may make a request in writing to SHIAC for that arbitrator's withdrawal. In the request, the facts and reasons on which the request is based shall be stated with supporting evidence. The aforesaid challenge of arbitrator shall be made in writing within fifteen (15) days upon the date of receipt of the Notice of the Constitution of the Tribunal. Where a party becomes aware of the facts and reasons for a challenge after that time, the party may challenge the arbitrator in writing within fifteen (15) days after such facts and reasons become known to the party, but no later than the conclusion of the last hearing.
3. The Secretariat shall communicate the challenge promptly to the other party, the arbitrator being challenged and the other members of the tribunal, who subsequently may all provide their comments on such challenge.
4. Where an arbitrator is challenged by one party and the other party agrees to the challenge, or the arbitrator being challenged withdraws from his/her office, such arbitrator shall no longer act as an arbitrator. Neither circumstance shall imply that the challenge made by the party is sustainable.
5. In circumstances other than those specified in Article 32.4, the Chairman of SHIAC shall render a decision on the challenge with or without stating the reasons therefor.
6. An arbitrator who has been challenged shall continue to perform his/her functions as arbitrator until a decision on the challenge has been made by the Chairman of SHIAC.

Article 33 Replacement of Arbitrator(s)

1. In the event that an arbitrator is prevented *de jure* or *de facto* from performing his/her functions, or he/she fails to perform his/her functions in accordance with the requirements in these Rules or within the period of time specified in these Rules, the Chairman of SHIAC has the discretion to decide whether to replace such arbitrator. Such arbitrator may also withdraw from his/her office.
2. In the event that an arbitrator is unable to perform his/her functions owing to his/her health reasons, removal from the Panel of Arbitrators, withdrawal, resignation or any other reasons, a substitute arbitrator shall be appointed according to Article 28.7.

3. After the replacement of the arbitrator(s), the tribunal shall decide whether to resume the proceedings that have been wholly or partially conducted.
4. The Chairman of SHIAC shall make the decision on whether or not an arbitrator should be replaced with or without stating the reasons therefor.

Article 34 Remaining Arbitrators to Continue Arbitration

In the event that, after the conclusion of the last hearing, an arbitrator in a three-arbitrator tribunal is unable to participate in the deliberation and/or render the award owing to his/her health reasons, or removal from the Panel of Arbitrators, the remaining arbitrators may request the Chairman of SHIAC to replace the arbitrator pursuant to Article 33. After consulting with the parties and upon the approval of the Chairman of SHIAC, the remaining arbitrators may continue the arbitration proceedings and make decisions or render the award. The Secretariat shall notify the parties of the matters above.

Chapter V Hearings

Article 35 Conduct of Hearing

1. The tribunal shall examine the case in any manner that it deems appropriate unless otherwise agreed to by the parties. Under any circumstance, the tribunal shall act impartially and fairly and shall provide reasonable opportunities to all parties for them to present and argue their cases.
2. The tribunal shall hold hearings when examining the case. However, hearings may be omitted and the case shall be examined on the basis of documents only if the parties so request or agree to and the tribunal also deems that hearings are unnecessary.
3. The tribunal may hold the deliberations at any place or in any manner that it deems appropriate.
4. Unless otherwise agreed to by the parties, the tribunal may, if it considers necessary, issue procedural directions and lists of questions, hold pre-hearing meetings and preliminary hearings, and produce terms of reference, and may also make an arrangement for the exchange and/or examination of evidence.

Article 36 Consolidation of Arbitrations

1. The tribunal may, on the application of any party and with the consent of all other parties concerned, order the consolidation of related arbitrations or arbitrations involving same or same sort of subject matter.
2. Unless otherwise agreed to by the parties, cases shall be consolidated into the case that has commenced first. Unless the parties otherwise jointly request for a single award, the tribunal shall render separate awards on the consolidated cases.
3. This Article shall not apply to cases where the arbitrators of the tribunals are different.

Article 37 Joinder of Other Parties under Same Arbitration Agreement

1. Where the Claimant or the Respondent requests another party under the same arbitration agreement to be joined into the arbitration proceedings, before the constitution of the tribunal, it shall submit a written application. The Secretariat shall make a decision on the application. In the case that the Secretariat has made a decision to permit such joinder, the multiple Claimants and/or, as the case may be, the multiple Respondents have failed to jointly appoint an respective arbitrator, the Chairman of SHIAC shall appoint all the arbitrators regardless of whether the parties have previously appointed the arbitrators.
2. Where the tribunal has been constituted and any Claimant or Respondent requests another party under the same arbitration agreement to be joined into the arbitration proceedings as a Respondent, the tribunal may decide whether to permit such application and such party has waived its right to re-appoint arbitrator and accepted the arbitration proceedings.

Article 38 Joinder of Third Parties

The Claimant and the Respondent may request a third party to be joined in arbitration with its consent by a joint written application. A third party may also apply in writing to become a party in arbitration with the written consent of both parties. The tribunal shall decide on the joinder of a third party, or, if the tribunal has not been constituted, the Secretariat shall make such decision.

Article 39 Notice of Hearing

1. The date of the first hearing shall be fixed by the tribunal and notified to the parties by the Secretariat at least twenty (20) days in advance of the date of hearing. For cases involving disputes referred to in Article 4.3 of these Rules, parties shall be notified by the Secretariat at least fifteen (15) days in advance of the date of hearing.
2. A party with justifiable reasons may request a postponement of the hearing. However, such request must be communicated to the tribunal in writing at least seven (7) days in advance of the date of hearing. The tribunal shall decide whether to postpone the hearing or not.
3. If a party having justifiable reasons fails to request a postponement of the hearing within the time limit in Article 39.2, the tribunal shall decide whether to accept such request or not.
4. A notice of hearing subsequent to the first hearing and a notice of a postponed hearing shall not be subject to the time limit in Article 39.1.

Article 40 Place of Hearing

1. Where the parties have agreed on the place of hearing, the case shall be heard at that agreed place except for circumstances stipulated in Article 82.2 of these Rules.

2. Unless otherwise agreed to by the parties, a case accepted by SHIAC shall be heard in Shanghai, or if the tribunal considers it necessary, at other places with the approval of the Secretary General of SHIAC.

Article 41 Confidentiality

1. Hearings shall be held in camera. Where both parties request an open hearing, the tribunal shall make such decision.
2. For cases heard in camera, the parties, their representatives, witnesses, interpreters, mediators, arbitrators, experts, appraisers and the relevant staff-members of the Secretariat shall not disclose to any outsiders any substantive or procedural matters of the case.

Article 42 Default

1. If the Claimant fails to appear at a hearing without showing justifiable reasons for such failure, or withdraws from an on-going hearing without the permission of the tribunal, the Claimant may be deemed to have withdrawn its Request for Arbitration. In such a case, if the Respondent has filed a counterclaim, the tribunal shall proceed with the hearing of the counterclaim and render a default award.
2. If the Respondent fails to appear at a hearing without showing justifiable reasons for such failure, or withdraws from an on-going hearing without the permission of the tribunal, the tribunal may proceed with arbitration and render a default award. In such a case, if the Respondent has filed a counterclaim, the Respondent may be deemed to have withdrawn its counterclaim.

Article 43 Record of Hearing

1. During the hearing, excluding that for mediation, the tribunal shall make written record of the hearing, and may arrange a stenographic and/or audio-visual record of the hearing.
2. The written record and the stenographic and/or audio-visual record of the hearing shall be available for the use and reference by the tribunal.
3. Any party or participant in the arbitration may apply for a rectification of any omission or error in the minutes of its own statement. If the request for rectification is refused by the tribunal, the application shall nevertheless be recorded into the file.
4. The written record shall be signed or sealed by the arbitrator(s), the recorder, the parties, and other participants in arbitration, if any.

Article 44 Evidence

1. Each party is under the burden of proving the facts on which its claim, defense or counterclaim is based.
2. The tribunal may specify a period of time for the parties to submit evidence and the parties shall produce evidence within the specified period of time. The tribunal may refuse to admit any evidence produced beyond the period. If a party has difficulties in submitting evidence within the specified period of time,

it may apply for an extension before the expiration of the period. The tribunal shall decide whether or not to extend the period of time.

3. Parties that bear the burden of proof shall bear the consequences for their failure to produce evidence within the specified period of time, or for the produced evidence is insufficient to support its claim or counterclaim.
4. Where the parties have agreed on matters or rules relating to evidence, the parties' agreement shall prevail except where such agreement is inoperative.

Article 45 Investigation by Tribunal

1. The tribunal may, on its own initiative, undertake investigations and collect evidence as it considers necessary.
2. When investigating and collecting evidence by itself, the tribunal shall promptly notify the parties to be present at such investigation if it considers it necessary. In the event that one or both parties fail to be present, the investigation and collection shall proceed without being affected.
3. The tribunal shall, through the Secretariat, transmit the evidence collected by itself to the parties and provide them with an opportunity to comment.

Article 46 Expert Opinion and Appraiser Report

1. The parties may request for consultation or appraisal on specific issues of a case. The tribunal has the discretion to decide whether to grant the aforesaid request. The tribunal may consult or appoint expert(s) and/or appraiser(s) for clarification on specific issues of a case as it considers necessary. Such expert(s) or appraiser (s) may either be a Chinese or foreign organization or natural person.
2. Such an expert or appraiser may be appointed jointly by the parties, who may make the joint appointment with reference to Article 28.3 and Article 28.4. If the parties fail to reach an agreement on the appointment, the tribunal shall make the appointment.
3. The parties shall pay in advance the consultation/appraisal fees according to the percentage agreed to or specified by the tribunal. Where the parties fail to pay such fees in advance within the specified period of time, the tribunal has the discretion to decide not to conduct the relevant consultation or appraisal.
4. The tribunal has the discretion to request the parties to deliver or produce to the expert or appraiser relevant materials, documents, or properties and goods for examination, inspection and/or appraisal. The parties are obliged to comply with such request.
5. The expert opinion and/or the appraiser report shall be transmitted to the parties by the Secretariat. The parties shall be given an opportunity to respond. At the request of either party and with the approval of the tribunal, the expert or the appraiser may be heard at a hearing where, if considered necessary and appropriate by the tribunal, he/she may give explanations on their reports.

Article 47 Examination of Evidence

1. Unless otherwise agreed to by the parties, all evidence submitted by a party shall be filed with the Secretariat for transmission to the other party and the tribunal.

2. Unless otherwise agreed to by the parties, where a case is examined by way of hearing, the evidence shall be exhibited at the hearing and examined by the parties.
3. In the event that evidence is submitted after the hearing and the tribunal decides to admit the evidence without holding further hearings, the tribunal may request the parties to submit their opinions thereon in writing within a specified period of time.

Article 48 Suspension of Proceedings

1. The arbitration proceedings may be suspended when the parties so request, or if other circumstances occur during the proceedings which make such suspension necessary.
2. The decision to suspend the arbitration proceedings shall be made by the tribunal, or it shall be made by the Secretary General of SHIAC in the event that the tribunal is not constituted.

Article 49 Withdrawal and Dismissal

1. A party may submit a request to withdraw its claim or counterclaim in its entirety. In the event that the Claimant withdraws its claim in its entirety, the tribunal shall proceed with its examination of the counterclaim and render the award thereon. In the event that the Respondent withdraws its counterclaim in its entirety, the tribunal shall proceed with the examination of the claim and render the award thereon.
2. Where a case is to be dismissed before the constitution of the tribunal, the decision shall be made by the Secretary General of SHIAC. Where the case is to be dismissed after the constitution of the tribunal, the decision shall be made by the tribunal.

Chapter VI Combination of Arbitration with Mediation

Article 50 Mediation by Mediator

1. Any party may apply for mediation upon the consent of the other party during the period after an arbitration case has been accepted and before the tribunal is constituted. The Chairman of SHIAC shall, within three (3) days upon the receipt of consent to mediate in writing, appoint a mediator from the Panel of Mediators.
2. Mediation shall not affect the arbitration proceedings. During mediation, if one party requests the postponement of the constitution of the tribunal, to which the other party agrees, the Secretariat may postpone the process of constituting the tribunal.
3. The mediator upon appointment shall disclose in writing to SHIAC any facts or circumstances which may give rise to justifiable doubts as to his/her impartiality or independence, of which the Secretariat shall notify the parties promptly. A party may request the withdrawal or change of the mediator by a written application. The Chairman of SHIAC shall decide on the application with or without stating the reasons therefor.

4. A mediator may use methods he/she considers appropriate for facilitating the parties to reach a settlement including but not limited to:
   (a) meeting with the parties and their representatives separately or jointly;
   (b) asking the parties to put forward settlement proposals in writing or verbally; and
   (c) suggesting settlement proposals to the parties under the principle of *ex aequo et bono*.
5. Where a settlement agreement is reached through mediation, the Claimant may withdraw its Application for Arbitration, or ask the tribunal to be subsequently constituted to render the award on the basis of the terms of the settlement agreement.
6. The mediator shall terminate mediation if either party requests such termination in the mediation proceedings. In any event, the mediation proceedings shall be terminated on the date of constitution of the tribunal.
7. Unless otherwise agreed to by the parties in writing, a mediator shall not act as an arbitrator in the subsequent arbitration proceedings.

Article 51 Mediation by Tribunal

1. After the constitution of the tribunal, where both parties have the desire for mediation or one party so desires and the other party agrees when approached by the tribunal, the tribunal may mediate the case during the course of the arbitration proceedings.
2. The tribunal may mediate the case in the manner it considers appropriate.
3. The tribunal shall terminate mediation and continue the arbitration proceedings, until rendering the award, if either party requests such termination or if the tribunal believes that further efforts to mediate will be futile.
4. A settlement agreement reached between the parties in mediation by the tribunal but without the involvement of the tribunal shall be deemed as one reached through the mediation by the tribunal.
5. Where settlement is reached through mediation by the tribunal, the parties shall sign a written settlement agreement. The parties may withdraw their requests for arbitration or counterclaims, or request the tribunal to render the award on the basis of the terms of the settlement agreement.

Article 52 Settlement not in Arbitration Commission

Where the parties have reached a settlement agreement by themselves through negotiation or mediation without involving SHIAC, the parties may, based on an arbitration agreement concluded between them that provides for arbitration by SHIAC and the settlement agreement, request SHIAC to constitute a tribunal to render the award on the basis of the terms of the settlement agreement. Unless otherwise agreed by the parties, the Chairman of SHIAC shall appoint a sole arbitrator to constitute such tribunal, which shall examine the case using the procedures it considers appropriate and render the award. The specific procedures and the time limit for rendering the award shall not be subject to other Articles in these Rules.

Article 53 No Reference to Contents in Mediation

Where mediation fails, any opinion, view or statement, and any proposal or proposition expressing acceptance or opposition, by either party or by the mediator or by the tribunal in the process of mediation shall not be invoked as grounds for any claim, defense or counterclaim in the subsequent arbitration proceedings, judicial proceedings or any other proceedings.

Chapter VII The Award

Article 54 Time Limit for Rendering Award

1. For cases involving disputes referred to in Article 4.1 and Article 4.2 of these Rules, the tribunal shall render the award within six (6) months upon the date the tribunal is constituted.
2. For cases involving disputes referred to in Article 4.3 of these Rules, the tribunal shall render the award within four (4) months upon the date the tribunal is constituted.
3. Upon the request of the tribunal, the Secretary General of SHIAC may extend aforesaid time limit if he/she considers it necessary with justifiable reasons.
4. The following periods of time shall not be counted within the aforesaid time limit:

   (a) the period of time during which a consultation or appraisal is conducted, as provided in Article 46 of these Rules; and
   (b) the period of time during which any arbitration proceedings is suspended in accordance with laws and/or these Rules.

Article 55 Rendering Award

1. The tribunal shall fairly and reasonably render the award on the basis of facts and in accordance with laws.
2. The tribunal shall state in the award the claims, the facts of the dispute, the reasons on which the award is based, the result of the award, the allocation of the arbitration costs and the date on which and the place at which the award is rendered. The facts of the dispute and the reasons on which the award is based may not be stated in the award if the parties have agreed so, or if the award is rendered in accordance with the terms of a settlement agreement between the parties. The tribunal has the discretion to determine in the award the specific period of time for the parties to execute the award and the liabilities to be borne by a party failing to execute the award within the specified time limit.
3. SHIAC shall affix its seal to an award rendered in an arbitration which is agreed to be submitted to SHIAC or to the China (Shanghai) Pilot Free Trade Zone Court of Arbitration, or to SHIAC and arbitration is conducted in the China (Shanghai) Pilot Free Trade Zone Court of Arbitration.

4. Where a case is examined by a three-arbitrator tribunal, the award shall be rendered by all three arbitrators or a majority of the arbitrators. A written dissenting opinion shall be docketed into the file and may be attached to the award, but it shall not constitute a part of the award.
5. Where the tribunal cannot reach a majority opinion, the award shall be rendered in accordance with the presiding arbitrator's opinion. The written opinion of other arbitrators shall be docketed into the file and may be attached to the award, but it shall not constitute a part of the award.
6. Unless the award is rendered with the opinion of the presiding arbitrator or the sole arbitrator, the award shall be signed by a majority of arbitrators. An arbitrator who has a dissenting opinion may or may not sign his/her name on the award.
7. The date on which the award is rendered shall be the date on which the award comes legally effective.
8. The award is final and binding upon both parties. Neither party may bring a suit before a court or make a request to any other organization for revising the award.

Article 56 Award *ex aequo et bono*

If the parties have so agreed in the arbitration agreement, or have made a written application upon agreement consensus during thc arbitration proceedings, the tribunal may render the award *ex aequo et bono*, under the condition that such an award shall not violate any mandatory provisions of laws and public policies.

Article 57 Partial Award

A partial award may be rendered by the tribunal during arbitration but before the final award is rendered if it considers it necessary, or if the parties so request and the tribunal accepts. Failure to perform the partial award by any one of the parties will neither affect the continuation of the arbitration proceedings nor prevent the tribunal from rendering the final award.

Article 58 Allocation of Costs

1. The tribunal has the discretion to determine in the award the arbitration fees and other expenses to be paid by the parties to SHIAC.
2. The tribunal has the discretion to decide in the award, according to the specific circumstances of the case, that the losing party shall compensate the winning party for the expenses reasonably incurred by it in pursuing its case. The tribunal shall consider the factors such as the outcome and complexity of the case, the workload of the winning party and/or its representative(s), and the amount in dispute, etc.

Article 59 Scrutiny of Draft Award

The tribunal shall submit its award draft to SHIAC for scrutiny before signing the award. SHIAC may remind the tribunal of issues in the award on condition that the tribunal's independence in rendering the award is not affected.

Article 60 Rectification of Award

Within thirty (30) days upon its receipt of the award, either party may request in writing for a rectification of any clerical, typographical, or calculation error or errors of a similar nature contained in the award; if such errors do exist in the award, the tribunal shall make a rectification in writing within thirty (30) days upon the receipt of the written request for the rectification. The tribunal may rectify any such errors in writing on its own initiative within a reasonable time after the award is rendered. Such rectification in writing shall constitute a part of the award.

Article 61 Supplementary Award

Within thirty (30) days upon the receipt of the award, either party may request the tribunal in writing for a supplementary award which was advanced in the arbitration proceedings but was omitted from the award. If such omission does exist, the tribunal shall render a supplementary award within thirty (30) days upon the date of receipt of the written request. The tribunal may also render a supplementary award on its own initiative within a reasonable period of time after the award is rendered. Such supplementary award shall constitute a part of the award previously rendered.

Article 62 Execution of Award

1. The parties must execute the award within the period of time specified in the award. If no time limit is specified in the award, the parties shall execute the award immediately.
2. Where one party fails to execute the award, the other party may apply to a competent court for enforcement of the award pursuant to laws.

Chapter VIII Summary Procedures

Article 63 Application of Summary Procedures

1. Unless otherwise agreed to by the parties, the Summary Procedures shall apply to any dispute referred to in Article 4.1 and Article 4.2 and the amount in dispute thereof does not exceeds RMB 100,000, or to any dispute referred in Article 4.3 and the amount in dispute thereof exceeds RMB 100,000 but does not exceed RMB 1,000,000, or to any dispute where the amount in dispute exceeds RMB 1,000,000 where one party applies for arbitration under these Summary Procedures and the other party agrees in writing.
2. Where no monetary claim is specified or the amount in dispute is not clear, SHIAC shall determine whether or not to apply the Summary Procedures after a full consideration of such factors as the complexity of the case and the interests involved, etc.

Article 64 Constitution of Tribunal

A sole-arbitrator tribunal shall be constituted in accordance with Article 29 under the Summary Procedures.

Article 65 Defense and Counterclaim

1. Within twenty (20) days upon the receipt of the Notice of Arbitration, the Respondent shall submit its Defense and relevant evidence, documents certifying the party's identity and other supporting documents to the Secretariat; counterclaims, if any, from the Respondent shall also be filed with supporting evidence within the aforesaid period of time.
2. Within twenty (20) days upon the receipt of the counterclaim and its attachments, the Claimant shall submit its Statement of Defense to the Respondent's counterclaim.
3. If the party does have justifiable reasons to request for an extension of the aforesaid time period, the tribunal shall decide whether to extend the time limit or not; and such decision shall be made by the Secretariat in the event that the tribunal has not been constituted.

Article 66 Conduct of Hearing

The tribunal may hear the case in the manner it considers appropriate. The tribunal may in its full discretion decide to hold hearings or examine the case only on the basis of the written materials and evidence submitted by the parties.

Article 67 Notice of Hearing

1. For a case examined by way of a hearing, the Secretariat shall, after the tribunal has fixed a date for the hearing, notify the parties of the date at least ten (10) days in advance of the date of hearing. A party having justifiable reasons may request the tribunal for a postponement of the hearing. However, such request must be submitted to the tribunal at least five (5) days in advance of the date of hearing. The tribunal shall decide whether to postpone the hearing or not.
2. If the party does have justifiable reasons for failure to request for a postponement of the hearing within the time limit provided in Article 67.1, the tribunal will decide whether to accept its request for postponement or not.
3. A notice of the subsequent hearing and a notice of a postponed hearing shall not be subject to the time limit provided in Article 67.1.

Article 68 Time Limit for Rendering Award

1. The tribunal shall render the award within three (3) months upon the date the tribunal is constituted.
2. Upon the request of the tribunal, the Secretary General of SHIAC may extend the time limit if he/she considers it necessary with justifiable reasons.

Article 69 Change of Procedures

1. The application of the Summary Procedures shall not be affected by any amendment to the claim, or by the filing of or any amendment to a counterclaim.

2. Where the amount in dispute of the amended claim or filing of or amendment of counterclaim exceeds RMB 1,000,000, the procedures of the case shall be changed from the Summary Procedures to the procedures provided for in Chapters II–VII of these Rules unless the parties have agreed to the continuous application of the Summary Procedures.

Article 70 Application of Other Articles in These Rules

As to matters not covered in this chapter, the relevant Articles in the other chapters of these Rules shall apply.

Chapter IX Procedures for Small Claims

Article 71 Application of Procedures for Small Claims

The Procedures for Small Claims shall apply to disputes as referred to in Article 4.3 of these Rules and the amount of such disputes does not exceed RMB 100,000.

Article 72 Constitution of Tribunal

Unless otherwise agreed to by the parties, the Chairman of SHIAC shall appoint one arbitrator to constitute a sole-arbitrator tribunal to hear a case under the Procedures for Small Claims.

Article 73 Defense and Counterclaim

1. Within ten (10) days upon the date of receipt of the Notice of Arbitration, the Respondent shall submit its Statement of Defense attaching with the evidence on which its defense is based, documents certifying the Respondent' identity, and other supporting documents, to the Secretariat; counterclaims, if any, from the Respondent shall also be filed with supporting evidence within the aforesaid time limit.
2. Within ten (10) days upon the date of receipt of the counterclaim and its attachments, the Claimant shall submit its written Statement of Defense to the Secretariat.

Article 74 Conduct of Hearing

The tribunal may hear any arbitration case in the manner it considers appropriate. The tribunal may in its sole discretion decide to hold hearings or to examine the case only on the basis of the written materials and evidence submitted by the parties.

Article 75 Notice of Hearing

1. For a case examined by way of hearing, the Secretariat shall, after the tribunal has fixed a date for the hearing, notify the parties of the date at least seven (7) days in advance of the date of hearing. Either party having justifiable reasons may request the tribunal for a postponement of the hearing, provided, however, that such request must be communicated to the tribunal at least five (5) days in advance of the date of hearing. The tribunal shall decide whether to postpone the hearing or not.

2. If one party has justifiable reasons for failing to request for a postponement of the hearing within the time limits provided in Article 75.1, the tribunal shall decide whether to accept its request for postponement or not.
3. A notice of the subsequent hearing and a notice of a postponed hearing shall not be subject to the time limit in Article 75.1.

Article 76 Time Limit for Rendering Award

1. The tribunal shall render the award within forty five (45) days upon the date the tribunal is constituted.
2. Upon the request of the tribunal, the Secretary General of SHIAC may extend the time limit if he/she considers it necessary with justifiable reasons.

Article 77 Change of Procedures

1. The application of the Procedures for small claims shall not be affected by any amendment to the claim, or by the filing of or any amendment to a counterclaim.
2. Where the amount in dispute of the amended claim or filing of or amendment of the counterclaim exceeds RMB 100,000 but does not exceed RMB 1,000,000, the procedures of the case shall be changed from Procedures for Small Claims to the Summary Procedures unless the parties have agreed to continue to use the Procedures for Small Claims.
3. Where the amount in dispute of the amended claim or filing of or amendment of the counterclaim exceeds RMB 1,000,000, the procedures of the case shall be changed from the Procedures for Small Claims to the procedures provided for in Chapters II–VII of these Rules unless the parties have agreed to continue to use the Procedures for Small Claims.

Article 78 Application of Other Articles in These Rules

Matters that are not covered in Chapter IX shall be referred to the relevant Articles in other chapters of these Rules.

Chapter X Supplementary Provisions

Article 79 Language

1. Where the parties have agreed on the language for arbitration, their agreement shall prevail. Absent such an agreement, the Chinese language shall be the working language of arbitration. The tribunal may, based on the mutual agreement of parties, decide to use other language as the working language for arbitration, taking the working language of arbitration agreement, the language of the contract and other factors in arbitration into account.
2. At a hearing, a party or its representative(s) or witness(es) may employ interpreter(s) if it/they requires, or may ask the Secretariat to employ the interpreter (s) on their behalf.
3. The tribunal and/or the Secretariat may, if it considers necessary, request the parties to submit a corresponding version of the documents and evidence by the parties in Chinese or in other languages.

Article 80 Service

1. Unless otherwise agreed to by the parties, documents, notices and written materials in relation to arbitration may be sent to the parties and/or their representatives in person, or by registered mail or express mail, facsimile, telex, cable, or by any other means considered appropriate by the Secretariat.
2. Documents, notices and written materials in relation to arbitration to a party and/or its representative(s) shall be deemed to have been properly served on the party if delivered to the parties in person or delivered at its place of business, registration, domicile, habitual residence or mailing address, or where, after reasonable inquiries by the other party, none of the aforesaid addresses can be found, the written correspondence is sent by the Secretariat to its last known place of business, domicile, habitual residence or mailing address by registered mail or by any other means that provides a record of the attempt of delivery.

Article 81 Calculation of Time Limit

1. A time limit specified in or fixed in accordance with these Rules shall commence to run on the day after the date on which such period commences. The day from which a time limit commences shall not be counted as within such time limit.
2. If the day after the date on which the time limit falls on a public holiday or non-business day at the place of the addressee, then the time limit shall commence from the first subsequent business day. The public holiday and the non-business day occurring within such period shall be included in calculating the period of time. If the expiration date of a time limit falls on a public holiday or a non-business day, then the period of time shall expire on the first subsequent business day.

Article 82 Arbitration Fees and Actual Expenses

1. Apart from charging arbitration fees to the parties according to the Schedules of Arbitration Fees, SHIAC may collect from the parties other additional, reasonable and actual expenses including arbitrators' special remuneration and their travel and accommodation expenses incurred when hearing a case, as well as the costs and expenses for experts, appraisers and interpreters appointed by the tribunal, etc.
2. Where the parties have agreed to hold a hearing at a place other than SHIAC's domicile, extra expenses including travel and accommodation expenses incurred thereby shall be paid in advance as a deposit by the parties. In the event that the parties fail to do so, the hearing shall be held at the domicile of SHIAC.

Article 83 Interpretation of These Rules

1. SHIAC reserves the right to interpret these Rules.
2. The headings of Articles in these Rules shall not serve as interpretations of the contents of the Articles contained herein.

3. Unless stated otherwise, other documents issued by SHIAC shall not constitute a part of these Rules.

Article 84 Official Versions of These Rules

All the versions of these Rules as published by SHIAC in Chinese, English and other languages are the official versions. In the event of any discrepancies among different versions, the Chinese version shall prevail.

Article 85 Coming into Force

These Rules shall be effective as from January 1, 2015. For cases accepted by SHIAC before these Rules become effective, the Arbitration Rules effective at the time of acceptance shall apply.

Shanghai International Economic and Trade Arbitration Commission (Shanghai International Arbitration Center) Schedule of Arbitration Fee I

(This Schedule of Arbitration Fee applies to the arbitration cases accepted under Article 4.1, Article 4.2 of these Rules, and is effective as from January 1, 2015)

Amount of claim (RMB Yuan)	Amount of fee (RMB Yuan)
1,000,000 or less	3.5 % of the claimed amount, minimum 10,000
1,000,001–5,000,000	35,000 plus 2.5 % of the amount above 1,000,000
5,000,001–10,000,000	135,000 plus 1.5 % of the amount above 5,000,000
10,000,001–50,000,000	210,000 plus 1 % of the amount above 10,000,000
50,000,001 or more	610,000 plus 0.5 % of the amount above 50,000,000

Each case, when being accepted, shall be charged an additional amount of RMB 10,000 as a Registration Fee which includes the expenses for examining the application for arbitration, initiating the arbitral proceedings, computerizing management and filing the documents.

Where the amount of the claim is not ascertained at the time when application for arbitration is handed in, or there exists special circumstances, the amount of arbitration fee shall be determined by the Secretariat.

If the arbitration fee is charged in foreign currency, an amount of foreign currency equivalent to the corresponding RMB value specified in this Schedule shall be paid.

Apart from charging arbitration fee according to this Schedule, SHIAC may collect other extra, reasonable and actual expenses pursuant to the relevant provisions of these Rules.

Shanghai International Economic and Trade Arbitration Commission (Shanghai International Arbitration Center) Schedule of Arbitration Fee II

(This Schedule of Arbitration Fee applies to the arbitration cases accepted under Article 4.3 of these Rules, and is effective as from January 1, 2015.)

In accordance with the Notice of the Measures for the Charging of Arbitration Fee by the Arbitration Commissions with the reference number of Guo Ban Fa No. 44/1995 issued by the

General Office of the State Council, the arbitration fee for cases accepted by SHIAC under Article 4.3 of these Rules are charged in the following way:

I. Registration Fee

Amount of claim (RMB Yuan)	Amount of fee (RMB Yuan)
100,000 or less	100
100,001–200,000	4550 plus 3 % of the amount above 100,000
200,001–500,000	7550 plus 2 % of the amount above 200,000
500,001–1,000,000	13,550 plus 1 % of the amount above 500,000
1,000,001 or more	18,550 plus 0.5 % of the amount above 1,000,000

II. Handling Fee

Amount of claim (RMB Yuan)	Amount of fee (RMB Yuan)
100,000 or less	1250
100,001–200,000	5000
200,001–500,000	5000 plus 2 % of the amount above 200,000
500,001–1,000,000	11,000 plus 1.5 % of the amount above 500,000
1,000,001–3,000,000	18,500 plus 0.5 % of the amount above 1,000,000
3,000,001–6,000,000	28,500 plus 0.45 % of the amount above 3,000,000
6,000,001–10,000,000	42,000 plus 0.4 % of the amount above 6,000,000
10,000,001–20,000,000	58,000 plus 0.3 % of the amount above 10,000,000
20,000,001–40,000,000	88,000 plus 0.2 % of the amount above 20,000,000
40,000,001 or more	128,000 plus 0.15 % of the amount above 40,000,000

The Amount of Claim referred to in this Schedule shall be based on the sum of money claimed by the Claimant. If the amount claimed is different from the actual amount in dispute, the actual amount in dispute shall be the basis for calculation.

Where the amount of claim is not ascertained at the time when application for arbitration is handed in, or there exists special circumstances, the amount of arbitration fee deposit shall be determined by the Secretariat in consideration of the specific rights and interests involved in the disputes.

Apart from charging arbitration fee according to this Schedule, SHIAC may collect other extra, reasonable and actual expenses pursuant to the relevant provisions of these Rules.

Shanghai International Economic and Trade Arbitration Commission (Shanghai International Arbitration Center) Schedule of Arbitration Fee III

(This Schedule of Arbitration Fee applies to the arbitrations under or involved in Article 21 of these Rules, and is effective as from January 1, 2015.)

The arbitration fee for either party applies for constituting an emergency tribunal to decide interim measure(s), and/or the counterparty applies for interim measure(s) to such emergency tribunal, is charged as follows:

Interim measure(s) claimed	Amount of fee (RMB Yuan)
Apply for one (1) interim measure	10,000
Apply for more than one (1) interim measures	$10{,}000 + (n - 1) \times 2000$

SCIA Arbitration Rules[6]

South China International Economic and Trade Arbitration Commission Arbitration Rules

Effective as from December 1, 2012

Chapter I General provisions

Article 1—Organization and Name

1. South China International Economic and Trade Arbitration Commission (also known as Shenzhen Court of International Arbitration, formerly known as China International Economic and Trade Arbitration Commission South China Subcommission, China International Economic and Trade Arbitration Commission Shenzhen Subcommission) is an arbitral institution established in Shenzhen, China for resolving contractual disputes and other disputes over

[6]http://www.sccietac.org/web/doc/view_rules/743.html.

rights and interests in property between natural persons, legal persons and other organizations.

2. Where an arbitration agreement provides for arbitration by the South China International Economic and Trade Arbitration Commission (hereinafter the "SCIA"), or by the Shenzhen Court of International Arbitration, the China International Economic and Trade Arbitration Commission South China Sub-commission or the China International Economic and Trade Arbitration Commission Shenzhen Sub-commission, or where the name of the arbitration institution agreed in the arbitration agreement can be inferred as the SCIA, it shall be deemed that the parties have agreed to arbitration by the SCIA.

Article 2—Jurisdiction

The SCIA accepts the following cases:

1. international or foreign-related arbitration cases;
2. arbitration cases related to the Hong Kong Special Administrative Region, the Macao Special Administrative Region and the Taiwan region; and
3. Chinese Mainland arbitration cases.

Article 3—Scope of Application

1. Unless otherwise agreed, the parties shall be deemed to have agreed to arbitration in accordance with the Rules where they have agreed to arbitration by the SCIA.
2. Where the parties agree to refer their dispute to arbitration under the Rules without providing for the name of the specific arbitration institution, they shall be deemed to have agreed to refer the dispute to arbitration by the SCIA.
3. Where the parties agree to refer their dispute to the SCIA for arbitration but have agreed on the application of other arbitration rules or have agreed on a modification of the Rules, the parties' agreement shall prevail unless such agreement cannot be implemented or is in conflict with a mandatory provision of the law as it applies to the arbitration proceedings. Where the parties have agreed on the application of other arbitration rules, the SCIA shall perform the relevant functions of the administrative authority under those arbitration rules. Where the parties agree to arbitration under the UNCITRAL Arbitration Rules, the SCIA shall be the appointing authority and shall perform other relevant administrative functions in accordance with the provisions of the UNCITRAL Arbitration Rules or the agreement of the parities.
4. The specialized arbitration rules adopted by the SCIA otherwise for a specific business sector shall prevail insofar as their provisions differ from the Rules. As to matters not covered in those specialized arbitration rules for a specific business sector, the relevant provisions in the Rules shall apply.

Article 4—Place of Arbitration

1. Where the parties have agreed on the place of arbitration, the parties' agreement shall prevail.
2. Where the parties have not agreed on the place of arbitration, the place of arbitration shall be the domicile of the SCIA. The SCIA may also determine the place of arbitration to be a location other than the domicile of the SCIA having regard to the circumstances of the case.
3. The arbitral award shall be deemed to be made at the place of arbitration.

Article 5—Notifications and Time Limits

1. All written documents, notices and materials in relation to the arbitration may be delivered in person or sent by mail, fax, or by any other means considered proper by the Secretariat of the SCIA or the arbitral tribunal.
2. Any written pleadings/submissions and all other correspondence submitted by any party, as well as all documents annexed thereto, shall be supplied in a number of copies sufficient to provide one copy for each party, plus one for each arbitrator, and one for the Secretariat of the SCIA.
3. Any arbitration documents, correspondence or materials to a party or its representative(s) shall be deemed to have been properly delivered to the party if delivered to the addressee in person or sent to the addressee's place of business, registration, domicile, habitual residence or other mailing address provided by the addressee or the other party. Where, after reasonable inquiries, none of the aforesaid addresses can be found, arbitration documents, correspondence or materials shall be deemed to have been properly delivered if sent to the addressee's last known place of business, registration, domicile, habitual residence or other mailing address by mail or by any other means that provides a record of the attempt at delivery.
4. Periods of time specified in or fixed under the Rules shall start to run on the day following the date a notification or communication is deemed to have been made. When the day next following such date is a public holiday, or a non-business day in the country where the notification or communication is deemed to have been made, the period of time shall commence on the first following business day. Public holidays and non-business days within the period concerned are included in the calculation of the period of time. If the last day of the relevant period of time is a public holiday or a non-business day, the period of time shall expire at the end of the first following business day.
5. If a party breaches a time limit because of force majeure events or other justifiable reasons, it shall inform the SCIA within a reasonable time period and may apply for an extension of time within 10 days of the removal of the obstacle. The arbitral tribunal shall decide on the request. Where the arbitral tribunal has not yet been formed, such decision shall be made by the Secretary General of the SCIA.

Article 6—Language of Arbitration

1. Where the parties have agreed on the language of arbitration, their agreement shall prevail. In the absence of such agreement, the arbitral tribunal shall determine the language or languages of the arbitration, due regard being given to the language of the arbitration agreement or the contract concerned and all other relevant circumstances.
2. If a party or its representative(s) or witness(es) requires interpretation at an oral hearing, the party shall provide or request the tribunal to provide the interpreter.
3. The arbitral tribunal or the Secretariat of the SCIA may, if it considers it necessary, require the parties to submit a corresponding translation of their documents and evidence in the language or languages agreed upon by the parties or determined by the arbitral tribunal.

Article 7—Confidentiality

1. Hearings shall be confidential. Where all parties request an open hearing, the arbitral tribunal shall make a decision.
2. For the case heard in camera, the parties and their representatives, the witnesses, the interpreters, the arbitrators, the experts consulted by the arbitral tribunal, the appraisers appointed by the arbitral tribunal, the staff of the SCIA and other relevant persons shall not disclose to any outsider any substantive or procedural matters relating to the case.

Article 8—Waiver of Right to Object

A party shall be deemed to have waived its right to object where it knows or should have known that any provision of, or requirement under, the Rules or arbitration agreement has not been complied with and yet participates in or proceeds with the arbitration proceedings without promptly submitting its objection in writing to such non-compliance.

Chapter II Arbitration Agreements and Jurisdiction

Article 9—Arbitration Agreements

1. An arbitration agreement means an arbitration clause in a contract or any other form of written agreement concluded between the parties providing for arbitration. An arbitration agreement may be concluded between the parties either before or after the occurrence of the dispute.
2. An arbitration agreement shall be deemed to exist where its existence is asserted by one party and not denied by the other during the exchange of the Request for Arbitration and the Statement of Defence.
3. An arbitration agreement shall be deemed to have concluded where one party undertakes in writing to submit the dispute to the SCIA for arbitration and the other party submits the dispute to the SCIA for arbitration.

Article 10—Independence of Arbitration Agreements

An arbitration clause contained in a contract or an arbitration agreement attached to a contract shall be treated independent and separate from all other clauses of the contract. The validity of an arbitration agreement shall not be affected by any modification, cancellation, termination, transfer, expiry, invalidity, ineffectiveness, rescission or non-existence of the contract.

Article 11—Objection to Validity of an Arbitration Agreement

1. An objection to an arbitration agreement and/or jurisdiction over an arbitration case shall be raised in writing before the first oral hearing is held by the arbitral tribunal. Where a case is to be decided on the basis of documents only, such objection shall be raised in writing before the expiry of the time limit for the submission of the first defence. If a party fails to raise such objections, it shall be deemed to have no objection. The above objection to the validity of the arbitration agreements includes the objection to whether the arbitration agreement exists, whether it is null and void or ceases to have effect, and whether it cannot be implemented.
2. Any objection to the validity of an arbitration agreement raised by the parties may be decided by the SCIA or by the arbitral tribunal authorized by the SCIA with such power. The decisions by the arbitral tribunal may be made in the form of interlocutory award or in the final award.
3. Where the SCIA is satisfied by *prima facie* evidence that an arbitration agreement providing for arbitration by the SCIA exists, it may make a decision that it has jurisdiction over the arbitration case. Such a decision based on *prima facie* evidence shall not prevent the arbitral tribunal from making a new decision on jurisdiction based on facts and evidence found by the arbitral tribunal during the arbitration proceedings that is inconsistent with the initial decision.

Article 12—Other Objections to Jurisdiction

Decisions concerning objections to jurisdiction other than those stipulated in Article 11 shall be made by the arbitral tribunal in the form of an interlocutory award or in the final award.

Article 13—Objections to Jurisdiction not Affecting the Proceedings

The arbitration shall proceed notwithstanding an objection to jurisdiction.

Chapter III Request for Arbitration, Defence and Counterclaim

Article 14—Commencement of Arbitration

The arbitration proceedings shall commence on the day on which the SCIA receives a Request for Arbitration.

Article 15—Request for Arbitration

A party applying for arbitration under the Rules shall:

1. Submit a Request for Arbitration in writing signed and/or sealed by the Claimant or its authorized representative(s), which shall, *inter alia*, include:

   (a) The names and addresses, telephone and fax numbers, and email addresses of the parties and of their representatives;
   (b) A reference to the arbitration agreement that is relied upon;
   (c) The statement of claim; and
   (d) The facts and grounds on which the claim is based.

2. Attach to the Request for Arbitration the relevant evidentiary materials of the facts on which the statement of claim is based.

Article 16—Multiple Contracts

Claims arising out of or in connection with more than one contract between the Claimant and the Respondent may be made in a single arbitration.

Article 17—Acceptance of a Case

1. Upon a written application of a party, the SCIA shall accept a case in accordance with an arbitration agreement concluded between the parties either before or after the occurrence of the dispute.
2. Upon receipt of a Request for Arbitration and its attachments, if the Secretariat of the SCIA finds the formalities required for arbitration application to be complete, it shall send a Notice of Arbitration to the parties together with one copy of each of the Rules and the SCIA's Panel of Arbitrators, and the Request for Arbitration and its attachments submitted by the Claimant to the Respondent.
3. Where the Secretariat of the SCIA finds the formalities required for the arbitration application to be incomplete, it may request the Claimant to complete them within a specified time period.

Article 18—Statement of Defence

1. The Respondent shall file a Statement of Defence in writing within thirty (30) days from the date of receipt of the Notice of Arbitration. Where the Respondent applies for an extension of time, if the arbitral tribunal deems any justified reasons exist, the arbitral tribunal shall decide to grant an extension. Where the arbitral tribunal has not yet been formed, the decision on whether to grant the extension of the time period shall be made by the Secretary General of the SCIA.
2. The Statement of Defence shall be signed and/or sealed by the Respondent or its authorized representative(s), and shall, *inter alia*, include:

   (a) The names and addresses, telephone and fax numbers, and email addresses of the Respondent and of their representatives;

(b) The defence to the Claimant's Request for Arbitration, setting forth the facts and grounds on which the defence is based; and
(c) The relevant evidentiary materials on which the defence is based.

3. The arbitral tribunal has the power to decide whether to accept a Statement of Defence submitted after the expiration of the above time limit.
4. Failure by the Respondent to file a Statement of Defence shall not affect the conduct of the arbitration proceedings.

Article 19—Counterclaim

1. The Respondent shall file a counterclaim, if any, in writing within thirty (30) days from the date of receipt of the Notice of Arbitration. Where the Respondent applies for an extension of time, if the arbitral tribunal deems any justified reasons exist, the arbitral tribunal shall decide to grant an extension. Where the arbitral tribunal has not yet been formed, the decision on whether to grant the extension of the time period shall be made by the Secretary General of the SCIA.
2. When filing its counterclaim, the Respondent shall specify its counterclaim in the Statement of Counterclaim and state the facts and grounds on which its counterclaim is based with the relevant evidentiary materials attached thereto.
3. Where the formalities required for filing a counterclaim are found to be complete, the Secretariat of the SCIA shall send a Notice of Acceptance of Counterclaim to the parties. The Claimant shall submit its Statement of Defence to the counterclaim in writing within thirty (30) days from the date of receipt of the Notice. If the Claimant has justified reasons to request an extension of the time period, the arbitral tribunal shall decide whether to grant such an extension. Where the arbitral tribunal has not yet been formed, the decision on whether to grant the extension of the time period shall be made by the Secretary General of the SCIA.
4. The arbitral tribunal has the power to decide whether to accept a Statement of Counterclaim and Statement of Defence thereto submitted after the expiration of the above time limit.
5. Failure by the Claimant to file a Statement of Defence to the Respondent's counterclaim shall not affect the proceedings of the arbitration.

Article 20—Amendment to the Claim, Defence or Counterclaim

Any party may apply to amend its claim, defence or counterclaim in writing during the arbitral proceedings, and that request may be granted unless the arbitral tribunal considers that the amendment will delay the arbitration proceedings, be unfair to the other party or result in other circumstances that may not be appropriate for such amendments.

Article 21—Advance Payment of Arbitration Fees

A party making claims, counterclaims or amendments thereof shall pay the arbitration fee in advance in accordance with the Schedule of Fees and Costs of Arbitration adopted by the SCIA.

Article 22—Submission of Documents

1. When submitting the Request for Arbitration, the Statement of Defence, the Statement of Counterclaim, evidentiary documents, and other arbitration documents, the parties shall make their submissions in quintuplicate. Where there are multiple parties, additional copies shall be provided accordingly. Where the arbitral tribunal is composed of a sole arbitrator, the number of copies submitted may be reduced by two.
2. Electronic versions may be submitted simultaneously when submitting the above documents.

Article 23—Representatives

A party may be represented by its authorized representative(s) including but not limited to the counsel from the Chinese Mainland or from jurisdictions outside the Chinese Mainland, in handling matters relating to the arbitration. In such a case, a Power of Attorney specifying the matters and scope of authorization shall be forwarded to the Secretariat of the SCIA.

Chapter IV Interim Measures

Article 24—Preservation

1. Any party may apply for preservation before the commencement of or during the arbitration proceedings if, due to emergency, the applying party's legitimate interests may suffer irreparable damages without immediate preservation, or if the other party's acts or some other circumstances may render the arbitral award impossible or difficult to enforce.
2. If any party applies for preservation during the arbitration proceedings, the SCIA shall submit the application for preservation to a competent court.

Article 25—Other Interim Measures

At the request of a party, or if the arbitral tribunal considers it necessary, the arbitral tribunal may order any other interim measure it deems appropriate. Any such measure may take the form of a procedural order or of an interlocutory award. The arbitral tribunal may order the requesting party to furnish appropriate security.

Chapter V Arbitral Tribunal

Article 26—Independence and Impartiality

Every arbitrator must be and remain impartial and independent of the parties involved in the arbitration.

Article 27—Number of Arbitrators

1. The arbitral tribunal shall be composed of one or three arbitrators.
2. Unless otherwise agreed by the parties or provided by the Rules, an arbitral tribunal shall be composed of three arbitrators.

Article 28—Appointment of Arbitrator

1. The SCIA establishes a Panel of Arbitrators. The parties shall appoint arbitrators from the Panel of Arbitrators provided by the SCIA.
2. Parties may agree on the means of appointing arbitrators, unless such agreement cannot be implemented or is in conflict with a mandatory provision of the law as it applies to the arbitration proceedings.
3. Parties may agree to appoint arbitrators from outside the SCIA's Panel of Arbitrators. An arbitrator appointed in accordance with such agreement from outside the SCIA's Panel of Arbitrators may serve as arbitrator of the arbitration in dispute if he/she meets the conditions prescribed by law for arbitrator subject to the confirmation by the Chairman of the SCIA.
4. Where there are multiple Claimants and/or multiple Respondents in arbitration case, the multiple Claimants, jointly, and/or the multiple Respondents, jointly, shall appoint or entrust the Chairman of the SCIA to appoint an arbitrator.

Article 29—Arbitral Tribunal of Three Arbitrators

1. Unless otherwise agreed by the parties, within fifteen (15) days from the date of receipt of the Notice of Arbitration, the Claimant and the Respondent shall each appoint, or entrust the Chairman of the SCIA to appoint, an arbitrator, failing which the arbitrator shall be appointed by the Chairman of the SCIA.
2. Unless otherwise agreed by the parties, within fifteen (15) days from the date of the Respondent's receipt of the Notice of Arbitration, the parties shall jointly appoint or jointly entrust the Chairman of the SCIA to appoint the presiding arbitrator, failing which the presiding arbitrator shall be appointed by the Chairman of the SCIA.
3. In the alternative the parties may agree that the presiding arbitrator to be appointed jointly by the two appointed arbitrators. Unless otherwise agreed by the parties, where the two appointed arbitrators fail to appoint the presiding arbitrator within five (5) days from the date of the determination of the second arbitrator, the presiding arbitrator shall be appointed by the Chairman of the SCIA.
4. With the consent of each party, the Chairman of the SCIA may recommend a list of candidates for the presiding arbitrator for the parties to select from.

Article 30—Arbitral Tribunal of a Sole Arbitrator

Where the arbitral tribunal is composed of a sole arbitrator, the sole arbitrator shall be appointed pursuant to the procedures stipulated in Article 29, paragraphs 2 or 4, of the Rules.

Article 31—Disclosure

1. A prospective arbitrator shall sign a Declaration, disclosing in writing to the SCIA any facts or circumstances likely to give rise to justifiable doubts as to his/her impartiality or independence.
2. If circumstances that need to be disclosed arise during the arbitration proceedings, the arbitrator shall promptly disclose to the SCIA such circumstances in writing.
3. The Declaration and/or the disclosure of the arbitrator shall be communicated to each party and other members of the arbitral tribunal if any.

Article 32—Challenge of Arbitrators

1. A party wishing to challenge the arbitrator on the grounds of the information disclosed by the arbitrator shall forward the challenge in writing within ten (10) days from the date of such receipt. Failing to file a challenge within the above time period, the party may not subsequently challenge the arbitrator on the grounds of the information disclosed by the arbitrator.
2. A party which has justifiable doubts as to the impartiality or independence of an arbitrator may challenge that arbitrator in writing and shall state the facts and reasons on which the challenge is based and provide supporting evidence.
3. The challenge by one party shall be promptly communicated to the other party, the arbitrator being challenged and the other members of the arbitral tribunal if any.
4. Where an arbitrator is challenged by one party and the other party agrees to the challenge, or the arbitrator being challenged voluntarily withdraws from his/her office, such arbitrator shall no longer be a member of the arbitral tribunal. However, in neither case shall it be implied that the reasons for the challenge are sustained.
5. In circumstances other than those specified in the preceding Paragraph 4, the Chairman of the SCIA shall make a final decision on the challenge.
6. An arbitrator who has been challenged shall continue to serve on the arbitral tribunal until a final decision on the challenge has been made by the Chairman of the SCIA.

Article 33—Replacement of Arbitrator

1. Where an arbitrator is unable to fulfill his/her functions due to, inter alia, being challenged or voluntary withdrawal from his/her office, a substitute arbitrator shall be appointed following the original procedure within the specified period of time.
2. Where an arbitrator is prevented *de jure* or *de facto* from fulfilling his/her functions, or fails to fulfill his/her functions in accordance with the requirements of the Rules, the Chairman of the SCIA shall have the power to replace the arbitrator. The arbitrator may also withdraw from his/her office. In the event that an arbitrator is unable to fulfill his/her functions due to the above reasons, a substitute arbitrator shall be appointed following the original procedure within the specified period of time.

3. After the appointment of substitute arbitrator, the arbitral tribunal shall determine whether and to what extent the previous proceedings in the case shall be repeated.

Chapter VI The Hearing Proceedings

Article 34—Conduct of Hearing

1. Unless otherwise agreed by the parties, the arbitral tribunal shall have the power to decide procedural matters, and examine the case in such a manner as it considers appropriate. Under all circumstances, the arbitral tribunal shall act fairly and shall afford a reasonable opportunity to all parties to make submissions and arguments.
2. The parties may agree to adopt an inquisitorial, adversarial or other approach in the hearing of the case.
3. Where the arbitral tribunal cannot reach consensus over procedural matters, the arbitration proceedings shall be conducted in accordance with the opinion of a majority of the arbitrators. Where the arbitral tribunal cannot reach a majority opinion, the arbitration proceedings shall be conducted in accordance with the presiding arbitrator's opinion.
4. Unless otherwise provided by the Rules or agreed by the parties, the arbitral tribunal shall hold oral hearings when examining the case. However, the arbitral tribunal may examine the case on the basis of documents only if the arbitral tribunal deems that oral hearings are unnecessary and the parties so agree.
5. Unless otherwise agreed by the parties, the arbitral tribunal may, if it considers it necessary, issue procedural orders or question lists, hold pre-hearing conferences, produce terms of reference, and require pre-hearing exchange of evidence or discovery of relevant documents by the parties.

Article 35—Joinder of Additional Parties and Participation of Third Parties

1. After the commencement of the arbitral proceedings, a party may apply in writing to join an additional party under the same arbitration agreement to the arbitration. The arbitral tribunal shall decide whether to grant such joinder. Where the arbitral tribunal has not yet been formed, such decision shall be made by the Secretary General of the SCIA.
2. With the agreement in writing of each party and each third party, the arbitral tribunal has the power to permit one or more third parties to participate in the arbitration proceedings as Claimant or Respondent. Where the arbitral tribunal has not yet been formed, such decision shall be made by the Secretary General of the SCIA.

Article 36—Consolidation of Arbitrations

1. With the agreement in writing by all parties, the SCIA may consolidate two or more arbitrations pending under the Rules into a single arbitration decided by one arbitral tribunal.

2. In deciding whether to consolidate the arbitrations in accordance with the preceding Paragraph 1, the SCIA shall consider the relevance between the different arbitrations concerned.
3. Unless otherwise agreed by all the parties, the arbitrations shall be consolidated into the arbitration that commenced first.

Article 37—Notice of Hearing

1. Where a case is to be examined by way of an oral hearing, the parties shall be notified of the date of the first oral hearing at least twenty (20) days prior to the oral hearing. A party having justified reasons may request a postponement of the oral hearing. However, such request must be communicated in writing to the arbitral tribunal at least ten (10) days prior to the fixed oral hearing date. The arbitral tribunal shall decide whether or not to postpone the oral hearing.
2. Where a party has justified reasons for failure to submit a request for a postponement of the oral hearing within the time period specified in the preceding Paragraph 1, the arbitral tribunal shall decide whether or not to accept the request.
3. A notice of a subsequent oral hearing and a notice of a postponed oral hearing shall not be subject to the time periods specified in the preceding Paragraph 1.

Article 38—Place of Hearing

1. Unless otherwise agreed by the parties, the place of oral hearings shall be the domicile of the SCIA, or if the arbitral tribunal considers it necessary and with the approval of the Secretary General of the SCIA, at another location.
2. Where the parties have agreed to hold an oral hearing at a place other than the domicile of the SCIA, such agreement shall prevail.

Article 39—Default

1. If the Claimant fails to appear at an oral hearing without showing sufficient cause, or withdraws from an on-going oral hearing without the permission of the arbitral tribunal, the Claimant shall be deemed to have withdrawn its Request for Arbitration. In such a case, if the Respondent has fi led a counterclaim, the arbitral tribunal shall proceed with the hearing of the counterclaim.
2. If the Respondent fails to appear at an oral hearing without showing sufficient cause, or withdraws from an on-going oral hearing without the permission of the arbitral tribunal, the arbitral tribunal shall make a default hearing, and proceed with the arbitration. In such a case, if the Respondent has filed a counterclaim, the Respondent shall be deemed to have withdrawn its counterclaim.

Article 40—Record of Hearing

1. The arbitral tribunal shall arrange for a written and/or an audio-visual record to be made of an oral hearing, which shall be available for use and reference by the arbitral tribunal.
2. Arbitrators, parties and/or their representatives, witnesses and/or other persons involved are required to sign to the written record. If the parties or other

participants to the arbitration consider that the record has omitted a part of their statement or is incorrect in some respect, they shall have the right to request correction thereof with the approval of the arbitral tribunal.

Article 41—Evidence

1. Each party shall bear the burden of proving the facts upon which its claims, defences or counterclaims are based.
2. The arbitral tribunal may specify a time period for the parties to produce evidence and the parties shall produce evidence within the specified time period. The arbitral tribunal may refuse to admit any evidence produced after that time period. If a party experiences difficulties in producing evidence within the specified time period, it may apply for an extension before the end of the period. The arbitral tribunal shall decide whether or not to extend the time period.
3. If a party bearing the burden of proof fails to produce evidence within the specified time period, or if the produced evidence is not sufficient to support its claim or counterclaim, it shall bear the consequences thereof.
4. Where a party applies to produce witness in the oral hearing, it shall notify in its application to the arbitral tribunal the identity information of the witness, the witness statement and language to be used by the witness.
5. As to the law and other professional issues, the parties may engage an expert witness on such relevant issues to provide written submissions and/or testify in the oral hearing.
6. Where the parties have an agreement specifying the applicable evidence rules, their agreement shall prevail, unless the agreement cannot be implemented or is in conflict with a mandatory provision of the law as it applies to the arbitration proceedings.

Article 42—Examination of Evidence

1. Unless otherwise agreed by the parties, the evidence shall be produced at the hearing and may be examined by the parties.
2. Where a case is to be decided on the basis of documents only, or where the evidentiary materials are to be submitted after the hearing, and the parties agree to examine the evidentiary materials in writing, the parties shall submit their written opinions on the evidentiary materials within the time period specified by the arbitral tribunal.

Article 43—Investigation by the Arbitral Tribunal

1. Where the arbitral tribunal considers it necessary, or where a party so requests and the arbitral tribunal agrees, the arbitral tribunal may undertake investigations and collect evidence on its own initiative.
2. When investigating and collecting evidence at site, the arbitral tribunal shall notify the parties to be present. In the event that the parties fail to be present after being notified, the investigation and collection of evidence shall proceed without being affected.

3. Information investigated or evidence collected by the arbitral tribunal shall be forwarded to the parties for their comments.

Article 44—Expert's Report

1. Where the arbitral tribunal considers it necessary, or where a party so requests and the arbitral tribunal agrees, the arbitral tribunal may appoint experts for, inter alia, appraisal, audit, evaluation, testing or consultancy to produce expert's report.
2. Copies of the expert's report shall be communicated to the parties for their comments. At the request of either party and with the approval of the arbitral tribunal, the expert shall participate in an oral hearing and give explanations on the report.

Article 45—Evidence Preservation

1. Any party may apply for evidence preservation before the commencement of or during the arbitration proceedings if the evidence might be destroyed or if it would be difficult to obtain the evidence later afterwards.
2. If any party applies for evidence preservation during the arbitration proceedings, the SCIA shall submit the application for evidence preservation to a competent court.

Article 46—Suspension of the Arbitration Proceedings

1. Where parties request a suspension of the arbitration proceedings, or under circumstances where such suspension is necessary pursuant to relevant law or provisions of the Rules, the arbitration proceedings may be suspended by the arbitral tribunal. Where the arbitral tribunal has not yet been formed, such decision shall be made by the Secretary General of the SCIA.
2. The arbitration proceedings shall resume as soon as the reason for the suspension no longer exists.

Article 47—Withdrawal and Dismissal

1. A party may withdraw its claim or counterclaim in its entirety. In the event that the Claimant withdraws its claim in its entirety, the arbitral tribunal shall proceed with its examination of the counterclaim and render an arbitral award thereon. In the event that the Respondent withdraws its counterclaim in its entirety, the arbitral tribunal shall proceed with the examination of the claim and render an arbitral award thereon.
2. A case shall be dismissed by the arbitral tribunal if the claim and counterclaim have been withdrawn in their entirety. Where a case is to be dismissed prior to the formation of the arbitral tribunal, the Secretary General of the SCIA shall make a decision on the dismissal.

Chapter VII Mediation and Settlement

Article 48—Mediation by the Arbitral Tribunal

1. Where the parties wish to mediate, the arbitral tribunal may conduct the mediation. In this case, the parties shall agree on whether the arbitrator(s) participating the mediation shall resign from their office as arbitrator in the subsequent proceedings if the mediation fails. The arbitral tribunal shall have the discretion to decide whether the mediation shall be conducted.
2. The arbitral tribunal may mediate the case in a manner it considers appropriate.
3. During the process of mediation, the arbitral tribunal shall terminate the mediation if either party so requests or if the arbitral tribunal believes that further mediation efforts would be futile.
4. Where a settlement is reached through mediation, the parties may withdraw their claim or counterclaim. The parties may also request the arbitral tribunal to render an arbitral award or a mediation statement in accordance with the terms of the settlement agreement.
5. Where mediation fails, any opinion, view or statement, and any proposal or proposition expressing acceptance or opposition by either party or by the arbitral tribunal in the process of mediation, cannot be invoked by either party as grounds for supporting any claim, defence or counterclaim in the subsequent arbitration proceedings, judicial proceedings, or any other proceedings.

Article 49—Settlement between the Parties and Mediation by the Mediation Institution

1. The parties may reach a settlement agreement of the dispute by themselves, or apply to the Mediation Centre attached to the SCIA or other mediation institutions for mediation.
2. Where a settlement agreement is reached, the parties may apply to the arbitral tribunal for rendering an arbitral award in accordance with the terms of the settlement agreement or apply to withdraw the arbitration case. In the event the parties have not commenced arbitration proceedings or the arbitral tribunal has not yet been formed, and the parties apply for rendering an arbitral award in accordance with the terms of the settlement agreement, unless otherwise agreed by the parties, the Chairman of the SCIA shall appoint a sole arbitrator to form the arbitral tribunal and examine the case in the procedures it considers appropriate and render an award in due course. The specific procedures and time limits shall not be subject to other provisions of the Rules.

Chapter VIII Arbitral Award

Article 50—Time Limit for the Final Award

1. For cases under Article 2, paragraphs 1 and 2, of the Rules, the arbitral tribunal shall render an arbitral award within six (6) months from the date on which the arbitral tribunal is formed.

2. For cases under Article 2, paragraphs 3, of the Rules, the arbitral tribunal shall render an arbitral award within four (4) months from the date on which the arbitral tribunal is formed.
3. Upon the request of the arbitral tribunal, the Secretary General of the SCIA may extend the time limit if he/she considers it necessary and the reasons for the extension are justified.
4. The following period shall be excluded when calculating the time limit in the preceding Paragraphs.

   (a) Period of appointing experts for, *inter alia*, appraisal, audit, evaluation, testing, expert consultancy pursuant to Article 44 of the Rules;
   (b) Any period of mediation pursuant to Article 48 and Article 49 of the Rules;
   (c) Any suspension period pursuant to relevant provisions of law and the Rules.

Article 51—Making of the Award

1. The arbitral tribunal shall independently and impartially make an arbitral award based on the facts, in accordance with the law and the principles of fairness and reasonableness, and with reference to international practices.
2. Where the parties have agreed on the law as it applies to the merits of their dispute, the parties' agreement shall prevail. In the absence of such an agreement or where such agreement is in conflict with a mandatory provision of the law of the place of arbitration, the arbitral tribunal shall determine which law is applicable to the merits of the dispute.
3. The arbitral tribunal shall state in the award the claims/counterclaims, the facts of the dispute, the reasons on which the award is based, the decision on the claims/counterclaims, the allocation of the arbitration costs, and the date on which and the place at which the award is made. The facts of the dispute and the reasons on which the award is based may not be stated in the award if the parties have so agreed, or if the award is made in accordance with the terms of a settlement agreement between the parties. The arbitral tribunal has the power to determine the specific time period for the parties to carry out the award and the liabilities for failure to do so within the specified time period
4. Where a case is arbitrated by a tribunal composed of three arbitrators, the award shall be made by all three arbitrators or a majority of the arbitrators. A written dissenting opinion shall be kept with the file and may be notified to the parties together with the award. Such dissenting opinion shall not form a part of the award. Where the arbitral tribunal cannot reach a majority opinion, the arbitral award shall be made in accordance with the presiding arbitrator's opinion. The written opinions of the other arbitrators shall be kept with the file and may be notified to the parties together with the award. Such written opinions shall not form a part of the award.
5. The arbitral award shall be signed by arbitrators. An arbitrator who has a dissenting opinion may or may not sign his/her name on the award.

6. The date on which the award is made shall be the date on which the award comes into legal effect.
7. The seal of the SCIA shall be affixed on the arbitral award.
8. The arbitral award is final and binding upon the parties.

Article 52—Interlocutory Award

Where the arbitral tribunal considers it necessary, or where a party so requests and the arbitral tribunal agrees, the arbitral tribunal may make an interlocutory award on any procedural issues or other related issues before rendering the final award. The making and implementation or non-implementation of an interlocutory award shall not affect the arbitration proceedings, nor shall it prevent the arbitral tribunal from making the final award.

Article 53—Partial Award

Where the arbitral tribunal considers it necessary, or where a party so requests and the arbitral tribunal agrees, the arbitral tribunal may render a partial award on any part of the claim before rendering the final award. A partial award is final and binding upon the parties.

Article 54—Scrutiny of the Draft Award

The arbitral tribunal shall submit its draft award to the SCIA for scrutiny before signing the award. The SCIA may suggest modifications as to the form of the award and, without affecting the independence of the tribunal, may also draw its attention to substantive issues.

Article 55—Correction of the Award

1. Within thirty (30) days from its receipt of the arbitral award, either party may request the arbitral tribunal in writing for a correction of any clerical, typographical or computational errors, or any errors of a similar nature contained in the award. If such an error does exist in the award, the arbitral tribunal shall make a correction in writing within thirty (30) days of receipt of the written request for the correction.
2. The arbitral tribunal may, on its own initiative, make corrections in writing of any clerical, typographical or computational errors, or any errors of a similar nature contained in the award within a reasonable period of time after the award is made.
3. Such correction of award shall form a part of the arbitral award.

Article 56—Additional Award

1. Either party may, within thirty (30) days from its receipt of the arbitral award, request the arbitral tribunal in writing for an additional award on any claim or counterclaim which was advanced in the arbitration proceedings but was omitted from the award. If such an omission does exist, the arbitral tribunal shall make an additional award within thirty (30) days of receipt of the written request.

2. Where any matter which should have been decided by the arbitral tribunal was omitted from the arbitral award, the arbitral tribunal may, on its own initiative, make an additional award within a reasonable period of time after the award is made.
3. Such additional award shall form a part of the arbitral award.

Chapter IX Summary Procedure

Article 57—Application

1. Unless otherwise agreed by the parties, Summary Procedure shall apply to any case where the amount in dispute does not exceed RMB 1,000,000 Yuan; or to any case where the amount in dispute exceeds RMB 1,000,000 Yuan, yet the parties agree in writing that the Summary Procedure shall apply.
2. Where no monetary claim is specified or the amount in dispute is not clear, the SCIA shall determine whether or not to apply the Summary Procedure after a full consideration of relevant factors, including but not limited to the complexity of the case and the interests involved.

Article 58—Formation of Arbitral Tribunal

Unless otherwise agreed by the parties, the arbitral tribunal of a sole arbitrator shall be formed in accordance with Article 30 of the Rules to hear a case under the Summary Procedure.

Article 59—Defence and Counterclaim

1. The Respondent shall submit its Statement of Defence and evidentiary materials within twenty (20) days of receipt of the Notice of Arbitration; counterclaim, if any, shall also be filed with evidentiary materials within the time period.
2. The Claimant shall file its Statement of Defence to the Respondent's counterclaim within twenty (20) days of receipt of the counterclaim.
3. If the arbitral tribunal considers there is justified reason(s), it shall decide to grant an extension of the above time limit. Where the arbitral tribunal has not yet been formed, such decision shall be made by the Secretary General of the SCIA.

Article 60—Conduct of Hearing

The arbitral tribunal may examine the case in the manner it considers appropriate. The arbitral tribunal may decide whether to examine the case solely on the basis of the written materials and evidence submitted by the parties or to hold an oral hearing.

Article 61—Oral Hearing

1. For a case examined by way of an oral hearing, after the arbitral tribunal has fixed a date for oral hearing, the parties shall be notified at least ten (10) days prior to the oral hearing. A party having justified reasons may request a postponement of the oral hearing. However, such request shall be communicated in writing to the arbitral tribunal at least seven (7) days prior to the fixed oral

hearing date. The arbitral tribunal shall decide whether or not to postpone the oral hearing.

2. Where a party has justified reasons for failure to submit a request for a postponement of the oral hearing within the time period specified in the preceding Paragraph 1, the arbitral tribunal shall decide whether or not to accept the request.
3. A notice of a subsequent oral hearing, as well as a notice of a postponed oral hearing, shall not be subject to the time limit specified in the preceding Paragraph 1.

Article 62—Time Limit for the Final Award

1. The arbitral tribunal shall make an arbitral award within three (3) months from the date on which the arbitral tribunal is formed.
2. Upon the request of the arbitral tribunal, the Secretary General of the SCIA may extend the time period if he/she considers it necessary and the reasons for the extension justified.

Article 63—Change of Procedure

The application of Summary Procedure shall not be affected by any amendment to the claim or by the filing of a counterclaim. Where the amount in dispute of the amended claim or that of the counterclaim exceeds RMB 1,000,000 Yuan, upon one of the parties' request or where the SCIA considers necessary, the Summary Procedure may be changed to the general procedure by the SCIA.

Article 64—Other Provisions

The relevant provisions in the other chapters of the Rules shall apply to matters not covered in this chapter.

Chapter X Miscellaneous

Article 65—Arbitration Fees and Costs

1. The parties shall pay the arbitration fees and costs in advance to the SCIA according to the applicable provisions in the Schedule of Fees and Costs of Arbitration.
2. Where the parties agree to submit to other arbitration rules, schedule of fees and costs of arbitration stipulated by other arbitration rules may apply. If those other arbitration rules lack such schedule, the Schedule of Fees and Costs of Arbitration adopted by the SCIA may apply.
3. During the course of the arbitral proceedings, where the parties fail to pay in advance the relevant fees and costs as required, the SCIA shall so inform the parties in order that one or another of them may make the required payment. If such payment is not made, the SCIA may order the suspension of the arbitral proceedings or continue with the proceedings on such basis as it sees fit.
4. The Schedule of Fees and Costs of Arbitration which is attached hereto forms an integral part of the Rules.

Article 66—Allocation of Fees

1. The arbitral tribunal has the power to determine in the arbitral award the arbitration fees and other expenses to be borne by the parties. Such fees and other expenses include fees and actual expenses payable under Schedule of Fees and Costs of Arbitration, and the reasonable legal fees and other expenses incurred by the parties for conducting the arbitration.
2. The arbitration fees and expenses shall in principle be borne by the losing party. However, the arbitral tribunal may apportion such fees and expenses between the parties in appropriate proportion, taking into account the relevant circumstances of the case.

Article 67—Interpretation

1. The headings of the articles in the Rules shall not be construed as interpretations of the contents of the provisions contained therein.
2. The Rules shall be interpreted by the SCIA.
3. Unless otherwise stated, other documents issued by the SCIA shall not constitute integral parts of the Rules.

Article 68—Coming into Force

The Rules shall be effective as from December 1, 2012. For cases administered by the SCIA before the Rules come into force, the Arbitration Rules effective at the time of acceptance shall apply, or where the parties agree, the Rules shall apply.

Appendix: Schedule of Fees and Costs of Arbitration

Article 1—Provisions as to Fees and Costs of Arbitration for International and Foreign-related Cases and Arbitration Cases related to the Hong Kong Special Administrative Region, the Macao Special Administrative Region and the Taiwan Region

Arbitration Fee Schedule 1

This fee schedule applies to the arbitration cases accepted under Article 2, paragraphs 1 and 2, of the Arbitration Rules.

Amount in dispute (in RMB)	Amount of fees (in RMB)
1,000,000 Yuan or less	3.5 % of the claimed amount, minimum 10,000 Yuan
1,000,001 Yuan to 5,000,000 Yuan	35,000 Yuan plus 2.5 % of the amount above 1,000,000 Yuan
5,000,001 Yuan to 10,000,000 Yuan	135,000 Yuan plus 1.5 % of the amount above 5,000,000 Yuan
10,000,001 Yuan to 50,000,000 Yuan	210,000 Yuan plus 1 % of the amount above 10,000,000 Yuan
50,000,001 Yuan or more	610,000 Yuan plus 0.5 % of the amount above 50,000,000 Yuan

Each case, when being accepted, shall be charged an additional amount of RMB 10,000 Yuan as a Registration Fee which includes the expenses for examining the application for arbitration, initiating the arbitration proceedings, computerizing management, filing the documents and correspondence.

The Amount in dispute referred to in this schedule shall be based on the sum of money claimed by the parties.

Where no monetary claim is specified or the amount in dispute is not clear, the amount of arbitration fee shall be determined by the SCIA in consideration of the specific rights and interests involved in the disputes.

If the arbitration fee is charged in a foreign currency, an amount of the foreign currency equivalent to the corresponding RMB value specified in this schedule shall be paid.

Apart from charging arbitration fee according to the above Schedule, the SCIA may collect other reasonable and actual expenses.

Article 2—Provisions as to Fees and Costs of Arbitration for Chinese Mainland Arbitration Cases

Arbitration Fee Schedule 2

The schedules, adopted in accordance with the Notice of the General Office of the State Council on the Measures Regarding Arbitration Fees of Arbitration Commissions, apply to the Fees for arbitration cases accepted under Article 2, paragraph 3, of the Arbitration Rules, including Case Acceptance Fee and Case Handling Fee.

1. Case Acceptance Fee Schedule

Amount in dispute (in RMB)	Case acceptance fee (in RMB)
1,000 Yuan or less	100 Yuan
1,001 Yuan to 50,000 Yuan	100 Yuan plus 5 % of the amount above 1000 Yuan
50,001 Yuan to 100,000 Yuan	2550 Yuan plus 4 % of the amount above 50,000 Yuan
100,001 Yuan to 200,000 Yuan	4550 Yuan plus 3 % of the amount above 100,000 Yuan
200,001 Yuan to 500,000 Yuan	7550 Yuan plus 2 % of the amount above 200,000 Yuan
500,001 Yuan to 1,000,000 Yuan	13,550 Yuan plus 1 % of the amount above 500,000 Yuan
1,000,001 Yuan or more	18,550 Yuan plus 0.5 % of the amount above 1,000,000 Yuan

2. Case Handling Fee Schedule

Amount in dispute (in RMB)	Case handling fee (in RMB)
200,000 or less	5000 Yuan
200,001 Yuan to 500,000 Yuan	5000 Yuan plus 2 % of the amount above 200,000 Yuan
500,001 Yuan to 1,000,000 Yuan	11,000 Yuan plus 1.5 % of the amount above 500,000 Yuan
1,000,001 Yuan to 3,000,000 Yuan	18,500 Yuan plus 0.5 % of the amount above 1,000,000 Yuan
3,000,001 Yuan to 6,000,000 Yuan	28,500 Yuan plus 0.45 % of the amount above 3,000,000 Yuan
6,000,001 Yuan to 10,000,000 Yuan	42,000 Yuan plus 0.4 % of the amount above 6,000,000 Yuan
10,000,001 Yuan to 20,000,000 Yuan	58,000 Yuan plus 0.3 % of the amount above 10,000,000 Yuan
20,000,001 Yuan to 40,000,000 Yuan	88,000 Yuan plus 0.2 % of the amount above 20,000,000 Yuan
40,000,001 Yuan or more	128,000 Yuan plus 0.15 % of the amount above 40,000,000 Yuan

The Amount in dispute referred to in this schedule shall be based on the sum of money claimed by the parties.

Where no monetary claim is specified or the amount in dispute is not clear, the amount of arbitration fee shall be determined by the SCIA in consideration of the specific rights and interests involved in the disputes.

Apart from charging arbitration fee according to the above Schedules, the SCIA may collect other reasonable and actual expenses.

Article 3—Provisions as to Advance Payment of Arbitration Fees in Installments

For an arbitration case with large amount of arbitration fees to pay or there exists special circumstances, at the request of the party, the SCIA may decide to allow the party to pay the advance payment of the arbitration fee in installments. Arbitration fees paid in advance by the parties to the SCIA at the stage of arbitration application shall not be less than one-third of the full amount of the arbitration fees; not less than half of the full amount before the constitution of the arbitral tribunal; the full amount shall be paid prior to the hearing. The above fees do not include the Registration Fee provided for in the preceding Article 1.

Article 4—Provisions as to Arbitration Fees for Applying UNCITRAL Rules

1. Where the parties have agreed to submit to UNCITRAL Rules, and the parties apply to the
   SCIA for the appointment of arbitrators pursuant to UNCITRAL Rules, they shall pay an arbitrator appointing fee to the SCIA which is 0.1 % of the amount in dispute, the minimum of which shall be no less than RMB 20,000 Yuan. The

arbitrator appointment fee is non-refundable. For additional service the SCIA will determine Administrative Fees depending on the circumstances.

2. Where the parties have agreed upon the application of UNCITRAL Arbitration Rules and the SCIA to be the appointing authority, the arbitrator's fees and expenses may be determined in accordance with the fee arrangements agreed between the party or parties and the arbitrator.

Article 5—Provisions as to Arbitration Fees for Applying Other Arbitration Rules

Where parties have agreed to arbitrate at the SCIA applying other arbitration rules, if those other arbitration rules to be applied lack provisions on arbitration fees and costs, the arbitrator's fees and expenses may be determined in accordance with the fee arrangements agreed between the party or parties and the arbitrator, subject to the following provisions:

(a) When applying for arbitration, the applicant shall pay a Registration Fee of RMB 10, 000 Yuan;
(b) The Administrative Fee of the SCIA shall be calculated and paid by the party in accordance with the following Schedule:

Administrative Fee Schedule

Amount in dispute (in RMB)	Administrative fee (in RMB)
1,000,000 Yuan or less	1.4 % of the claimed amount, minimum 4000 Yuan
1,000,001 Yuan to 5,000,000 Yuan	14,000 Yuan plus 1 % of the amount above 1,000,000 Yuan
5,000,001 Yuan to 10,000,000 Yuan	54,000 Yuan plus 0.6 % of the amount above 5,000,000 Yuan
10,000,001 Yuan to 50,000,000 Yuan	84,000 Yuan plus 0.4 % of the amount above 10,000,000 Yuan
50,000,001 Yuan or more	244,000 Yuan plus 0.2 % of the amount above 50,000,000 Yuan

Where no monetary claim is specified or the amount in dispute is not clear, the amount of arbitration fee shall be determined by the SCIA in consideration of the specific rights and interests involved in the disputes.

Apart from charging arbitration fee according to the above Schedule, the SCIA may collect other reasonable and actual expenses.

Article 6—Provisions as to Fees of Arbitrators Determined in accordance with the Fee Arrangements between Parties and Arbitrators

1. The allocation of the fees and expenses of arbitrators determined in accordance with the fee arrangements agreed between the party or parties and the arbitrator shall be decided by arbitral tribunal pursuant to the applicable arbitration rules and the relevant provisions of this Schedule.

2. The fees and expenses of arbitrators determined in accordance with the fee arrangements shall be reasonable in amount, taking into account the amount in dispute, the complexity of the subject matter, the time spent by the arbitrators and any other relevant circumstances of the case. According to the above circumstances, the SCIA shall have the power to make any necessary adjustment to the fees and expenses of arbitrators, which will be binding upon the arbitral tribunal.

BAC Arbitration Rules[7]

Beijing Arbitration Commission Arbitration Rules

(Revised and adopted at the Fourth Meeting of the Sixth Session of the Beijing Arbitration Commission on July 9, 2014, and effective as of April 1, 2015)

Table of Contents

Chapter I: General Provisions

Article 1: The Beijing Arbitration Commission

(1) The Beijing Arbitration Commission **(the "BAC")** is an arbitral institution, registered in Beijing, China, to resolve contractual disputes and other disputes over property rights and interests between natural persons, legal persons and other organisations.
(2) The BAC is also known as the Beijing International Arbitration Center **(the "BIAC")**. Where the parties designate the BIAC as the arbitral institution in their arbitration agreement [Article 4(1)], the arbitration shall be administered by the BAC.

---

[7]http://arbitrator.bjac.org.cn/en/Arbitration/index.html.

(3) The Chairman of the BAC **(the "Chairman")** or, with the authorisation of the Chairman, one of the Vice-Chairmen or the Secretary-General of the BAC, shall perform the functions and duties vested in the Chairman by the BAC Arbitration Rules **(the "Rules")**.

(4) The Secretariat of the BAC **(the "Secretariat")** shall handle the day-to-day affairs of the BAC. For each case, the Secretariat shall designate a member of its staff as the case manager **(the "Case Manager")**, who shall attend to the procedural administration and the provision of services relating to the case.

Article 2: Scope of Application

(1) The Rules shall apply where the parties have agreed to submit their dispute to the BAC for arbitration. Where the parties have agreed on certain procedural matters or the application of a different set of arbitration rules, their agreement shall prevail, unless the agreement is unenforceable or in conflict with the mandatory rules of law of the seat of arbitration. Where the parties have agreed to the application of a different set of arbitration rules, the BAC shall perform the corresponding administrative functions and duties.

(2) Where the parties have agreed to apply the Rules, but have not designated an arbitral institution, they shall be deemed to have agreed to submit their disputes to the BAC for arbitration.

(3) In respect of any matters not expressly provided for in the Rules, the BAC may administer and the Arbitral Tribunal may conduct the arbitration in such manner as it considers appropriate, to ensure the efficient and fair resolution of disputes between the parties.

(4) When applying the Rules, the BAC, the Arbitral Tribunal, the parties and their representatives shall act in accordance with the principles of good faith, collaboration, and appropriate resolution of the dispute.

Article 3: Waiver of Right to Object

A party who knows or ought reasonably to know of a failure to comply with any provision of the Rules or any term of the arbitration agreement, but nevertheless take part in or continues to take part in the arbitral proceedings without promptly raising its objection to such non-compliance in writing to the BAC or the Arbitral Tribunal, shall be deemed to have waived its right to object to such non-compliance.

Chapter II: Arbitration Agreements

Article 4: Definition and Form of Arbitration Agreements

(1) An arbitration agreement is an agreement by the parties to submit any dispute which has arisen or which may arise from or in connection with an arbitrable legal relationship between the parties to arbitration [Article 1(1)]. An arbitration agreement may take the form of an arbitration clause included in a contract or any other written arbitration agreement.

(2) An arbitration agreement shall be in written form. "Written form" includes, but is not limited to, contractual instruments, letters and electronic data messages (including telexes, facsimiles, electronic data interchange, and e-mails), and any other form where the contents are retrievable.

(3) Where, during exchange of the Application for Arbitration [Article 7(1)(b)] and the Statement of Defence [Articles 9 and 10(1)(a)], one party asserts the existence of an arbitration agreement but the other party does not deny this, a written arbitration agreement between the parties shall be deemed to exist.

Article 5: Separability of Arbitration Agreements

An arbitration agreement shall be independent of the contract in which it is contained. The validity of the arbitration agreement shall be determined separately, and shall not be affected by the fact that the contract has been concluded, modified, terminated, rescinded or avoided, or is null and void, no longer effective or not yet in force.

Article 6: Objection to Jurisdiction

(1) If a party objects to the existence or validity of an arbitration agreement [Article 4 and 5] or to jurisdiction, it may raise an objection to jurisdiction with the BAC. Any objection shall be raised in writing before the first hearing. Where the parties have agreed to a documents-only arbitration [Article 24(2)], any written objection shall be raised within the time limit for the submission of the defence [Article 10(1)].

(2) If a party fails to raise any objection to jurisdiction pursuant to Article 6(1), it shall be deemed to have accepted that the BAC has jurisdiction.

(3) The raising of any objection to jurisdiction by any party with the BAC shall not affect the progress of arbitral proceedings.

(4) The BAC, or the Arbitral Tribunal as authorised by the BAC, may determine an objection as to jurisdiction. The Arbitral Tribunal may make its decision on jurisdiction either during the arbitral proceedings or in the arbitral award.

(5) Where the BAC, or the Arbitral Tribunal as authorised by the BAC, determines that it has no jurisdiction, an order for dismissal of the case shall be made by the Arbitral Tribunal, or if no Arbitral Tribunal has been constituted, by the BAC.

Chapter III: Application for Arbitration, Defence and Counterclaim

Article 7: Application for Arbitration

(1) A party applying for arbitration **(the "Claimant")** shall submit:

  (a) the arbitration agreement;

  (b) its application for arbitration **(the "Application for Arbitration")**, containing the following information:

    (i) the names, addresses, postcodes, telephone numbers, facsimile numbers, email addresses and details of any other effective means of communication with the Claimant and the Respondent; where a party concerned is a legal person or other organisation, the name, position, address, postcode, telephone number, facsimile number, email address and details of any other effective means of communication with the legal representative or the person in charge;

(ii) its claim for relief (**the "Claim"**), and the facts and grounds on which the Claim is based;

(c) the evidence and/or other supporting documents on which the Application for Arbitration is based; and

(d) proof of the Claimant's identity.

(2) The Claimant shall deposit an advance on the arbitration fees in accordance with the provisions of the *Case Acceptance Fee Schedule of the Beijing Arbitration Commission* and the *Case Handling Fee Schedule of the Beijing Arbitration Commission* [Annex 1]. Where the amount in dispute is not specified in the Application for Arbitration, the BAC shall determine the amount in dispute or the amount of the arbitration fees that shall be deposited in advance.

(3) If a party experiences difficulties with depositing the required advance on the arbitration fees, it may apply to the BAC for an extension of time, and the BAC shall determine such application. If a party has neither deposited the required advance nor applied for an extension of time, or has failed to deposit the full amount of the advance on arbitration fees within an extended time limit granted by the BAC, it shall be deemed not to have submitted or to have withdrawn its Application for Arbitration, as the case may be.

Article 8: Acceptance

(1) After receiving the Application for Arbitration [Article 7], the BAC shall, if it finds that the requirements for acceptance have been met, accept the Application for Arbitration within 5 days from the date of deposit by the Claimant of its advance on the arbitration fees.

(2) Where the Application for Arbitration does not comply with the requirements of Article 7(1), the Claimant shall rectify it within the time limit specified by the BAC, failing which the Claimant shall be deemed not to have submitted an Application for Arbitration.

(3) The arbitral proceedings shall be deemed to commence on the date of acceptance of the Application for Arbitration by the BAC.

Article 9: Notice of Arbitration

Within 10 days of the acceptance of the Application for Arbitration, the BAC shall send to the Claimant a notice of acceptance **(the "Notice of Acceptance")**, a copy of the Rules, and a list of the BAC's Panel of Arbitrators [Article 18] **(the "Panel of Arbitrators")**. The BAC shall send to the Respondent a request for submission of the defence **(the "Request for Submission of Defence")**, as well as a copy of the

Application for Arbitration, together with its attachments, a copy of the Rules and a list of the Panel of Arbitrators.

Article 10: Defence

(1) Within 15 days of receiving the Request for Submission of Defence, the Respondent shall submit:

(a) its statement of defence **(the "Statement of Defence")**, containing the following information:

(i) the name, address, postcode, telephone number, facsimile number, email address and details of any other effective means of communication with the Respondent; where a party concerned is a legal person or other organisation, the name, position, address, postcode, telephone number, facsimile number, email address and details of any other effective means of communication with the legal representative or the person in charge;

(ii) its defence to the Claim, and the facts and grounds on which the defence is based;

(b) the evidence and/or other supporting documents on which the defence is based; and

(c) proof of the Respondent's identity.

(2) Within 10 days of receiving the Statement of Defence, the BAC shall send to the Claimant a copy of the Statement of Defence, together with its attachments.

(3) Failure by the Respondent to submit its Statement of Defence shall not affect the progress of the arbitral proceedings.

Article 11: Counterclaim

(1) The Respondent shall file its counterclaim (the "Counterclaim"), if any, by submitting a written application for counterclaim (the "Application for Counterclaim") within 15 days from the date of receiving the Request for Submission of Defence. If the Counterclaim is raised after the expiration of the time limit (a "late Counterclaim"), the decision on whether or not to accept a late Counterclaim shall be made by the Arbitral Tribunal, or if no Arbitral Tribunal has been constituted, by the BAC.

(2) When determining whether or not to accept a late Counterclaim, the BAC or the Arbitral Tribunal, as the case may be, shall take into account the necessity to hear the late Counterclaim and the Claim at the same time in a single arbitration, the extent of the delay in lodging the Application for Counterclaim, unnecessary delay that will be caused to the arbitral proceedings and any other relevant factors.

(3) The provisions of Articles 7 and 8 of the Rules shall apply *mutatis mutandis* to the submission and acceptance of the Counterclaim.

(4) Within 10 days of accepting the Counterclaim, the BAC shall send to the Claimant a request for submission of its defence to the Respondent's Counterclaim **(the "Request for Submission of Defence to Counterclaim")**, as well as the Application for Counterclaim together with its attachments.
(5) The provisions of Article 10 shall apply to submission by the Claimant of its statement of defence to the Counterclaim **(the "Statement of Defence to Counterclaim")**.
(6) Any other matters concerning the Counterclaim which are not expressly provided for in these Rules shall be dealt with by reference to provisions concerning the Application for Arbitration [Article 7], insofar as they are relevant.

Article 12: Amendments to Claim or Counterclaim

(1) A party may apply to amend its Claim or Counterclaim. The application to amend **(the "Application to Amend")** shall be in writing and will be determined by the Arbitral Tribunal or, if no Arbitral Tribunal has been constituted, by the BAC.
(2) Where an Application to Amend is unreasonably delayed and may adversely affect the ordinary course of the arbitral proceedings, the BAC or the Arbitral Tribunal may refuse such amendment.
(3) The provisions of Articles 7–10 of the Rules shall apply *mutatis mutandis* to the submission of, acceptance of and response to an Application to Amend.

Article 13: Joinder of Additional Parties

(1) Before the Arbitral Tribunal is constituted, the parties may apply to join an additional party to the arbitration under the same arbitration agreement, subject to approval by the BAC.
(2) A party applying to join an additional party to the arbitration shall submit an application for arbitration against the additional party **(the "Application for Joinder")**. The provisions of Articles 7–10 of the Rules shall apply *mutatis mutandis* in respect of the content of such application, its acceptance and the submission of a defence.
(3) No Application for Joinder will be accepted after the Arbitral Tribunal has been constituted, unless the Claimant, the Respondent and the party to be joined otherwise agree.

Article 14: Claims between Multiple Parties

(1) Where there are two or more Claimants or Respondents in a single arbitration, or any additional party is joined to the arbitration [Article 13], any party may raise claims against any other party under the same arbitration agreement. The decision on whether or not to accept such claims shall be made by the Arbitral Tribunal, or if no Arbitral Tribunal has been constituted, by the BAC.
(2) The provisions of Articles 7–10 and Article 12 shall apply *mutatis mutandis* to the submission and acceptance of, defence(s) to and amendment of claims raised under this Article.

Article 15: Submission of Documents and Number of Copies

(1) Unless otherwise agreed by the parties, the parties shall submit to the BAC documents in the arbitration, which the BAC shall forward to the Arbitral Tribunal and to the other parties. If the parties agree to submit documents in the arbitration directly to the Arbitral Tribunal, copies of such documents shall be filed with the BAC.

(2) The Application for Arbitration [Article 7], the Statement of Defence [Article 10], the Application for Counterclaim [Article 11], evidence and any other written documents shall be submitted in quintuplicate. Where there are more than two parties, additional copies shall be provided accordingly. If the Arbitral Tribunal comprises a sole arbitrator, the number of copies shall be reduced by two.

Article 16: Preservation Measures

(1) In the event that enforcement of any award is likely to become difficult or if any other detriment is likely to be caused to one party as a result of the conduct of the other party or of the existence of any other relevant factors, a party may apply for an order to preserve property or assets of the other party's, or to require that party to take or to refrain from taking certain actions.

(2) A party may apply for an order to preserve evidence if there is a risk that such evidence might be lost, destroyed or might subsequently become difficult to obtain.

(3) Where a party submits an application to the BAC under Article 16(1) or (2), the BAC shall forward the application to the competent court for determination.

(4) In urgent circumstances, such as where a party's lawful rights and interests would be irreparably damaged, or evidence might be lost, destroyed or subsequently become difficult to obtain if no preservation measure is applied for immediately, a party may file an application for preservation measures before submitting its Application for Arbitration under Article 7.

Article 17: Representation

Where a party engages one or more representatives for the arbitration, it shall submit to the BAC a power of attorney setting out the matters specifically entrusted to each representative and the scope of each representative's authority.

Chapter IV: The Arbitral Tribunal

Article 18: Panel of Arbitrators

The BAC shall establish a Panel of Arbitrators. The parties shall choose arbitrators from the Panel of Arbitrators maintained by the BAC.

Article 19: Composition of the Arbitral Tribunal

(1) Unless otherwise agreed by the parties or provided for in the Rules, the Arbitral Tribunal shall comprise 3 arbitrators.

(2) Within 15 days of receiving the Notice of Arbitration [Article 9], each party shall nominate or request the Chairman to appoint an arbitrator from the Panel of Arbitrators [Article 18]. If a party fails to nominate an arbitrator or fails to request the Chairman to appoint an arbitrator within the time limit, the arbitrator shall be appointed by the Chairman.

(3) Within 15 days of receiving by the Respondent of the Notice of Arbitration, the parties shall jointly nominate or jointly request the Chairman to appoint the presiding arbitrator. The parties may each nominate between 1 and 3 arbitrator (s) as candidate(s) for the role of presiding arbitrator within the time limit. Where the parties agree or make an application to the BAC, the BAC may also provide a list of between 5 and 7 candidates from which the parties may each select between 1 and 4 candidates within the time limit fixed by Article 19(2) as the presiding arbitrator. Where there is only one common candidate on both parties' lists for nomination or selection, that candidate shall be deemed to have been jointly nominated by both parties as presiding arbitrator. If there are two or more common candidates, the Chairman shall, taking into consideration the particular circumstances of the case, appoint one of those candidates as the presiding arbitrator, who shall be deemed to have been jointly nominated by the parties. If there are no common candidates, the Chairman shall appoint an arbitrator who is not on the list of nomination or the list of selection as the presiding arbitrator, as the case may be.

(4) If the parties fail to nominate the presiding arbitrator jointly, in accordance with Article 19(2) and (3), the presiding arbitrator shall be appointed by the Chairman.

(5) Where there are two or more Claimants or Respondents, each set of Claimants or Respondents shall, by agreement, jointly nominate or jointly request the Chairman to appoint an arbitrator. If no joint nomination or joint request has been made within 15 days of receiving the Notice of Arbitration by the last party, the Chairman shall then appoint the arbitrator.

(6) In the event of a joinder [Article 13], the joined party shall nominate the arbitrator jointly with either the Claimant or the Respondent, as the case may be. If no such a nomination has been made, all members of the Arbitral Tribunal shall be appointed by the Chairman.

(7) Where a party nominates an arbitrator who resides outside Beijing, that party shall bear the necessary travel and accommodation expenses incurred by that arbitrator for hearing the case. If that party has not deposited the advance on such expenses within the period specified by the BAC [Article 7(2)], it shall be deemed not to have nominated that arbitrator. In this event, the Chairman may appoint another arbitrator for that party in accordance with this Article.

(8) Where an arbitrator declines to accept a party's nomination or is unable to participate in the arbitration, due to illness or any other relevant factors that may prevent him or her from performing an arbitrator's usual functions and duties, that party shall nominate another arbitrator within 5 days of receipt of notice of re-nomination **(the "Notice of Re-nomination")**. If that party fails to nominate another arbitrator within the time limit, the arbitrator shall be appointed by the Chairman.

Article 20: Notice of Constitution of the Arbitral Tribunal

Within 5 days of the constitution of the Arbitral Tribunal, the BAC shall notify the parties accordingly. The Case Manager [Article 1(4)] shall forward the case file to the Arbitral Tribunal promptly thereafter.

Article 21 Disclosure by Arbitrators

(1) Upon accepting appointment, each arbitrator shall sign a statement of independence and impartiality, a copy of which shall be forwarded to each party by the Case Manager.
(2) If, at any time, an arbitrator becomes aware of circumstances relating to either party or its authorised representatives, that are likely to lead any party to have reasonable doubts about his or her independence or impartiality, the arbitrator shall disclose such circumstances in writing.
(3) Within 10 days of receiving a written disclosure under Article 21(2), either party shall state in writing whether it intends to challenge the arbitrator.
(4) The provisions of Article 22(1), (2), (4), (5) and (6) shall apply to the challenge to an arbitrator on the basis of circumstances disclosed by the arbitrator under Article 21(2).
(5) A party who fails to challenge an arbitrator within the period of time specified in Article 22(3) shall not be permitted to challenge the arbitrator at a later time during the arbitral proceedings on the basis of the circumstances already disclosed by the arbitrator.

Article 22: Challenge to the Arbitrator

(1) A party may challenge any arbitrator on the basis of its reasonable doubts as to the independence or impartiality of the arbitrator.
(2) A challenge shall be made in writing and accompanied by the grounds of the challenge and supporting evidence.
(3) A challenge shall be raised before the first oral hearing. A challenge based on circumstances that become known after the first oral hearing may be raised prior to the closure of the final oral hearing. Without prejudice to Article 21(3), where no further oral hearing will be conducted, or in a documents-only arbitration, a challenge shall be raised within 10 days after the challenging party becomes aware of the circumstances giving rise to a challenge.
(4) The Case Manager shall promptly forward the application for challenge **(the "Application for Challenge")** to the other party and to each member of the Arbitral Tribunal.

(5) Where a party challenges an arbitrator and the other party concurs with the challenge, or the challenged arbitrator withdraws voluntarily upon being informed of the challenge, that arbitrator shall no longer participate in the arbitration. Neither of these circumstances shall imply that the grounds on which the challenge is based are established.
(6) Unless Article 22(5) applies, the Chairman shall decide on the challenge. The decision of the Chairman shall be final. The Chairman may decide, according to the particular circumstances of the case and as a matter of discretion, whether or not to provide reasons for the decision.
(7) A party who, after becoming aware of the composition of the Arbitral Tribunal, appoints authorised representatives [Article 17] whose appointment may give rise to grounds for the challenge of any arbitrator, shall be deemed to have waived its right to challenge the arbitrator on those grounds; the right of the other party to challenge the arbitrator shall not, however, be affected. Additional costs resulting from any delay caused to the arbitral proceedings in these circumstances shall be borne by the party responsible for giving rise to the grounds for challenge.

Article 23: Replacement of the Arbitrator

(1) An arbitrator shall be removed if he or she becomes unable to conduct the arbitration as a result of death, or illness, or withdraws from the arbitration, or the Chairman decides that he or she is to withdraw from the arbitration [Article 22(6)], or is requested by all the parties to withdraw from the arbitration [Article 22(5)].
(2) An arbitrator may also be removed on the initiative of the Chairman if the Chairman decides that the arbitrator is prevented *de jure* or *de facto* from fulfilling his or her functions and duties as an arbitrator, or is not fulfilling his or her functions and duties as required by the Rules.
(3) Before making any decision pursuant to the provisions of Article 23(2), the Chairman shall provide the parties and all members of the Arbitral Tribunal with an opportunity to comment thereon in writing.
(4) If the arbitrator to be removed was nominated by a party, that party shall nominate a substitute arbitrator within 5 days of its receipt of the notice of removal. If the arbitrator to be removed was appointed by the Chairman, the Chairman shall appoint a substitute arbitrator. Within 5 days of such nomination or appointment of the substitute arbitrator, the BAC shall send a notice of reconstitution of the Arbitral Tribunal to the parties. After the reconstitution of the Arbitral Tribunal, either party may request the previous arbitral proceedings to be repeated and the Arbitral Tribunal shall determine whether such repetition is necessary. The Arbitral Tribunal may also, on its own initiative, decide whether and to what extent the previous arbitral proceedings shall be repeated. If the Arbitral Tribunal decides to repeat the arbitral proceedings in their entirety, the time limit provided for in Articles 47, 58 and 68 shall be recalculated from the date of the reconstitution of the Arbitral Tribunal.

Chapter V: The Arbitral Proceedings

Article 24: Mode of Proceeding

(1) The Arbitral Tribunal shall hold an oral hearing.
(2) If the parties agree on a documents-only arbitration, or if the Arbitral Tribunal considers a oral hearing unnecessary and the parties so agree, the Arbitral Tribunal may decide the arbitration on the basis of the documents submitted by the parties.
(3) Regardless of the mode of proceeding adopted, the Arbitral Tribunal shall treat the parties fairly and impartially and give each party a reasonable opportunity to make submissions and arguments.

Article 25: Confidentiality

(1) All arbitration hearings shall be conducted in private. If the parties agree on a public hearing, the arbitration hearing may proceed in public, except where the case involves state secrets, any third party's commercial secrets, or any relevant circumstances in which the Arbitral Tribunal considers that a public hearing is inappropriate.
(2) Where an arbitration is conducted in private, neither the parties, nor their authorised representatives, nor any witnesses, arbitrators, experts consulted by the Arbitral Tribunal and appraisers appointed by the Arbitral Tribunal, nor the staff of the BAC shall disclose to third parties any information concerning the arbitration, whether substantive or procedural.

Article 26: Seat of Arbitration

(1) Unless otherwise agreed by the parties, the seat of arbitration shall be the location of the BAC. The BAC may also determine the seat of arbitration according to the particular circumstances of the case.
(2) The arbitral award shall be deemed to have been rendered at the seat of the arbitration.

Article 27: Place of Hearing

(1) Unless the parties otherwise agree, hearings shall be held at the BAC's premises.
(2) If the parties agree upon a hearing at any other location, the resulting additional costs shall be borne by the parties. The parties shall deposit an advance on such additional costs in accordance with the proportion agreed by them or decided upon by the Arbitral Tribunal within a period specified by the BAC. If such deposit is not made, the hearing shall be held at the BAC's premises.

Article 28: Concurrent Hearings

(1) The Arbitral Tribunal may, upon meeting all of the following conditions, order concurrent hearings:

    (a) the arbitrations concerned involve the same or related subject-matter;

(b) a party applies for concurrent hearings with the consent of all other parties concerned; and

(c) the composition of the Arbitral Tribunals in the arbitrations concerned is identical.

(2) The Arbitral Tribunal may, according to the particular circumstances of the case, decide on the detailed procedure for the arbitral proceedings as a result of its order.

Article 29: Consolidation of Arbitrations

(1) Where the parties so agree, or where one party applies and the BAC, in its discretion, considers it necessary, the BAC may decide to consolidate two or more arbitrations pending under the Rules into a single arbitration. Where an order for consolidation is made, arbitrations shall be consolidated into the arbitration that commenced first, unless otherwise agreed by the parties.

(2) In deciding whether or not to order consolidation, the BAC shall take into account the specific circumstances of arbitration agreements on which the relevant arbitrations are based, the nexus between those arbitrations, the stage that each set of arbitration proceedings has reached, the arbitrators already nominated or appointed in the relevant arbitrations and any other relevant factors.

Article 30: Notice of Hearing

(1) Where an arbitration is to be conducted by way of an oral hearing, the Arbitral Tribunal shall notify the parties of the date of the first hearing at least 10 days in advance. The first hearing may be rescheduled to an earlier date by the Arbitral Tribunal with the agreement of the parties. A party may, no less than 5 days in advance of the hearing, request a postponement of the first hearing, provided that there are grounds justifying the postponement. The Arbitral Tribunal shall, in its discretion, decide whether or not to postpone the first hearing, having regard to all relevant circumstances.

(2) A notification of the date of any subsequent hearing, or of the date of a postponed hearing, shall not be subject to the 10-day time limit in Article 30(1).

Article 31: Default

(1) Having been duly notified in writing of the hearing under Article 30, if the Claimant fails to appear at the hearing without any justification, or withdraws from an ongoing hearing without the permission of the Arbitral Tribunal, the Claimant may be deemed to have withdrawn its Application for Arbitration. Where the Respondent has raised a Counterclaim, the Claimant's default shall not affect the hearing of the Counterclaim by the Arbitral Tribunal.

(2) Having been duly notified in writing of the hearing, if the Respondent fails to appear at the hearing without any justification, or withdraws from an ongoing hearing without the permission of the Arbitral Tribunal, the Arbitral Tribunal may proceed with the arbitration. Where the Respondent has raised a Counterclaim, such Counterclaim shall be deemed to have been withdrawn.

Article 32: Production of Evidence

(1) Each party shall bear the burden of proving the facts relied upon to support its claim or defence.
(2) The Arbitral Tribunal may require the parties to produce their evidence within a specified period of time and the parties shall comply with any such order. The Arbitral Tribunal may reject any evidence not produced within the specified period of time, unless the parties agree otherwise or the Arbitral Tribunal considers it necessary to accept the evidence.
(3) If a party having the burden of proof fails to produce evidence within the specified period of time, or if the evidence produced is insufficient to discharge its burden of proof, it shall bear the adverse consequences of such failure.
(4) Each party shall properly bind, number, and paginate the evidence it produces. The file of evidence shall be accompanied by a list stating briefly the title of each piece of evidence and the purpose of producing it. The evidence list shall be signed, sealed and dated.
(5) Any reproduction, photograph, duplicate, or abridged version of any document or any item produced by one party to another party shall be deemed to be identical to the original copy, unless the other party challenges its authenticity.
(6) Unless otherwise agreed by the parties or otherwise provided for in the Rules, evidence and written documents submitted in a foreign language shall be accompanied by a Chinese translation. The Arbitral Tribunal may, if necessary, require the parties to provide a translation of the evidence and of any written documents in another language or languages.

Article 33: Investigation and Collection of Evidence by Arbitral Tribunal

(1) If a party makes an application and the Arbitral Tribunal considers it necessary, or there is no such application but the Arbitral Tribunal considers it necessary according to the particular circumstances of the case, the Arbitral Tribunal may undertake investigations and/or collect evidence on its own initiative. If the Arbitral Tribunal considers it necessary to require the parties to be present when it undertakes investigations or collects evidence, it shall notify the parties in a timely fashion. Provided that the parties have been duly notified, the Arbitral Tribunal may proceed with the investigations or the collection of evidence even if they fail to appear.
(2) Evidence collected by the Arbitral Tribunal on its own initiative shall be forwarded to both parties for their comments in a timely fashion before an award is made.

Article 34: Appraisal

(1) If a party requests an appraisal and the Arbitral Tribunal agrees with the request, or neither party makes an application but the Arbitral Tribunal considers it necessary to conduct an appraisal, the Arbitral Tribunal may notify the parties to nominate an appraiser jointly within a period of time specified by the

Arbitral Tribunal. If the parties fail to do so, the appraiser shall be appointed by the Arbitral Tribunal.

(2) The parties shall deposit an advance on the appraisal costs in accordance with a proportion agreed by them or decided upon by the Arbitral Tribunal. The Arbitral Tribunal may decide not to conduct the appraisal if the parties do not deposit an advance.

(3) The Arbitral Tribunal may require the parties, and the parties shall be under an obligation, to provide or present to the appraiser any relevant document, data, property or any other goods required for the appraisal. The Arbitral Tribunal shall decide upon any disagreement between any party and the appraiser as to whether a document, data, property or any other goods required for the appraisal is relevant to the case.

(4) The appraiser shall provide an appraisal report in writing. A copy of the appraisal report shall be sent to each party. Each party may express opinions on the appraisal report.

(5) If the Arbitral Tribunal considers it necessary or if any party so requests, the Arbitral Tribunal may notify the appraiser to attend the hearing. The parties may, with the permission of the Arbitral Tribunal, question the appraiser on relevant aspects of the appraisal report.

(6) Any period of time taken to conduct an appraisal shall not be taken into account for the purposes of calculating the time limits provided for in Articles 47, 58 and 68 of these Rules.

Article 35: Procedural Orders

The Arbitral Tribunal may, according to the particular circumstances of the case, make procedural orders, including but not limited to the preparation of the procedural timetable for the hearing, issuing lists of questions, holding pre-hearing conferences, and producing terms of reference. The Arbitral Tribunal may authorise the presiding arbitrator to make any of these procedural orders.

Article 36: Examination of Evidence

(1) The Arbitral Tribunal may, according to the particular circumstances of the case, require the parties to take appropriate steps to verify the authenticity of the copies of the evidence. The Arbitral Tribunal may delegate the Case Manager to coordinate this process.

(2) Where an oral hearing is to be held, evidence exchanged between the parties prior to the hearing shall be presented by them for examination during the hearing. Evidence produced by a party may be admitted and accepted as the basis of fact finding without being presented at the hearing for examination if the other party has acknowledged its admissibility and the Arbitral Tribunal has, during the hearing, confirmed the other party's acknowledgement of this.

(3) Where evidence is produced by any party during or after the hearing and the Arbitral Tribunal decides to admit the evidence without holding any further hearings, the Arbitral Tribunal may require the other party to comment on such evidence in writing within a specified period of time.

Article 37: Assessment of Evidence

(1) The Arbitral Tribunal shall have the authority to assess the evidence. It shall also decide on whether or not to adopt an appraiser's opinion.
(2) When assessing any evidence, the Arbitral Tribunal may, in addition to referring to relevant laws, regulations and judicial interpretations, conduct its assessment by taking into consideration factors such as industry practices and trade usages, and shall consider the case in its totality.

Article 38: Presentation of Arguments

Each party may present oral arguments during the hearing [Article 24(3)]. The Arbitral Tribunal may also require the parties to submit written arguments on particular issues according to the circumstances of the case.

Article 39: Closing Statements

At the closing of the hearing, the Arbitral Tribunal shall invite closing statements from the parties, which may be presented either orally during the hearing or in writing within a period of time specified by the Arbitral Tribunal.

Article 40: Record of Hearing

(1) The Arbitral Tribunal shall make a written record of the hearing, except in the case of conciliation proceedings [Article 42 and 67].
(2) The Arbitral Tribunal may make an audio or video record of the hearing.
(3) A party or any other participant in the arbitration may request the rectification of any omission or error in the written record of their oral statement. The request shall be recorded if the Arbitral Tribunal does not allow the rectification.
(4) The Arbitral Tribunal, person who makes the recording, the parties and other participants in the arbitration shall sign or affix their seals on the written record.
(5) Upon a joint request by both parties, or a request by one party that has been approved by the BAC, the BAC may appoint one or more stenographers to record the hearing. The resulting additional costs shall be borne by the parties or the requesting party, as the case may be.

Article 41: Withdrawal of an Application for Arbitration and Dismissal of a Case

(1) The Claimant may withdraw the Application for Arbitration [Article 7]. Where the Respondent has raised a Counterclaim [Article 11], withdrawal of the Application for Arbitration shall not affect the hearing and determination of such counterclaim by the Arbitral Tribunal. The Respondent may withdraw its counterclaim. Withdrawal of the Counterclaim shall not affect the hearing and determination of the Claimant's claim by the Arbitral Tribunal.

(2) Where all claims and counterclaims (if any) have been withdrawn, the case can be dismissed. Dismissal of the case shall be decided by the Arbitral Tribunal, or if no Arbitral Tribunal has been constituted, by the BAC.
(3) Where it becomes unnecessary or impossible to continue the arbitral proceedings for any reason, the BAC or the Arbitral Tribunal, as the case may be, may dismiss the case.
(4) Where the case has been dismissed, the BAC may decide whether to refund the advance on the arbitration fees or any other fees paid in advance, as well as the specific amount of such refund, according to the circumstances of the case.

Article 42: Conciliation by the Tribunal

(1) The Arbitral Tribunal may, at the request or with the consent of the parties, conduct a conciliation of the case in such manner as it considers appropriate.
(2) If the conciliation leads to a settlement, the parties may withdraw their claims and counterclaims (if any), or may request the Arbitral Tribunal either to issue a Statement of Conciliation [Article 42(3)] or to render an award in accordance with the terms of the settlement agreement.
(3) The Statement of Conciliation shall state the claims and the terms of the resulting settlement agreement reached by the parties. It shall be signed by the arbitrators, sealed by the BAC, and served on all the parties. The Statement of Conciliation shall be legally binding after all the parties have acknowledged receipt of it in writing.
(4) The Arbitral Tribunal shall rectify any clerical and computational errors or similar errors in the Statement of Conciliation. The parties may request such rectification within 30 days from the date on which the parties sign the receipt of the Statement of Conciliation. Any such rectification shall become part of the Statement of Conciliation and shall take effect immediately after being served on the parties.
(5) If the conciliation fails to lead to a settlement, neither party shall be permitted to adduce evidence of or to refer to or use any statements, opinions, views or proposals expressed by the other party or by the Arbitral Tribunal during the conciliation as in support of any claim, defence, or counterclaim in the subsequent arbitral proceedings, or as grounds in any judicial or other proceedings.

Article 43: Independent Conciliation

(1) During the arbitral proceedings, the parties may enter into a voluntary settlement agreement or may apply to the Mediation Center of the BAC (**the "Mediation Center"**) for mediation by the mediators of the Mediation Center in accordance with the Mediation Rules of the Mediation Center of the BAC.
(2) Where a settlement agreement is concluded through an independent conciliation under this Article, the parties may jointly request the constitution of an Arbitral Tribunal either to issue a Statement of Conciliation or render an award in accordance with the terms of the settlement agreement. The parties shall bear the resulting additional costs.

Article 44: Suspension and Resumption of Arbitral Proceedings

(1) If the parties jointly request, or if one party requests and the other parties do not object, the arbitral proceedings may be suspended. The arbitral proceedings may be resumed if one party so requests or the BAC or the Arbitral Tribunal deems this necessary.
(2) The arbitral proceedings may be suspended if any exceptional circumstances occur that necessitate suspension. The arbitral proceedings shall be resumed once such circumstances cease to exist.
(3) The suspension and resumption of the arbitral proceedings shall be decided by the Arbitral Tribunal, or if no Arbitral Tribunal has been constituted, by the BAC. Any period of time during which the arbitral proceedings were suspended shall not be taken into account for the calculation of the time limits provided for in Articles 47, 58 and 68.

Article 45: Continuation of the Arbitral Proceedings with Majority of the Arbitral Tribunal

In the event that, after the conclusion of the last hearing, an arbitrator on a three-member Arbitral Tribunal is unable to participate in the deliberations and render an award as a result of his or her death or for other reasons, the Chairman may replace that arbitrator with a substitute arbitrator, pursuant to Article 23 of the Rules. Alternatively, provided that the parties consent and with the approval of the Chairman, the two remaining arbitrators may continue with the arbitral proceedings and make decisions, or an award.

Chapter VI: Decisions and Awards

Article 46: Decisions on Procedural Matters

(1) The Arbitral Tribunal may decide upon procedural matters during the arbitral proceedings.
(2) Any decision of an Arbitral Tribunal comprising 3 arbitrators shall be made by a majority of the arbitrators. If the Arbitral Tribunal fails to reach a majority decision, the decision of the presiding arbitrator shall prevail.
(3) The presiding arbitrator may, with the consent of the parties or with the authorisation of the Arbitral Tribunal, decide upon procedural matters.

Article 47: Time Limit for Rendering the Award

The Arbitral Tribunal shall render its award within 4 months of its constitution [Articles 19 and 20]. If there are special circumstances justifying an extension of this period, the Secretary-General may approve an appropriate extension of time at the request of the presiding arbitrator.

Article 48: Rendering the Award

(1) The award of an Arbitral Tribunal comprising 3 arbitrators shall be made by a majority of the arbitrators. The minority dissenting opinion may be recorded in writing. If the Arbitral Tribunal fails to reach a majority decision, the award shall be made in accordance with the opinion of the presiding arbitrator.
(2) The award shall state the claims, the facts associated with the dispute, the reasons upon which the award is based, operative directions disposing of the dispute, the allocation of arbitration fees [Article 51], the date of the award, and the seat of the arbitration. The Arbitral Tribunal shall not be required to state the facts associated with the dispute or the reasons upon which the award is based if the parties so agree, or if the award is made in accordance with the terms of a settlement agreement between the parties [Articles 42 and 43].
(3) The award shall be signed by each member of the Arbitral Tribunal. A dissenting arbitrator may elect not to sign the award. An arbitrator who elects not to sign the award shall issue a dissenting opinion in writing, which shall be sent by the BAC to the parties together with the award. A dissenting opinion shall not form part of the award.
(4) After an award has been signed by the arbitrator(s), the BAC's seal shall be affixed to it.

Article 49: Partial Award and Interim Award

(1) Where the Arbitral Tribunal considers it necessary, or where a party so requests and the Arbitral Tribunal approves, the Arbitral Tribunal may render a partial award disposing of particular claims before proceeding to render the final award.
(2) Where the Arbitral Tribunal considers it necessary, or where a party so requests and the Arbitral Tribunal approves, the Arbitral Tribunal may render an interim award on disputed procedural or substantive issues.
(3) The parties concerned shall perform any partial award and interim award. Failure by any party to perform a partial award or an interim award shall neither affect the subsequent arbitral proceedings nor prevent the Arbitral Tribunal from rendering the final award.

Article 50: Validity and Performance of the Award

(1) An award shall be legally binding from the date on which it is made.
(2) After an award has been made, the parties concerned shall perform the award in accordance with the time limit for performance specified in the award. Where an award does not specify the time limit for performance, it shall be performed immediately. Where any party fails to perform the award, the other party may apply to the competent court for enforcement.

Article 51: Allocation of Costs

(1) The Arbitral Tribunal may determine in its award how the arbitration fees and any expenses actually incurred shall be borne by the parties, including but not limited to appraisal fees, evaluation fees and audit fees.
(2) Unless otherwise agreed by the parties, the costs of the arbitration shall in principle be borne by the losing party. If either party is only partially successful, the Arbitral Tribunal shall determine the proportion of each party's share of the costs on the basis of the extent of liability of each party. If the parties reach a settlement either independently or as a result of conciliation by the Arbitral Tribunal [Article 42], they may agree upon the proportion of their respective shares.
(3) Where the circumstances described in Article 22(7) of the Rules apply, or there exist any other breaches of the Rules that cause delay in the arbitral proceedings, the allocation of arbitration costs to the party at fault shall not be limited by the provisions in Article 51(2). Where other costs are incurred or increased due to such delay in the arbitral proceedings, the party causing the delay shall also bear the costs so incurred or increased.
(4) The Arbitral Tribunal may, pursuant to a party's request, order that the losing party shall bear the winning party's reasonable costs and expenses for the conduct of the arbitration, including but not limited to attorney's fees, the costs of preservation measures, travel and accommodation expenses, and notarial fees. Where the Arbitral Tribunal determines the amount of these costs and expenses, it shall take into consideration the outcome of the case, its complexity, the actual workload of the parties or their attorneys, the amount in dispute and any other relevant factors.

Article 52: Correction of the Award and Supplementary Award

(1) The Arbitral Tribunal shall correct any clerical error or computational error, and address any omission of issues that have been raised by a party in its claim and decided upon by the Arbitral Tribunal but omitted in the operative directions disposing of the dispute. In the event that any claim is omitted entirely from the award, the Arbitral Tribunal shall render a supplementary award thereon.
(2) Upon discovering the existence of any of the circumstances described in Article 52(1), a party may, within 30 days of the date of receiving the award, request in writing that the Arbitral Tribunal rectify the award or render a supplementary award.
(3) Any rectification by or supplementary award of the Arbitral Tribunal shall form part of the original arbitral award.

Chapter VII: Expedited Procedure

Article 53: Scope of the Application of Expedited Procedure

(1) Unless otherwise agreed by the parties, the expedited procedure set out in this chapter (**the "Expedited Procedure"**) shall apply if the amount in dispute does not exceed RMB 1,000,000.
(2) The parties may also agree to apply the Expedited Procedure where the amount in dispute exceeds RMB 1,000,000. In such a case, the arbitration fees shall be reduced accordingly.
(3) If the parties agree to apply the ordinary procedure **(the "Ordinary Procedure")** when the amount in dispute does not exceed RMB 1,000,000, they shall bear any resulting additional arbitration fees.
(4) Where Chapter VIII of the Rules makes special provisions for the Expedited Procedure, such provisions shall apply.

Article 54: Composition of the Arbitral Tribunal

(1) Arbitrations conducted in accordance with the Expedited Procedure shall be heard by a sole arbitrator.
(2) Within 10 days of receipt of the Notice of Arbitration [Article 9] by all parties, the parties shall jointly nominate a sole arbitrator or jointly request the Chairman to appoint a sole arbitrator from the Panel of Arbitrators. The sole arbitrator may be selected in the manner prescribed by Article 19(3). If the parties fail jointly to nominate a sole arbitrator or request the Chairman to appoint a sole arbitrator within the specified period, the Chairman will appoint the sole arbitrator.

Article 55: Time Limit for Defence and Counterclaim

Within 10 days of receipt of the Request for Submission of Defence [Article 9], the Respondent shall submit to the BAC its Statement of Defence [Article 10], together with any relevant supporting documents. A Counterclaim [Article 11], if any, shall also be submitted within 10 days of receipt of the Request for Submission of Defence, together with any relevant supporting documents.

Article 56: Notice of Hearing

(1) Where an oral hearing [Article 24(1)] is to be held, the Arbitral Tribunal shall notify the parties of the date of the hearing at least 3 days in advance.
(2) If the Arbitral Tribunal decides to hear the case by way of oral hearing, it shall hold one hearing only. Where necessary, however, the Arbitral Tribunal may on its own initiative decide to hold further hearings. Notification of the date of any further hearing shall not, however, be subject to the 3-day time limit under Article 56(1).

Article 57: Expedited Procedure Converted into Ordinary Procedure

(1) Proceedings under the Expedited Procedure may be converted into proceedings under the Ordinary Procedure upon the joint request of the parties or upon the request of one party with the approval of the other parties.
(2) Proceedings under the Expedited Procedure shall not be affected by reason of any amendment to the Claim, the submission of a Counterclaim or any amendment causing the amount in dispute to exceed RMB 1,000,000. If a party is of the opinion that the proceedings under the Expedited Procedure may be so affected, it may request the Chairman to convert the proceedings into proceedings under the Ordinary Procedure. The Chairman shall decide whether or not to approve such application.
(3) The parties shall agree upon their respective proportions of the advance on the additional arbitration fees arising from the conversion of proceedings from the Expedited Procedure into the Ordinary Procedure. Where the parties fail so to agree, such proportions shall be determined by the BAC. Where the parties fail to deposit an advance on the resulting additional costs in accordance with the requirements of the BAC, no conversion of procedure shall be ordered.
(4) In the event of conversion of proceedings from the Expedited Procedure into the Ordinary Procedure after the constitution of the Arbitral Tribunal, the parties shall, within 5 days of receipt of a notice of the conversion of the procedure (**"Notice of Conversion of Procedure"**), respectively nominate or respectively request the Chairman to appoint their arbitrators in accordance with Article 19 of the Rules. Unless otherwise agreed by the parties, the sole arbitrator originally appointed shall become the presiding arbitrator. The reconstituted Arbitral Tribunal shall decide whether and to what extent the arbitral proceedings conducted prior to the reconstitution shall be repeated. Where the reconstituted Arbitral Tribunal decides to repeat the arbitral proceedings in their entirety, the time limit provided for in Articles 47 and 68 of the Rules shall be recalculated from the date of the reconstitution of the Arbitral Tribunal.
(5) The Expedited Procedure shall cease to apply to the arbitral proceedings from the date of conversion.

Article 58: Time Limit for Rendering the Award

The Arbitral Tribunal shall render its award within 75 days from the date of its constitution. If there are special circumstances justifying an extension of this period, the Secretary-General may approve an appropriate extension of time at the request of the sole arbitrator.

Article 59 Reference to Other Provisions of the Rules

In respect of matters not provided for in this chapter, other relevant provisions of the Rules shall apply.

Chapter VIII: Special Provisions for International Commercial Arbitration

Article 60: Scope of Application of this Chapter

(1) Unless otherwise agreed by the parties, the provisions of this chapter shall apply to international commercial arbitrations. In respect of matters not provided for in this chapter, the other relevant provisions of the Rules shall apply.
(2) Arbitrations relating to the Hong Kong Special Administrative Region (**"SAR"**), the Macao SAR and the Taiwan region may be conducted by reference to the provisions of this chapter.
(3) Any dispute between the parties as to the existence of international elements shall be referred to the Arbitral Tribunal for a decision. The decision of the Arbitral Tribunal shall not affect arbitral proceedings already conducted. This chapter shall apply if the Arbitral Tribunal decides that international elements exist in the case.

Article 61: Arbitration Fees

In respect of an international commercial arbitration case, the parties may agree to pay arbitration fees in accordance with the *Arbitration Fee Schedule for International Commercial Arbitration* set out in Annex 2 to these Rules.

Article 62: Interim Measures

(1) At the request of the parties, the Arbitral Tribunal may order any interim measures it deems appropriate in accordance with the applicable law. An order for interim measures may take the form of a decision of the Arbitral Tribunal, an interim award [Article 49], or any other form permitted by the applicable law. Where necessary, the Arbitral Tribunal may require the requesting parties to provide appropriate security.
(2) The parties may also directly apply for interim measures to the competent court in accordance with the applicable law.

Article 63: Emergency Arbitrator

(1) After the acceptance of the case by the BAC [Articles 8 and 9] and before the constitution of the Arbitral Tribunal [Article 19 or Article 64], any party that wishes to apply for interim measures may submit a written application to the BAC for the appointment of an emergency arbitrator in accordance with the applicable law. The BAC shall decide whether or not to approve such application.
(2) Where the BAC approves the appointment of an emergency arbitrator, it shall appoint an emergency arbitrator from the Panel of Arbitrators within 2 days after the parties concerned pay the corresponding fees in accordance with the Schedule set out in Annex 3 to these Rules, and shall notify the parties of such appointment.
(3) The provisions of Articles 21 and 22 shall apply, *mutatis mutandis,* to disclosure by and challenge to an emergency arbitrator and the procedures applicable to these matters.

(4) An emergency arbitrator shall consider the application for interim measures in such manner as he or she deems appropriate, and shall ensure that the parties have a reasonable opportunity to present their cases.
(5) The emergency arbitrator shall issue a decision, order or award, stating the grounds on which the interim measures are based, within 15 days after his or her appointment. Such decision, order or award shall be sent to the parties after being signed by the emergency arbitrator and affixed with the seal of the BAC.
(6) Where a party objects to a decision, order or award made by the emergency arbitrator, it may apply to the emergency arbitrator for an amendment to or the suspension or revocation of such decision, order or award within 3 days of receipt of such decision, order or award. The emergency arbitrator will decide whether or not to approve such application.
(7) Unless otherwise agreed by the parties, the emergency arbitrator shall not subsequently act as an arbitrator in the proceedings to which the application for interim measures relates.
(8) Any decision, order or award made by an emergency arbitrator [Article 63(5)] will not be binding upon the Arbitral Tribunal. The Arbitral Tribunal may amend, suspend or revoke such a decision, order or award.

Article 64: Composition of the Arbitral Tribunal

(1) Arbitrators may be selected by the parties from the Panel of Arbitrators maintained by the BAC [Article 18] or from amongst arbitrators who are not on the Panel of Arbitrators.
(2) Parties who wish to select arbitrators who are not on the Panel of Arbitrators shall submit their candidates' resumes and contact details to the BAC. A candidate selected from amongst arbitrators who are not on the Panel of Arbitrators may act as an arbitrator with the approval of the BAC.
(3) Within 20 days of receipt of the Notice of Acceptance [Article 9], the parties shall, pursuant to the provisions of Article 19, nominate or request the Chairman to appoint their arbitrators and jointly nominate or jointly request the Chairman to appoint the presiding arbitrator. If the parties fail to nominate or request the Chairman to appoint their arbitrators or the presiding arbitrator in accordance with those provisions, the arbitrators or the presiding arbitrator shall be appointed by the Chairman.
(4) Where a party agrees to an increased fee for a foreign arbitrator, that party shall deposit a corresponding advance on costs within the period specified by the BAC. If a party fails to deposit such advance on costs within the period specified, it shall be deemed not to have nominated the arbitrator. The Chairman may then appoint an arbitrator for that party in accordance with the Rules.
(5) Where Article 53 applies, the Arbitral Tribunal shall be constituted in accordance with Article 54 of the Rules.

Article 65: Defence and Counterclaim

Within 45 days (or 30 days where Article 53 applies) of receipt of the Request for Submission of Defence [Article 9], the Respondent shall submit to the BAC its Statement of Defence [Article 10], together with any relevant supporting documents. The Respondent shall also submit in writing the Application for Counterclaim [Article 11], if any, within the time limit.

Article 66: Notice of Hearing

(1) Where an oral hearing is to be held, the Arbitral Tribunal shall notify the parties of the date of the hearing at least 30 days (or 10 days where Article 53 applies) in advance of the hearing. The date of the first hearing may be brought forward by the Arbitral Tribunal with the agreement of the parties. A party may request in writing a postponement of the first hearing, no less than 12 days (or 5 days where Article 53 applies) in advance, provided that there are grounds justifying the postponement. The Arbitral Tribunal shall decide whether or not to order postponement.

(2) A notification of the date of any further hearing or postponed hearing shall not be subject to the 30-day or 10-day requirement under Article 66(1).

Article 67: Conciliation by the Tribunal

(1) The Arbitral Tribunal may, with the consent of the parties, conduct a conciliation of the case in such manner as it considers appropriate.

(2) If, upon the termination of unsuccessful conciliation proceedings, all parties request the replacement of an arbitrator on the ground that the outcome of the award may be affected by the conciliation proceedings, the Chairman may approve such request. The resulting additional costs shall be borne by all the parties.

Article 68: Time Limit for Rendering the Award

The Arbitral Tribunal shall render its award within 6 months (or 90 days where Article 53 applies) of the date of its constitution. If there are special circumstances justifying an extension of this period, the Secretary-General may approve an appropriate extension of time at the request of the presiding arbitrator or the sole arbitrator, as the case may be.

Article 69: Applicable Law

(1) The Arbitral Tribunal shall apply the law agreed upon by the parties to decide the dispute. Unless otherwise agreed by the parties, the agreed applicable law refers to the substantive rules of law but not to the rules of conflict of laws.

(2) In the absence of an agreed choice of law, the Arbitral Tribunal may determine the applicable law according to all the relevant circumstances of the case.

(3) By agreement of the parties, whether before or during the arbitral proceedings, the Arbitral Tribunal may render its award as *amiable compositeur* or *ex aequo et bono*. Such award shall not, however, violate the mandatory provisions of the applicable law and the public interest.
(4) In all cases, the Arbitral Tribunal shall render its award in accordance with the valid terms of the parties' agreement and take into account the relevant industry practices and trade usages.

Chapter IX: Supplementary Provisions

Article 70: Calculation of Time Limits

(1) Any period of time specified or determined in accordance with the Rules shall start to run on the day following the date on which such period commences. The day on which such period commences does not form part of the period of time.
(2) If the day following the date on which the period of time commences is an official holiday or a non-business day at the place of the service, the period of time shall begin to run on the first following business day. Official holidays or non-business days occurring within such period are included in the calculation of the period of time. If the last day of the relevant period of time falls on an official holiday or a non-business day, the period of time shall expire on the first following business day.
(3) Time for delivery shall not be included in the period of time. Any arbitral document, notice, or material that has been mailed or dispatched within the time limit shall be deemed to have been delivered in time.
(4) If a party exceeds a time limit because of *force majeure* events or other legitimate reasons, it may apply for an extension of that time limit within 10 days of the events or other reasons ceasing to have effect. The BAC or the Arbitral Tribunal, as the case may be, shall decide upon the application.

Article 71: Service

(1) Arbitral documents, notices and other materials may be served on the parties or their authorised representatives in person or by mail, courier, facsimile, email, or any other means that the BAC or the Arbitral Tribunal, as the case may be, considers appropriate.
(2) Arbitral documents, notices and materials shall be deemed to have been served if they have been delivered to the parties or their authorised representatives in person or by mail to the addressee's place of business, place of registration, place of residence, address indicated on ID card, *Hukou* address, address for service agreed by the parties or any other correspondence address provided by the addressee or the counterparty.
(3) If, despite reasonable inquiries, the addressee's place of business, place of registration, place of residence, address indicated on ID card, *Hukou* address, address for service agreed by the parties, or other correspondence address cannot be found, service shall be deemed to have been effected if the

document, notice or material is delivered to the addressee's last known place of business, place of registration, place of residence, address indicated on ID card, *Hukou* address, address for service agreed by the parties or other correspondence address, whether by mail, courier or by any other means of delivery which allows for a record of delivery.

Article 72: Language

(1) The parties may agree upon the language(s) to be used in the arbitral proceedings. Where the parties make no such agreement, the BAC or the Arbitral Tribunal, as the case may be, may determine that Chinese and/or any other language(s) shall be used in the arbitral proceedings according to the particular circumstances of the case.
(2) Where the parties have agreed upon the use of two or more languages in the arbitral proceedings, the Arbitral Tribunal may, upon obtaining consent from the parties, decide to adopt one language. If the parties fail to reach a unanimous agreement thereon, the arbitral proceedings may be conducted in multiple languages, in which case the resulting additional costs shall be borne by the parties.
(3) The BAC or the Arbitral Tribunal, as the case may be, may determine, in accordance with the particular circumstances of the case, whether or not written documents in international commercial arbitral proceedings shall be accompanied by a translation into Chinese or other language(s).
(4) If translation services are required by the parties or their authorised representatives or witnesses, translators may be provided either by the BAC or by the parties themselves. The parties shall bear the costs of translation.

Article 73: Interpretation of the Rules

(1) The Rules shall be interpreted by the BAC.
(2) Other documents issued by the BAC shall not constitute part of the Rules, unless the BAC states otherwise.

Article 74: Official Versions of the Rules

Each of the Chinese, English and other language versions of the Rules published by the BAC is an official version. In the event of any conflict between the different versions, the Chinese version shall prevail.

Article 75: Implementation of the Rules

The Rules shall take effect on April 1, 2015 and apply to all cases accepted by the BAC on or after that date. For cases accepted by the BAC before the Rules came into effect, the edition of the Arbitration Rules effective at the time of such acceptance shall apply. These Rules may, however, apply in such a case if the parties so agree and with the approval of the BAC.

Annex 1: Case Acceptance Fee Schedule of the Beijing Arbitration Commission

(Amended and adopted on September 16, 2003 at the fifth meeting of the third session of the Beijing Arbitration Commission and effective from March 1, 2004)

In accordance with the Notice of the State Council General Office on the Measures Regarding Arbitration Fees of Arbitration Commission (Guobanfa [1995] No. 44), and with the approval of the Beijing Price Bureau, the standard case acceptance fees of the Beijing Arbitration Commission are as follows:

Amount in dispute (RMB)	Rate (%)	Total fee (RMB)
Up to and including ¥1000		¥100
¥1000 to (and including) ¥50,000	5	¥100 plus 5 % of the amount in dispute exceeding ¥1000
¥50,000 to (and including) ¥100,000	4	¥2550 plus 4 % of the amount in dispute exceeding ¥50,000
¥100,000 to (and including) ¥200,000	3	¥4550 plus 3 % of the amount in dispute exceeding ¥100,000
¥200,000 to (and including) ¥500,000	2	¥7550 plus 2 % of the amount in dispute exceeding ¥200,000
¥500,000 to (and including) ¥1,000,000	1	¥13,550 plus 1 % of the amount in dispute exceeding ¥500,000
Above ¥1,000,000	0.3	¥18,550 plus 0.3 % of the amount in dispute exceeding ¥1,000,000

Notes

The amount claimed by the Claimant shall be deemed the amount in dispute as set forth in this Schedule. If there is a discrepancy between the amount claimed and the actual amount in dispute, the actual amount in dispute shall prevail

Where the amount in dispute is not specified, the acceptance fee shall be determined by the Secretariat of the Beijing Arbitration Commission

Case Handling Fee Schedule of the Beijing Arbitration Commission

(Amended and adopted on September 16, 2003 at the fifth meeting of the third session of the Beijing Arbitration Commission and effective from March 1, 2004)

In accordance with the Notice of the State Council General Office on the Measures Regarding Arbitration Fees of Arbitration Commission (Guobanfa [1995] No. 44), and with the approval of the Beijing Price Bureau, the standard case administration fees of the Beijing Arbitration Commission are as follows:

Amount in dispute (RMB)	Rate (%)	Total fee (RMB)
Up to and including ¥200,000		¥5000
¥200,000 to (and including) ¥500,000	2	¥5000 plus 2 % of the disputed amount exceeding ¥200,000
¥500,000 to (and including) ¥1,000,000	1	¥11000 plus 1 % of the disputed amount exceeding ¥500,000
¥1,000,000 to (and including) ¥5,000,000	0.4	¥16000 plus 0.4 % of the disputed amount exceeding ¥1,000,000
¥5,000,000 to (and including) ¥10,000,000	0.3	¥32000 plus 0.3 % of the disputed amount exceeding ¥5,000,000
¥10,000,000 to (and including) ¥20,000,000	0.25	¥47000 plus 0.25 % of the disputed amount exceeding ¥10,000,000
¥20,000,000 to (and including) ¥40,000,000	0.2	¥72,000 plus 0.2 % of the disputed amount exceeding ¥20,000,000
above ¥40,000,000	0.1	¥112,000 plus 0.1 % of the disputed amount exceeding ¥40,000,000

Notes

The amount claimed by the applicant shall be deemed the amount in dispute as set forth in the Case Handling Fee Schedule. If there is a discrepancy between the amount claimed and the actual amount in dispute, the actual amount in dispute shall prevail

Where the amount in dispute is not specified, the handling fee shall be determined by the Secretariat of the Beijing Arbitration Commission

Annex 2: Arbitration Fee Schedule for International Commercial Arbitration

Article 1 [Scope of Application] This Schedule shall apply where the parties to an arbitration of any international commercial case so agree.

Article 2 [Registration Fee] Where one party applies for arbitration, it shall pay a registration fee to the BAC of RMB 10,000 for each case. The BAC will not continue with the arbitration proceedings if that party fails to pay the registration fee within the time specified. The registration fee is not refundable.

Article 3 [Case Administration Fee] The parties shall prepay the case administration fee in accordance with the following Schedule:

Amount in dispute (RMB)	Rate (%)	Administration fee (RMB)
Up to and including ¥200,000		¥5000
¥200,000 to (and including) ¥500,000	2	¥5000, plus 2 % of the amount in dispute exceeding ¥200,000
¥500,000 to (and including) ¥1 million	1	¥11,000, plus 1 % of the amount in dispute exceeding ¥500,000
¥1 million to (and including) ¥5 million	0.4	¥16,000, plus 0.4 % of the amount in dispute exceeding ¥1 million
¥5 million to (and including) ¥10 million	0.3	¥32,000, plus 0.3 % of the amount in dispute exceeding ¥5 million
¥10 million to (and including) ¥20 million	0.25	¥47,000, plus 0.25 % of the amount in dispute exceeding ¥10 million

Article 4 [Determination of Amount in Dispute] The BAC will determine the amount in dispute based on the sum of claims and counterclaims. Where the amount in dispute is not specified, the BAC will determine such amount or the administration fee in accordance with the circumstances of the case.

Article 5 [Other Reasonable Expenses] The BAC may charge for other additional reasonable expenses in accordance with relevant provisions of the Rules.

Article 6 [Arbitrator's Fee] The Arbitrator's Fee will be determined in accordance with any one of the following methods:

(1) Calculation by hourly rate

   (a) For any arbitrator nominated by the parties, the arbitrator and the parties nominating this arbitrator shall negotiate and determine the rate applicable to such arbitrator.
   (b) The rate applicable to a sole arbitrator or the presiding arbitrator will be determined by the arbitrator and all the parties through negotiation.
   (c) If the parties fail to negotiate and determine a rate applicable to the arbitrator, the BAC will decide the rate.
   (d) The hourly rate of the arbitrator shall not exceed RMB 5000 Yuan in principle, regardless of the method of determination.

(2) Calculation based on the amount in dispute in accordance with the following table

Amount in dispute (RMB)	Arbitrator's fee (RMB)
No more than ¥400,000	11 % of the amount in dispute
¥400,001–¥800,000	¥44,000 + 10 % of the amount in dispute exceeding ¥400,000
¥800,001–¥4,000,000	¥84,000 + 5.3 % of the amount in dispute exceeding ¥800,000
¥4,000,001–¥8,000,000	¥253,600 + 3.78 % of the amount in dispute exceeding ¥4,000,000
¥8,000,001–¥16,000,000	¥404,800 + 1.73 % of the amount in dispute exceeding ¥8,000,000
¥16,000,001–¥40,000,000	¥543,200 + 1.06 % of the amount in dispute exceeding ¥16,000,000
¥40,000,001–¥80,000,000	¥797,600 + 0.44 % of the amount in dispute exceeding ¥40,000,000
¥80,000,001–¥240,000,000	¥973,600 + 0.25 % of the amount in dispute exceeding ¥80,000,000
¥240,000,001–¥400,000,000	¥1,373,600 + 0.228 % of the amount in dispute exceeding ¥240,000,000
¥400,000,001–¥600,000,000	¥1,738,400 + 0.101 % of the amount in dispute exceeding ¥400,000,000

(continued)

(continued)

Amount in dispute (RMB)	Arbitrator's fee (RMB)
¥600,000,001–¥800,000,000	¥1,940,400 + 0.067 % of the amount in dispute exceeding ¥600,000,000
¥800,000,001–¥4,000,000,00	¥2,074,400 + 0.044 % of the amount in dispute exceeding ¥800,000,000
More than ¥4,000,000,000	¥3,482,400 + 0.025 % of the amount in dispute exceeding ¥4,000,000,000, up to a maximum of ¥12,574,000

(a) The calculation method in the above table applies to only one arbitrator. Where the Arbitral Tribunal comprises 3 arbitrators, the maximum amount of the Arbitral Tribunal's fee will be 3 times the amount calculated in accordance with the method in the above table.
(b) The amount in dispute will be calculated on the basis of the sum of claims and counterclaims. Where the amount in dispute is not specified, the BAC will determine such amount or the arbitrator's fee in accordance with the circumstances of the case.

(3) The parties shall attempt to agree a method for calculating the arbitrator's fee. If thcy fail to agree the calculation method within 45 days after the Respondent receives the request for Submission of Defence, the arbitrator's fee will be calculated in accordance with paragraph (2) of this article of the Schedule

Article 7 [Payment of Fees]

(1) The registration fee will be paid in advance by the applicant to the BAC at the time of application.
(2) The parties may agree upon their respective proportions of the administration fee and arbitrator's fee, and then pay such fee in advance to the BAC. Where the parties fail to reach an agreement within the time limit specified by the BAC, the BAC will determine how the parties are to make advance payment and notify the parties.
(3) The parties shall be jointly and severally liable for payment of the fee of any arbitrator, regardless of whoever has appointed that arbitrator.
(4) Where the parties fail to pay in advance the administrative fee or arbitrator's fee, the BAC or the Arbitral Tribunal, as the case may be, may decide whether to continue with the arbitration proceedings in accordance with the particular circumstances of the case.

Article 8 [Other matters] The parties will agree upon any other matters not covered by this Schedule. If they fail to agree, the BAC will decide in accordance with the particular circumstances of the case.

Annex 3: Schedule of Fees for Appointing Emergency Arbitrators and Applications to Emergency Arbitrators for Interim Measures

Where parties apply to the BAC for the appointment of an emergency arbitrator in relation to interim measures in accordance with Article 63 of the Rules, and/or where parties apply to an emergency arbitrator for interim measures, the following charging Schedule will apply:

Application for interim measures	Fees (RMB)
Single measure	¥10,000
Multiple measures	¥10,000 + (n − 1) × ¥2000

Note

In this Schedule, "n" refers to the number of interim measures applied for by a party

Appendix II
Model Arbitration Clauses

International Chamber of Commerce[8]

All disputes arising out of or in connection with the present contract shall be submitted to the International Court of Arbitration of the International Chamber of Commerce and shall be finally settled under the Rules of Arbitration of the International Chamber of Commerce by one or more arbitrators appointed in accordance with the said Rules.

CIETAC[9]

Model Clause 1

Any dispute arising from or in connection with this Contract shall be submitted to China International Economic and Trade Arbitration Commission (CIETAC) for arbitration which shall be conducted in accordance with the CIETAC's arbitration rules in effect at the time of applying for arbitration. The arbitral award is final and binding upon both parties.

Model Clause 2

Any dispute arising from or in connection with this Contract shall be submitted to China International Economic and Trade Arbitration Commission (CIETAC) __________Sub-Commission (Arbitration Center) for arbitration which shall be conducted in accordance with the CIETAC's arbitration rules in effect at the time of applying for arbitration. The arbitral award is final and binding upon both parties.

[8] http://www.iccwbo.org/products-and-services/arbitration-and-adr/arbitration/standard-icc-arbitration-clauses/.

[9] http://www.cietac.org/index.cms.

G. Pisacane et al., *Arbitration in China*,
China Law, Tax & Accounting, DOI 10.1007/978-981-10-0684-5

SHIAC[10]

Model Clause 1

Any dispute arising from or in connection with this Contract shall be submitted to Shanghai International Economic and Trade Arbitration Commission/Shanghai International Arbitration Center for arbitration.

Model Clause for arbitration in the Shanghai Free Trade Pilot Zone

Any dispute arising from or in connection with this Contract shall be submitted to Shanghai International Economic and Trade Arbitration Commission/Shanghai International Arbitration Center for arbitration. The arbitration shall be held in The China (Shanghai) Pilot Free Trade Zone Court of Arbitration.

SCIA[11]

Model Clause 1

Any dispute arising from or in connection with this contract shall be submitted to South China International Economic and Trade Arbitration Commission (SCIA) for arbitration.

Model Clause 2

Any dispute arising from or in connection with this contract shall be submitted to Shenzhen Court of International Arbitration (SCIA) for arbitration.

BAC[12]

All disputes arising from or in connection with this contract shall be submitted to Beijing Arbitration Commission for arbitration in accordance with its rules of arbitration in effect at the time of applying for arbitration. The arbitral award is final and binding upon both parties.

---

[10]http://shiac.org/English/Guide.aspx?tid=13.
[11]http://www.sccietac.org/web/doc/view_guide/681.html.
[12]http://arbitrator.bjac.org.cn/en/.

Bibliography

Statutory, Judiciary and Administrative Provisions Quoted in the Text

1. PRC National People's

PRC Arbitration Law (中华人民共和国仲裁法), issued by PRC President Order No. 31 [1994] of August 31, 1994. English translation at http://www.wipo.int/wipolex/en/text.jsp?file_id=182634.

PRC Civil Procedure Law (中华人民共和国民事诉讼法), issued on April 9th, 1991; amended for the first time on October 28th, 2007; amended for the second time on August 31st, 2012.

PRC Law on the Laws Applicable to Foreign-Related Civil Relations (中华人民共和国涉外民事关系法律适用法), issued by PRC President Order No. 36 [2010] of October 28, 2010. English translation at http://www.wipo.int/wipolex/en/text.jsp?file_id=206611.

2. Supreme People's Court

Interpretation of the Supreme People's Court on Certain Issues Concerning the Application of the Arbitration Law of the People's Republic of China (最高人民法院关于适用《中华人民共和国仲裁法》若干问题的意见), issued by Fa Shi No. 7 [2006] of August 23, 2006. English translation at http://tradeinservices.mofcom.gov.cn/local/2007-11-22/11414.shtml.

Opinions of the SPC on Some Issues Concerning the Application of the Civil Procedure Law of the People's Republic of China (最高人民法院关于适用《中华人民共和国民事诉讼法》若干问题的意见), issued by Fa Fa No. 22 [1992] of July 14, 1992.

SPC Provisions on Recognition by the People's Courts of Civil Judgments Made by Courts in the Taiwan Region (最高人民法院关于人民法院认可台湾地区有关法院民事判决的规定), issued by Fa Shi No. 11 [1998] of May 22, 1998.

Regulations of the SPC on Certain Issues Concerning Enforcement by the People's Courts (for Trial Implementation) (最高人民法院关于人民法院执行工作若干问题的规定 (试行)), issued by Fa Shi No. 15 [1998] of June 27, 1998.

SPC Reply on Several Questions Regarding the Determination of the Validity of Arbitration Agreements (最高人民法院关于确认仲裁协议效力几个问题的批复), issued by Fa Shi No. 27 [1998] of October 26, 1998.

Certain Provisions of the SPC Regarding the Handling by the People's Courts of Cases Involving Foreign-Related Arbitrations and Foreign Arbitrations (Draft for Comment) (最高人民法院关于人民法院处理涉外仲裁及外国仲裁案件的若干规定(征求意见稿)), issued on December 31, 2003.

G. Pisacane et al., *Arbitration in China*,
China Law, Tax & Accounting, DOI 10.1007/978-981-10-0684-5

SPC Provisions on Some Issues concerning the Application of Law in Hearing Foreign-Related Contractual Dispute Cases Related to Civil and Commercial Matters (最高人民法院关于审理涉外民事或商事合同纠纷案件法律适用若干问题的规定), issued by Fa Shi No. 14 [2007] of July 23, 2007.

Provisions of the SPC on Case Guidance (最高人民法院关于案例指导工作的规定), issued by Fafa No. 51 [2010] of November 26, 2010.

Reply of the SPC regarding the Dispute on the Validity of an Arbitration Agreement between Anhui Longlide Packing and Printing Co., Ltd. and BP Agnati S.R.L. (最高人民法院关于申请人安徽省龙利得包装印刷有限公司与被申请人BP Agnati S.R.L.申请确认仲裁协议效力案的复函), [2013] Min Si Ta Zi No. 13, March 25, 2013; also in *Guide on Adjudication of Cases involving Commercial and Maritime Affairs*, Volume 26, 125–129.

SPC Notice on Certain Issues Relating to Correct Handling of Judicial Review of Arbitration Matters (最高人民法院关于正确审理仲裁司法审查案件有关问题的通知), issued by Fa No. 194 [2013] of September 4, 2013.

Reply to the Request for Instructions of Guangdong Province High People's Court on the Case of Zhaoqing United Nations Metal Products Factory Co., Ltd. Requesting not to Enforce Award No. D19 (2013) of the South China International Economic and Trade Arbitration Commission (关于广东省高级人民法院就肇庆国联金属制品厂有限公司申请不予执行华南国际经济贸易仲裁委员会(2013)D19号仲裁裁决一案请示的复函), [2014] Min Si Ta Zi No. 52.

3. Other People's Courts

Shanghai No. 2 Intermediate People's Court Opinions on Judicial Review and Enforcement of Arbitration Cases Applying China (Shanghai) Pilot Free Trade Zone Arbitration Rules (上海市第二中级人民法院关于适用《中国(上海)自由贸易试验区仲裁规则》仲裁案件司法审查和执行的若干意见) of May 4, 2014.

Shanghai No. 2 Intermediate People's Court Interpretation of the Opinions on Judicial Review and Enforcement of Arbitration Cases Applying the China (Shanghai) Pilot Free Trade Zone Arbitration Rules (上海市第二中级人民法院关于适用《自贸区仲裁规则》仲裁案件司法审查和执行的若干意见解读) of July 17, 2014.

4. PRC State Council

Notice of the General Office of the State Council on Some Notable Issues Concerning the Execution of the PRC Arbitration Law, issued by Guobanfa No. 22 [1996] of June 8, 1996.

Notice on Carrying out According to Law the Arbitration Work on Securities and Futures Contracts (关于依法做好证券、期货合同纠纷仲裁工作的通知), jointly issued by the Legal Affairs Bureau of the State Council and the China Securities Regulatory Commission on March 17, 2004 by Guofa No. 5 [2004].

Sources

G. CRESPI REGHIZZI, "L'arbitrato commerciale in Cina", in *Sulla Via del Catai*, Vol. 12, Centro Studio Martino Martini, Trento (Italy).

J. D'AGOSTINO, J. BOOTH, T. WU, "The Aftermath of the CIETAC Split: two years on, lower courts take clashing views on arbitration agreements and awards– but higher courts strive for consistency", published May 2, 2014 in *Kluwer Arbitration Blog*: http://kluwerarbitrationblog.com/blog/2014/05/02/the-aftermath-of-the-cietac-split-two-years-on-lower-courts-take-clashing-views-on-arbitration-agreements-and-awards-but-higher-courts-strive-for-consistency/.

A. FONG, "The New CIETAC Rules 2015", in *Hong Kong Lawyer*, March, 2015, 44–49.

GU Zhenlong, *Some Considerations on Parties' Self-Determination in the Arbitration Law* (关于仲裁法中当事人意思自治的几点思考), 2012, in the legal database *pkulaw.cn*, Ref. Code CLI.A.073818.

HUANG Tao, "Validity of Arbitration Agreements under Chinese Law", in M. J. MOSER (ed.), *Business Disputes in China*, 2011, JurisNet LLC, 111–122.
KUN Fan, *Arbitration in China: A Legal and Cultural Analysis*, Hart Publishing, 2013.
TANG Guoxiang, "A Brief Study on the Scope of Arbitration in Our Country" (我国仲裁的受案范围浅探), in *West China Development*, Vol. 6, 2012, 49.
TAO Jingzhou, M. ZHONG, "Picking the Right Arbitration Institution in China", in *China Law & Practice*, September/October 2014, 28–30.
WENFEI ATTORNEYS-AT-LAW LTD., *China Briefing*, No. 241, June, 2014.
WENFEI ATTORNEYS-AT-LAW LTD., *China Briefing*, No. 245, October, 2014.
ZHANG Shouzhi, HU Ke, TIAN Jing, *Onshore Arbitration by Offshore Institutions Recognized by China's Highest Court*, King & Wood Mallesons, August 11, 2014, at http://www.chinalawinsight.com/2014/08/articles/dispute-resolution/onshore-arbitration-by-offshore-arbitration-institutions-recognized-by-spc/.
ZHU Sanzhu, "Legal Aspects of Commodity and Financial Futures Market in China", in *The Brooklyn Journal of Corporate, Financial and Commercial Law*, 2009, 3 (2), 377–430.
J. M. ZIMMERMAN, *China Law Deskbook: A Legal Guide for Foreign-Invested Enterprises*, 3rd ed., 2010, ABA Books.

The manufacturer's authorised representative in the EU is Springer Nature Customer Service Centre GmbH, Europaplatz 3, 69115 Heidelberg, Germany. If you have any concerns regarding our products, please contact ProductSafety@springernature.com

Printed and bound by CPI Group (UK) Ltd, Croydon, CR0 4YY
22/09/2026
02221058-0012